SNOWDON
The Story of a Welsh Mountain

Jim Perrin

SNOWDON

The Story of a Welsh Mountain

Gomer

Published in 2012 by Gomer Press,
Llandysul, Ceredigion, SA44 4JL.

ISBN: 978-1-84323-574-3

A CIP record for this title is available from
the British Library.
Copyright: Jim Perrin © 2012

Jim Perrin asserts his moral right under the
Copyright, Designs and Patents Act, 1988
to be identified as author of this work.

This book is published with the financial
support of the Welsh Books Council.

Printed and bound in Wales at
Gomer Press, Llandysul, Ceredigion.

Contents

Cyflwynedig i

1.

Dyma'r Wyddfa a'i chriw; dyma lymder a moelni'r tir;
Dyma'r llyn a'r afon a'r clogwyn;
        'Hon' — T. H. PARRY-WILLIAMS

2.

Nid wy'n byw
Un amser nac yn unlle'n gyfan oll:
Mae darn o hyd ar grwydyr neu ar goll.
        'Anwadalwch' — T. H. PARRY-WILLIAMS

Epigraph

The most famous first: the view of Yr Wyddfa, Snowdon, the highest mountain in Wales, from the waters of Porthmadog Bay, looking over the artificial embankment which there crosses the estuary of the Glaslyn river. This grand prospect is like an ideal landscape, its central feature exquisitely framed, its balance exact, its horizontals and perpendiculars in splendid counterpoint. Cloud generally drifts obligingly around the crags of the mountain, and lies vaporously in its grey gulleys; in the green-and-blue foreground swans swim, cormorants dive, cattle really do stand up to their hocks in the shallows of the estuary, as in old water-colours, and the hussocked grass of the saltings is overlooked by gentle green woods on either side.

It is the classic illumination of Wales, being not much like anywhere else on earth. The bare Welsh mountains have few peers, and the illusory scale of them is peculiarly indigenous. That noble peak before us, one of the most celebrated of mountain forms, is only 3,500 feet high, and you could easily fit the whole landscape, its rocky eminences, its winding river, its woods and its salt-flats, into one of the lesser Alpine glaciers. It is a dream-view. It is as though everything is refracted by the pale, moist quality of the air, so that we see the mountain through a lens, heightened or dramatized. 'There is no corner of Europe that I know', wrote Hilaire Belloc, wondering at it from the deck of his yacht, 'which so moves me with the awe and majesty of great things as does this mass of the northern Welsh mountains seen from this corner of their silent sea.'[1]

— JAN MORRIS

1   Jan Morris, *The Matter of Wales: Epic Views of a Small Country* (Oxford University Press, 1984).

Foreword

Mountains are assemblies of rock, oftentimes carpeted in snow and ice, and in early summer in meadows, flowers. But they are, basically, assemblages of rock and if you feel compelled to climb the higher of them then that is what you will confront. They have no emotional radiance; they are not alive; they do not talk to you. They do not, like pets, respond to you. And they can kill you. Quite easily. And yet? And yet humans have related to their hills, universally, in profoundly respectful ways. Mountains galore are declared sacred, or glorified, or exploited. We all aspire to ascend them, or to appropriate them.

My mountain, whether it likes it or not, and Jim Perrin's as well, is Snowdon. I have lived with it for most, if not all, of my life. Let me explain: I grew up with Yr Wyddfa; by which I mean that we looked at each other from the moment I opened my eyelids in Llanfrothen until I decided to go and live in Brighton when I was seventeen. There it was, every clear day, every morning, every night: proud, relaxed, angry, glowing, inviting, forbidding and so starkly, undeniably beautiful in its symmetry and its languid, relaxed, challenging pose, arm draped across Lliwedd. There is no finer prospect of the mountain than that across the Traeth Mawr. And when I went to secondary school in Harlech there it was again – further away, but more finely drawn, stencilled against the pale sky.

Did I get into that rocky embrace? Curiously, for it was not the local custom, I did. A few years ago, on an extraordinarily chill and clear January morning, I stumbled up the Rhyd Ddu path over Llechog. On meandering across the 'saddle', I saw a sight which I had never seen before: there in front of me was an island onto which I felt I could almost step: Anglesey shouldn't be there – it was the Isle of Man! To the further reaches of the north there were the Cumbrian mountains; to the south Mynydd Preseli in Pembrokeshire: and of course to the west the Wicklow mountains in Ireland. I stood transfixed and, yes, Wordsworth's *Prelude* somehow flashed through my mind.

As I contemplated – could it be upon immortality? – a couple emerged from the depths of the Watkin Path. I told them, in what I thought was a hushed and respectful tone, that I had been coming up this mountain for fifty years and had never seen anything so clear and so astonishingly translucent: 'Well you'll never see it again then, will you mate?' was the down-to-bloody-earth Manchester reply.

Fifty years! Yes, I have been going up there for fifty years. My first serious encounter with the mountain was when I was ten or eleven – and I have the photos to prove it – when I climbed Crib Goch and Crib y Ddisgyl with the mountaineer John Earle. We followed the snow-plough up from Penygwryd so you can imagine what the conditions were like. Roped together on the ridge, John suggested that if he fell over one side the best thing I could do was jump over the other. Which was actually good, if life-threatening, advice. But then the problems started: the way up to the summit was, as so often in winter, encased in ice. Unfortunately, so was our way down. The zigzags were sheer ice. Jumping off the ridge was not an option. And so, with my uncle Herb's giant ice axe in my thin arm, I had patiently to cut steps down the whole face. We had no crampons so this was the only option. I must have been a tenth of John Earle's weight so I had to go first, for I couldn't possibly have held him had he fallen. I had to lead and cut the steps (a skill I still treasure and have used, despite crampons, in the Alps). It took hours.

Then there was the time we young tigers from our local climbing club, Clwb Dringo Porthmadog, camped near Llyn Llydaw, climbed all day on Y Lliwedd (we were old-fashioned even then, in the 1960s), and later, as the moon rose, we ascended Crib Goch and completed the Snowdon Horseshoe by its wan light; and the time I took Rhodri and Steffan, my sons, when they were ten and seven, up the Snowdon Ranger path where the snow was crisp and bright and then down the western ridge where the snow was shoulder-high and wet and they vowed never to climb a mountain again; or the time when – ah! Old men reminiscing . . .

I first came across Jim Perrin's work, and his style, when I acquired his 1971 *Climber's Club* guide to Cwm Silyn and Cwellyn, written with my neighbour in Dyffryn Nantlle, Mike Yates, in, yes, 1971. I clambered over many of the cliffs they described in such detail but followed few of the routes. To be in the mountains was enough for me. All along from Nantlle, one gazed at the same sight Richard Wilson had immortalized (several times, as it happens) in his pioneering landscape paintings referred to in these following pages.

Jim Perrin has stayed true to his mountains and has brought to them an exquisite and unique literary talent, redolent with challenge. Anyone who reads any of Jim's work – whether it be his biographies of mountaineers (and *Menlove*, his 1985 biography of Menlove Edwards, is one of the finest biographies ever written); or his Country Diaries in the *Guardian*; or his confessional and heart-rending *West: A Journey through the Landscapes of Loss* – as moving and profound an exploration of grief and the will to live as one is likely to find – will confront a literary talent full of inner, and writerly, japes and challenges; full of observation (what happened to that in contemporary literature?); and full of unquenchable energy and scholarship. And, when it comes to his subject here, Snowdon, full of intimate knowledge, respect and love.

I know each step of Jim's mountain circuit – the lie of the land – but have never relived it as clearly as in these pages. I hope this book makes Snowdon more alive and challenging and intellectually stimulating to those who pass over it in springtime and in summer. I hope it makes those of us who have lived with it all our lives revisit not only its grandeur and its hidden places but also its creative force and presence – in painting, in poetry, in English as well as – most powerfully and appropriately – in Welsh.

R. Merfyn Jones
August, 2012

Introduction

This mountain ahead is not only old, but with its uncovered
rock and broken boulders and hoary streams and twisted trees,
that look as if a child had gathered garlands and put them in
play upon the ancient stems, it declares mightily, if vaguely,
the immense past which it has seen.[2] — EDWARD THOMAS

A good friend of mine from north of Hadrian's Wall, during
one of the jousting conversations about the merits of our native
hills in which those of the Celtic Fringe delight, was kind
enough to concede recently that the 'Snowdon Horseshoe'[3] is
by far the finest ridge walk in Britain, if you exclude Skye from
consideration. That's some concession, coming from a proud
Scotsman, and even as an equally proud Welshman I didn't
jib at his assertion on behalf of the Black Cuillin. Unique
though the latter is, there is a comparison to be drawn here.
Both Snowdon[4] and the Cuillin have about them a similarity

2   Edward Thomas, *Wales* (Oxford, 1983), p. 148. Originally published as
Beautiful Wales, (A & C Black, 1905).
3   A circuit, starting and finishing at Pen-y-Pass and usually followed in
an anti-clockwise direction, which takes in Crib Goch, Crib y Ddysgl, Yr
Wyddfa and Y Lliwedd. Under winter conditions in particular – when proper
equipment and knowledge of its use are absolute necessities – this is certainly
one of the great mountain excursions in Britain.
4   Curiously, the Saxon name ('Snawdune') would appear to be of longer
provenance than the Welsh one of Yr Wyddfa, having been first recorded in
1095, the first appearance of the latter only occurring in 1284. The reason for
this may well be the same as for the Saxon name of Cnicht – purportedly for
its resemblance to a knight's helmet – having been bestowed on the fine peak

of architecture and mood. They are shapely and complex, bare-rocked, precipiced and glacier-hewn, architectonic in the swirl and scatter of their ridges, physically unlike any other British hills. The sea's proximity to both – the western gable of the Cuillin sheers out of the Hebridean Sea, and to the west or the north it is little more than seven miles from the summit of Snowdon to the great Traeth or to Aber Menai – adds to their sense of height, their light-play, their capricious atmospherics, their drama and perhaps even their occasionally stormy characters (devotees of Brandon Mountain down on the Dingle Peninsula of County Kerry will recognize the attraction of these qualities too).

Scafell Pike and Ben Nevis, as high points of their respective nations, have their devotees, but as any objective witness would aver, they're lumpen and uncouth masses in comparison with Snowdon. There are finer and more interesting peaks than either of these uncomfortably close at hand to them. Who would choose to walk on Ben Nevis when the more elegant ridges of the Mamores beckon, or stay on Scafell Pike with Scafell in prospect? Snowdon is by far the finest peak in our trio of national high points, and though the Cuillin may equal or even excel it in mountainous character, there are the aesthetics and the echoing richness of human story to be accounted on Snowdon's side. There is so much more to Snowdon than its mere physical fabric, however magnificent that may be. The Victorian writer Theodore Watts-Dunton, in his eccentric and oddly appealing novel of 1898 *Aylwin*, the crucial scenes

---

above Traeth Mawr (above which Snowdon is also dominant), the supposition being that it was bestowed by Saxon sailors, to whom the two would have been notable landmarks. Whatever the reason, I shall be using Snowdon to refer to the mountain as a whole, and Yr Wyddfa or Snowdon summit interchangeably to denote its top.

of which are set on the mountain, wrote of 'the mysterious magic of *y Wyddfa* [sic], that magic which no other mountain in Europe exercises'.

Like consciousness itself, that allure teases at, and yet remains beyond our complete understanding. The appeal of the mountain resists simple definition. Of all our native hills, Snowdon has the most astonishing wealth of cultural texture, which in itself argues long attraction.

From neolithic cairn-builders through the legendry out of which grew those Arthurian stories that, when they had migrated to mainland Europe, became known as 'The Matter of Britain', to the arduous industry of copper-miners and the travails, controversies and achievements of modern eco-management, by way of poets and novelists and travellers and the accounts of sporting participants in Welsh and in English, humanity has inscribed the sense of its own passage down through the ages on its stones and crags. No other mountain I know of – not Schiehallion nor Croagh Patrick nor Kailash; not Mount Olympus nor Mont Aiguille; not the magical Basque peak of La Rhune nor the Catalan one of Canigou at either end of the Pyrenees; not Shivling nor Bhagirathi, nor any other of humanity's holy and legendary hills – come with quite so much story attached.

'It is from its connection with romance that Snowdon derives its chief interest,' George Borrow wrote, grasping a part of the truth here. Physical form, association, myth and a long history of human awareness mingle cloudily about Snowdon and distil into the most heady and potent of mountain brews. It is a hill of many dimensions, one which we can approach from an extraordinary number of directions: the stilled foldings, the cleave and fracture of its rocks; the rich relict flora left behind on groined cliffs after the retreat of the ice; folk-tale echoes of an older race who inhabited here, and its religious beliefs; the scarcely-explored archaeology of stone circle, hut circle, fort and cairn; chronicled time, industry, sport – on all these levels, Snowdon has something to give to the effort of our understanding, and all of them will be touched upon in this book.

The mountain possesses also its own anthology of literature, and in two languages at that; one of them – the generally disregarded one – being perhaps the greatest treasure-house of all medieval European literatures. Snowdon's physical appeal and its wealth of tradition have ensured its popularity, and that in its turn for some has meant its ruin. There are times nowadays when it can seem trampled or managed to death – though those who criticize the National Park Authority for the latter seem unable to offer their own broadly acceptable and democratic proposals as to how else the sheer pressure of visitor-traffic this hill inspires might best be mediated.[5]

That visitor-traffic has been around for a very long time. Both Thomas Pennant and William Wordsworth climbed Snowdon's western flank to watch the dawn from its heights in the closing decades of the eighteenth century, and their writing about the experience helped stimulate an ever-increasing popularity for the ascent throughout the following centuries. The first time I climbed the mountain, by myself in the Easter snow of 1960 as a schoolboy just turned thirteen, I came up from the west as well, and still harbour an affection for the ascents from this side. Two hundred years before, when the head of the Llanberis lakes had to be reached by boat and there was no road up the Llanberis Pass, the approaches from

5   Even before its 2009 opening, for example, the new summit visitor centre, Hafod Eryri – which replaced Clough Williams-Ellis' drably utilitarian design of 1935 – had proved particularly controversial.

Nant Colwyn or Cwellyn to the west were the more accessible ones. I doubt if a tenth of the walkers who reach the summit these days go that way.

Certainly, one of the most glorious and affecting of all my hill-memories comes from the other, eastern side. It is of walking up through the close and obscuring drizzle of a pre-dawn into cloud-damped Cwm Glas, plodding heavily on, enveloped in a soaking mist, with no hint of anything other than this slow, wet suffocation of the senses to come, until suddenly, at Bwlch Coch, I burst through into a clearer world. The sky was palest blue. A white cloud-sea filled the Nant y Gwryd and shaded to rose in the east. Indigo slopes of island peaks, still air, and two sole points of movement completed the scene: from Bwlch y Saethau and Bwlch Ciliau opposite, pink cloud frothed in a slow fall, seething around the steeps of Cribau; on the ridge of Crib y Ddysgl above me, a fox flicked his brush, glanced down towards where I stood, and in a glisten of rich chestnut he was unconcernedly gone.

These are the kind of gifts that Snowdon can bring; and there is more. Charles Edward Mathews, one of the Victorian worthies who were yearly visitors to the Pen-y-Gwryd Hotel in training for their alpine endeavours of those long-gone summers – brought an eminent Swiss guide, Melchior Anderegg, to the summit of Crib Goch in the snowy Easter of 1888. Looking at the ridge ahead and the peak of Yr Wyddfa across the cwm, the erstwhile guide told his *Herr*,

'We must go back; we cannot climb the final peak in less than five or six hours.'

Mathews reassured him that they would be standing on the summit in an hour.

'That,' the gentleman-amateur was told by his professional companion, 'is quite impossible!'

They pressed on, and in five minutes over the hour were standing by the summit cairn.[6]

The anecdote is telling. This is the way that Snowdon works on the mind. This is its affect. It is a shape-shifter of a mountain; enchanting, not easily surrendering itself and its essence to the simple certainties on which humankind in the twenty-first century habitually insists. On a recent winter's day I met a boy up here following his GPS device, heading for the brink of a precipice.

'Turn it off,' I told him, 'and follow that path,' pointing to one that led at an angle of ninety degrees to his intended direction. 'And don't turn your GPS on again until you're down on the road.'

Maybe all this is why the mountain has shrunk by twelve feet in the last century, according to the Ordnance Survey. Or maybe they just have more accurate measuring now. In an earlier encounter, on the last stretch from Bwlch Glas to the summit I came across a young man in a garish anorak shambling down in mist and rain, eyes fixed on a bright yellow device of a kind I'd not seen before, which dangled from his neck where a compass would normally hang with hill-goers of the generations I'd known: 'It's a global positioning instrument,' the young man told me, with no other prompt than my interrogatory glance. 'You're at an altitude of 3,470 feet and 218 metres distant from the summit.'

He looked concerned, his eyes gliding over my antique apparel and equipment, as I climbed on into the mist, and he told me to take care. Arriving a few minutes later at the cairn, with all its then-litter of rusting stays and hooks from former

6 As recounted in 'Reminiscences of Pen-y-gwryd', *Climbers' Club Journal*, 1901.

shelters, its resonance and its mysterious grandeur, I thought that I do have a care of this mountain, and a sense of what endures here:

> Other the boys, other their transient fame,
> Snowdon remains the same.

For the whole of my outdoor life I've been under the spell cast by this most beautiful and redolent of British hills. If I were to look for clues that might lead me better to understand the nature of the enchantment, perhaps as preliminary they would lead me to the old church of Nant Peris, hard under the more easterly of the mountain's two northern ridges.

In high summer the churchyard here is a cool and wistful place. Above the riverside meadows are velvety green oakwoods, and glinting rock outcrops on slopes that rear up on every side to lead your eye towards distant red screes and spiky crests. The jagged triple peak of Tryfan – Snowdon has two versions of its own under this name – soars above the belfry of the medieval church, which stretches out long and low, sheltered by a thicket of ash and yew from gales that funnel up or down the Pass of Llanberis at their proper seasons. The churchyard itself is a secretive place, one of nettles and long grass and jackdaws calling from the ash trees. It's set back from the road, as though harbouring a mystery. The graves huddle in little clusters among hummocks and clearings. They are almost all of the local Dinorwig slate, muted purple speckled with greeny-blue ovals like two-dimensional thrushes' eggs. A social history of the region around the foot of the mountain is written here.

Between two of the graves passes a particular frisson. One of them is a squat slab which lies against the wall of the church itself. Its inscription reads thus:

Underneath lie the remains of William Williams, upwards
of 25 years botanical guide at the Royal Victoria Hotel, who
was killed by a fall from Clogwyn y Garnedd, June 13, 1861,
whilst pursuing his favourite vocation. This tombstone was
erected to his memory by a few friends.

Twenty yards away, on the other side of the path and between
two yew trees, is a large, flat slab, the ornate lettering on which
recounts the following story:

Sacred to the memory of the Reverend Henry Willington
Starr, B.A., Curate of All Saints, Northampton, who perished
on Snowdon while on a tour through North Wales, September
15, 1846, aged 32 years. And whose remains, discovered June
1, 1847, were interred beneath this stone June 7, 1847.

Here are the bones of a story that aches to be told, and
we will come to it when we arrive at the place where the
associated mystery adheres, in chapter five. Likewise there is
a story behind the epitaph by the poet Dafydd Ddu Eryri on
the grave near the lichgate of little John Closs, seven-year-old
son of the landlord at Nant Peris' inn, who was buried there
just before Christmas in 1805. He was lost in the snow as he
slipped away from his grandmother's house in Betws Garmon
to follow his mother back over the mountain to Nant Peris,
his crouched and frozen body found three days later after an
extensive search, high on the slopes of Moel Eilio.

All three graves underline another aspect of this mountain:
child, guide or man of God – for each of them, and for many
who have come after, this was the mortal place. Popularity and
mountains are a perilous mix, and we do well to remember
here our human smallness in the face of the mountain
elements. Even Pennant, in 1781, sounded his warning about
the disorientating swirl of cloud and mist:

It is very rare that the traveller gets a proper day to ascend the hill; for it often appears clear, but by the evident attraction of clouds by this lofty mountain, it becomes suddenly and unexpectedly enveloped in mist, when the clouds have just before appeared very remote, and at great heights. At times I have observed them lower to half their height, and notwithstanding they had been dispersed to the right and to the left, yet they have met from both sides, and united to involve the summit in one great obscurity.[7]

We do well to remember also the gifts an adventurous spirit will receive, and which a mountain like Snowdon – however small it may seem relative to Himalayan or Alpine scale – can bestow in full measure. You can dismiss that response of the alpine guide on Bwlch Coch as merely the falling for a natural *trompe l'œil;* or you can accept that this is the way Snowdon will feel at times – greater than its actual scale, capable of inducing still a respectful surprise, teasing always at an imagination prepared to explore its echoes and endured epochs.

On a simple topographical note, I have taken the territory of this hill – and hence of this book – as being all the high ground of very roughly rhomboidal shape, and including the satellite peaks of Garnedd Ugain, Crib Goch, Lliwedd, Yr Aran, Moel Eilio, Foel Gron, Foel Goch and Moel Cynghorion as well as Yr Wyddfa itself, which is contained within the A498 road running from Penygwryd to Beddgelert, the A4085 from Beddgelert through Rhyd Ddu and Betws Garmon to Waunfawr, the minor road from Waunfawr through Groeslon to Llanrug, and the A4086 from Llanrug by way of Llanberis and Nant Peris back to Penygwryd again.

---

7   Thomas Pennant, *A Tour in Wales*, vol. II (London, 1784). p. 173.

Here then, in the following chapters, is the life story of the British mainland's finest mountain. If you have already climbed to its top, I hope good memories will be invoked; if not, may these chapters lead you there, and the experience encompass everything for which you might hope.

I

The Lie of the Land

This is to know a mountain; to inch one's way up it from ledge to ledge; to break one's nails on its surface. To feel for handholds, for footholds, face pressed to its stone cheek. The long look at the traverse, the scrutiny of each fissure. And the thought that it has all been done before is of no help. There is the huge tug of gravity, the desire of the bone for the ground, with the dogged spirit hauling the flesh upward. Rare flowers tremble, waver, just out of reach. From the summit the voices fall, a careless garland. A girl stands with her back to the drop. A slim figure, she leads the mountain by a rope. It will not try to master her again? The next time there will be snow, ice. The mountain will digest her slowly.[8] — R. S. THOMAS

In the two dimensions of the 1:25,000 Ordnance Survey map it looks animated, starfish-like, pinky-beige, its radiating ridges decorative, crag-stippled and lake-enclosing, the suggestion of motion continually hovering about them as though they were limbs waving gently in the depths of a clear pool. None of the other mountains in Snowdonia, in Britain even, has this dynamic quality. They are no more than ragged and static in plan. But even in linear representation the symmetries of

---

8   *R. S. Thomas: Selected Prose*, ed. Sandra Anstey (Poetry Wales Press, 1986), 'The Mountains' (1968), pp. 98–9. Introduction by Ned Thomas.

Snowdon, radiating out from the focal point of Yr Wyddfa, draw you in. There is a sculpted beauty to its design, a right succession that whirls itself into your imagination. How best to approach it? If it can give the illusion of life even on a map, how much more powerful will its effect be in reality, in the five senses, and maybe even in the one beyond them?

It is no doubt futile to suggest this, because everyone on his or her first visit will succumb to summit fever and head for Yr Wyddfa itself – which is what I did as a schoolboy first visiting here. But once that necessity is dispensed with, I would propose another more comprehensive way to gain the acquaintance of this marvel of a hill, one which might make the experience of the summit even more memorable thereafter. It is to circle the mountain, and hence to catch at and come to understand the lie of the land. The late Showell Styles, one of this mountain region's most ardent and articulate devotees, in a charming, knowledgeable, garrulous book, *The Mountains of North Wales*,[9] proposed that you should do just this as 'a rapid, mind's-eye journey', a girdling of the mountain at a distance of a mile or a mile and a half (no kilometric nonsense for old Showell) more or less from the top, 'touching the tourist paths only to step across them'.

When I started to plan this book, Showell's idea grew on me. Why not follow the circuit of the peak not just rapidly and in the mind's eye, but lingeringly and in reality? Would it not be a good way initially to locate and to touch glancingly upon the themes more fully examined in later chapters? It would surely put me in the mood to attempt to evoke the unique atmosphere of Snowdon. A long day in good weather and the light months of the year might have sufficed, though it would

---

9   Showell Styles, *The Mountains of North Wales* (Gollancz, 1973).

THE LIE OF THE LAND

be better, I decided, to take it in more leisurely fashion – to contemplate, carry a stove and sleeping bag, watch at dawn and dusk for the transfiguring play of light across landscape, give myself time for close scrutiny, consideration, remembrance. And I wouldn't necessarily avoid all the tourist paths. I'd just make use of those sections that lent themselves naturally to the enterprise, and join them up in a way that suited my purpose. This literally roundabout excursion, I argued to myself, might best introduce the mountain's complexity, its physical and associative richness, to a degree that a hundred trips to the summit would not necessarily achieve.

There was the question of a detailed route to be decided, of course. I had no intention of holding strictly to the mind's-eye configuration put forward by Showell, much though I had esteemed his guidance in the mountains and his commentary on them throughout my hill-going life. His imagined journey missed out places and pathways that I hold dear, features which I find attractive but which always seem to lie somehow outside the main narrative of the place; and which lend themselves to an itinerary quite apart from those of the summit-fixated. But I thought in essence that his close circumscribing, his notion of summit-proximity was a good one. You can certainly construct a more wandering and expansive way than either Showell's or the one I had in mind – a Tour of Snowdon like the famous one of Mont Blanc, but miniaturized, which holds to footpaths through the redolent and lovely valleys of Llanberis and Nant Gwynen,[10] Colwyn and Cwellyn around the base,

---

10 'Nant Gwynant' is, like so many versions of Welsh names on the Ordnance Survey maps, an invented nonsense, as well as a tautology in this case. Its first official appearance was on the NW quarter of Sheet 75 in the *Old Series*, published on 1 May, 1840. If you want a view of the historical and colonialist process at work here, Brian Friel's play *Translations* (1980),

and crosses only the single low *bwlch* of Maesgwm between
Foel Goch and Moel Cynghorion; but that would not give you
the clearest or most advantageously close view of the structure
and fabric of the mountain. To gain that, you would need to
make some acquaintance with every one of those axial ridges,
and with every high cwm. And all this can be done, I argued
to myself, in the space of fifteen or so miles. I set to planning,
and waited on the weather through a bitter spring.

Both Showell's route and the one upon which, after much
canvassing of options, I eventually decided for this eccentric
clockwise circumambulation begin along the most popular
route of them all to the summit – the Miners' Track. So with
an anticyclone holding in the west and a May morning sun
clearing the last of the mist from Nant y Gwryd, I set off
from Gorffwysfa. A scene from more than forty years ago was
playing in my mind – myself when young, walking from Capel
Curig alongside Llynnau Mymbyr in the dawn, the dark lake
surface a glassy stillness, mist that was pink-tinged as candy
floss in the just-risen sun hanging down to the water on the
Moel Siabod shore, small trout flashing silver as they leapt, the
whole world that was apart from this scene simply suspended,

---

about the work of the Ordnance Survey in Donegal during the 1830s – the
same period as the Snowdon map's preparation – gives a very incisive one. The
correct name for the valley, Nant Gwynen (Nanhwynen or Nanhwynein are
older, mutated versions of this) – was still in common and popular use at the
beginning of the twentieth century, and in spite of what D. E. Jenkins in this
exact area refers to most fittingly as 'the tyranny of custom', it is the one I shall
use throughout in the – no doubt vain – hope that it will re-establish itself. I'll
content myself with raising at length this single early objection to Ordnance
Survey toponymy. If I were to go on in this vein it might fill the whole book
– as much reliance can be placed on the words on government maps as on
those of governments themselves. In cartographic rather than cultural terms,
of course, the OS maps perform their function perfectly well, and I wouldn't
advise you to throw them away too immediately. Just make sure that on this
mountain, where not all is as it seems on the map, you use them wisely.

and a heron in slow and creaking flight claiming the moments for timelessness. Memory fixes these gifts the hills bring, and perhaps today there would be more. With a light rucksack on my back I set off from the car-park along the track, which is sociable and gradual and eases a rhythm into your limbs to tune them for the exertions to come.

There was a flash of rusty red from among the screes above Llyn Teyrn. A chippy, urgent, reiterated call alerted me to the presence of a stonechat – one of the familiar little witching presences of the Welsh hills. I caught sight of him, white-collared and distinctly dapper, perching on a pointed rock and asserting his territory. Not against me, but at a stoat stuttering over the stones, still scruffed about with moulting ermine, for it had been a cold, late spring. The stonechat flew to a safer vantage point to continue volleying his unregarded warnings and aggressions at the stoat, and I walked on.

In all the hill areas of Britain there is no easier means of access to a mountain sanctum than that along the Miners' Track, which was built in the early decades of the nineteenth century to facilitate the transport of ore from the Glaslyn mines, production at which ceased for the last time during the Great War. Even as late as the onset of the Second World War, the Miners' Track for much of its length was a motorable road. I have a photograph, taken in 1938 during his work on the climbing guidebook to the thousand-foot-high cliff of Y Lliwedd above Llyn Llydaw, of the most significant of rock-climbing pioneers from that time, Menlove Edwards, coiling his ropes on the greensward by the valve-house for the Cwm Dyli power station, his Austin car parked alongside.

The rough and foot-worn track of the present day lays fair claim to be considered the country's greatest recreational highway. I reached the causeway across Llyn Llydaw, one of the largest lakes in the Welsh hills, and at an official depth of 190 feet, one of the deepest. I remembered winters and wet springs long gone, when crossing the causeway (breached and uneven in those days) meant wading waist- or chest-deep in freezing water at times – something better undertaken on the return journey than in the setting-out – or a very long diversion round the lake shore. In recent years the causeway has been built up again and repaired, and the lake level too is lower than it often was twenty or thirty years ago after prolonged spells of wet weather. You might be inclined to ponder whether this is from natural or unnatural causes, depending on your understanding and acceptance of 'climate change', but in fact it's just the result of a deliberate lowering by the National Park authority of the lake's overflow level, in response to the former flooding problem.

Two hundred years ago, in Thomas Pennant's day, the lake was considerably more substantial than it is now, but the mine captains at Glaslyn commissioned David Jones of the Prince Llewelyn Hotel in Beddgelert to drain off sixteen feet from it. His doing so revealed a remarkable archaeological curiosity – a Bronze Age craft, a dugout canoe that was sold as Roman to a Dr. Hughes from Ardudwy for the sum of £5, and that was still being auctioned around the gentry of the area eighty years later for vastly greater sums. When Pennant came to Llyn Llydaw in the 1770s, he reached it from Nant Gwynen by way of Cwm Dyli, where haymaking was in progress, and the shepherd in his *hafod* [11] entertained him with curds and whey, much as a nomadic Tibetan yak-herder might do for a twenty-

---

11   A summer-pasturing hut – transhumance lingered on as widespread practice in the Welsh hills until the early nineteenth century and those pernicious examples of wholesale land-theft by the gentry called the Enclosure Acts.

first century Western tourist itinerant in that country. Pennant described Llydaw in the following terms:

> . . . a fine lake, winding beneath the rocks, and vastly indented by rocky projections, here and there jutting into it. In it was one little island, the haunt of black-backed Gulls, which breed here, and, alarmed by such unexpected visitants, broke the silence of this sequestered place by their deep screams[12]

Herring gulls – latterly one of the mountain's permanent avian residents – inhabit here now, drifting low over the grey waves, their skirling cries re-echoing between Crib Goch and the 'vast, mural steeps' (Pennant's phrase) of Y Lliwedd. I much prefer the old, evocative name of 'silver-mew' for these handsome, resourceful birds. Hopeful of food, they kept me company as I hurried on up the abrupt rise to Glaslyn. Here's Pennant again:

> This brought us into the horrible crater, immediately beneath the great precipice of the Wyddfa, in which is lodged Ffynnon Las.[13] Its situation is the most dreadful . . . the waters had a greenish cast; but what is very singular, the rocks reflected into them seemed varied with stripes of the richest colours, like the most beautiful lute-strings; and changed almost to infinity. Here we observed the Wheat-ear, a small and seemingly tender bird; and yet it is almost the only small one . . . that frequents these heights: the reason evidently is the want of food.[14]

---

12 Pennant, op. cit. II. 180.
13 The old name for Glaslyn – the green lake – was Llyn Ffynnon Las – lake of the green spring.
14 Pennant, op. cit. II. 180–181.

Spot on cue, as I hopped from stone to stone across the outfall from the lake, a wheatear flitted and dipped across the grass slope in front of me like some revisiting and tutelary spirit, braiding my consciousness of this scene together with that of the great eighteenth-century naturalist and antiquary. After watching it for a while I stirred myself and set to climbing the ridge marked on the map as Cribau, but generally known to hill-goers as Y Gribin – one of the shorter and less well-known scrambling ascents on Snowdon, but pleasing, well-situated and worthwhile, with taxing and exposed moments here and there if you seek them out, and a particularly fine profile when seen from Glaslyn. The reflection of its ribbed risings in the lake below are Pennant's 'beautiful lute-strings'.

As a way to the summit, Y Gribin is hopeless, stranding you, as it does, on Bwlch y Saethau beneath the horrid top section of the Watkin Path – one of those few ascents on Snowdon which no one with foreknowledge and of sound mind would ever countenance.[15] But as an approach to Y Lliwedd (along with which it can be used for a short afternoon's circuit), and as a part of this circumambulation of the mountain, Y Gribin comes into its playful and enjoyable own. Put all the best bits on Helvellyn's Swirral and Striding Edges together, add in Sharp Edge from Blencathra, tilt them up twenty degrees, throw in a few scrambling moves as technical as any on Crib Goch opposite, take in the views to the left across the thousand-foot face of Lliwedd and a surprisingly rapid degree of exposure as you climb, and you would have a fair comparison. This is from

15   The upper section of the Watkin Path is also one of the winter accident black-spots on Snowdon, and there have been fatalities here over the years. In fairness, the section from Bwlch y Saethau up to the Bwlch Main ridge has been substantially improved in recent times. There are still ways I would find far preferable for reaching the top.

an entirely unbiased Welsh perspective, of course, and always remembering that you are not talking about the major league of mountain ridges in Eryri here.[16]

When my morning's sport was at all too sudden an end and the ridge gave out onto Bwlch y Saethau, I paced on through the sheaved flakes of rock along the saddle to Bwlch Ciliau. Here the Watkin Path angles off west on its long descent towards Cwm Tregalan before turning south and slanting across the skirts of Lliwedd into Cwm Llan. (This should really be Cwm Llam or Cwm Llem – the cwm of the leap, after the Afon Llem – leaping river – which is very apt for this cascading mountain stream; but since I've promised not to hold forth again at length about OS map names I'll leave the matter for some inevitable future Welsh Assembly official inquiry into colonialist attitudes of the Ordnance Survey as they affect Wales, at which I look forward to offering testimony.) The landscape here – Bwlch y Saethau, Cwm Tregalan, Y Lliwedd and Dinas Emrys down in the lower reaches of Nant Gwynen – is replete with Arthurian associations, which I'll come to in the chapter on folklore and legend. My way diverged to climb up onto Y Lliwedd's spiky dragon's crest, with Llŷn – the long

---

16   Don't worry too much about this flyting if you're a devotee of Cumbria – between your tribe and that of *Cambria* there has long existed a mutually amused antipathy. Remember Wordsworth's barbed assessment of Llyn Dinas in Nant Gwynen as 'the only Welsh lake which has any pretensions to compare with one of our own'? But then, despite all that hanging 'Above the raven's nest, by knots of grass | And half-inch fissures in the slippery rock | But ill sustained, and almost (as it seemed) | Suspended by the blast which blew amain', and despite his most profound mystical epiphany's taking place on the Bwlch Main ridge, William didn't quite make it to the top of Snowdon. So perhaps in this comment he was just expending some of the rancour consequent on that disappointment? And perhaps it's true that for all the shortcomings of its hills, Cumbria's lakes are at least rather *prettier* on the whole? I'd almost be prepared to concede that point.

western peninsula of Wales – far down there, curving gently as though to entice the sun in each day's decline, for the sun always shines on Llŷn.

On my left hand, the imposing buttresses above Llydaw were already enveloped in early afternoon shadow as I peered across from Lliwedd Bach after jumping, bounding and slithering down the stratified runnels from the East Peak. These buttresses were the birthplace of rock-climbing as a sport in Britain, and the huge ribbed and grooved, quartz-speckled north-east face of Y Lliwedd was associated with all the eminent names of its early days before the Great War. If you arrive at the col by Lliwedd Bach, having climbed up from Cwm Merch below and to the south, the sudden view down into Cwm Dyli and across to Glaslyn, with Clogwyn y Garnedd, Garnedd Ugain[17] and Crib Goch sentinel all around, is as startling and dramatic as any on the mountain. I left it behind and slipped down from the edge of the ridge, picked a careful path southwards by trickles of red scree among the sparse turf and the heather and made my way past trial levels, rifts and disused adits – a dangerous area, this, in mist – of Cwm Merch copper mine. The dismantled water wheel of this latter marks the high point and conclusion of one of the quiet delights of Snowdon – the softly-graded and perfectly-engineered green track that winds back down through stands of Scots Pine to cross the Afon Llem by a single-span stone bridge a mile or so above Pont Bethania.

The Afon Merch, which drains this cwm throughout its short course, is one of the loveliest of Welsh hill streams: winding, boisterous, jewelled with pools and brilliant falls. In

---

17   This is the correct name for the summit usually referred to as Crib y Ddysgl – that name properly belonging to the ridge rising from Bwlch Coch to Garnedd Ugain.

its lower reaches it flounces about, headlong and impetuous, in a series of torrents and cataracts through open woodland of ash and holly, the ground verdant, soft with vivid mosses, starred with wood anemones at the proper seasons, the branches of the trees too a luminous green, and the more open places shimmering with bluebells before the bracken croziers out across them in spring and cloaks them in summer verdure or autumn fire. This gnarled wood has a strong sense of enchantment. If Merlin were to appear here, as Welsh legend recounts that he did at Dinas Emrys, a mile down the valley from where you reach Nant Gwynen, I think it would scarcely be a surprise.[18] On this lower stretch of the river too you can find Ogof y Gŵr Blewog – the cave of the hairy man, which is another theme we'll be taking up in the chapter on the mountain's folklore. For today, I kept to the old green way, gently descending, watched warily by flocks of magnificent wild goats, the original inhabitants of these hills, that have roamed here for 10,000 years. When George Borrow passed through Eryri in 1854 he was moved to remark on what 'beautiful creatures they were, white and black with long silky hair, and long upright horns. They were of large size, and very different in appearance from the common race.'

Sadly, in our conservation-conscious times not everyone is so appreciative, and foremost in denunciations of these gorgeous rascals are the National Park 'conservationists' themselves. The goats' existence is now threatened by authority. Massive secret culls have taken place, notably in 2007 using official marksmen. Their crimes, apparently, and ones for which they

---

18 The 1981 John Boorman film *Excalibur*, with Nicol Williamson as a thoroughly eccentric Merlin, in fact was filmed in part in the woods of Nant Gwynen. And it has to be said that the visuals are the film's strongest point – its plot, characterisation and historicity are best classified under 'codswallop'.

had been tried and privily sentenced so that their numbers could be officially decimated or worse, are: their propensity for raiding the inappropriate cottage gardens of incomers to the area's valleys; their ability to climb to the cliff ledges where the rarest plants grow (though in fact they're very seldom to be seen there, the richest grazing being elsewhere); and their interference with the National Park Authority's managed woodland regeneration schemes. Personally, I'd rather goats than hollyhocks, countryside managers, impenetrable brush, and prissy Surrey retirees. The sight of these bold and playful anarchists of the hills is always a gladdening experience for me. The career-conservationists who can countenance the slaughter of indigenous species are, to my mind, the ones with cloven hooves – not to mention brimstone on their breath.

As if empathising with my thoughts, the goats wisely shunned my human presence, melting mysteriously into the trees and leaving only a healthy, animal pungency in the air. I crossed the clapper bridge, and sat quietly for a while before the next climb, revelling in glimpses of shapely hills beyond the shaggy skylines, and the sylvan nature of this landscape south of Snowdon – so unlike the bareness of the eastern and northern slopes, or the long, rushy cwms of the western approaches. After a few minutes I ambled along a brief stretch of the Watkin Path and began the long ascending traverse to Bwlch Cwm Llan, which gives another of the unexpected vistas, at once far-flung and intimate, with which Snowdon abounds. Above you here, the ridge rising towards Yr Wyddfa – one of the best approaches to the summit, and I'd strongly advise climbing up to it by this route rather than by the Watkin Path – arches over the line of splintery, broken cliffs called Clogwyn Du to join the Beddgelert Path from Ffridd Uchaf at Bwlch Main, a narrow saddle between Cwm Clogwyn and

Cwm Tregalan which often caused consternation among the earliest visitors to Snowdon, by whom this line of ascent was much used.

From just below the *bwlch* to the west a wide track which served the small quarrying enterprises dating from the 1840s on these southern flanks of Snowdon clatters its slaty way down to Rhyd Ddu in a couple of miles, with the Eifionydd hills which so enhance the views in that direction by their shapeliness and the almost melodic notation of their outline in front. With plenty of daylight left, I thought it would be a shame not to take in the fine and neglected little peak of Yr Aran to the south, which is so prominent from Nant Gwynen and most other locations south and west of Snowdon. I left my rucksack by a rocky miniature tarn at its foot and scrambled up the ridge, choosing the most entertaining line across rocky slabs to arrive at a pleasantly aloof greensward summit, which looks down Cwellyn to the north, very blue today between its crowding hills, the west coast of Anglesey glimpsed beyond through the gap between Mynydd Mawr and Moel Eilio. Westwards and close at hand were the elegant ridges surrounding Cwm Pennant, the hidden valley where I lived and worked as a shepherd for some of the most memorable years of my life in the 1970s – living out a youthful version of the famous lines from the sentimental early twentieth-century lyricist Eifion Wyn:

Pam, Arglwydd, y gwnaethost Gwm Pennant mor dlws
A bywyd hen fugail mor fyr?
(Why, lord, did you make Cwm Pennant so lovely
And an old shepherd's life so short?)

This was during the declining years of an industry that had been crucial and ubiquitous throughout the Welsh uplands for

200 years, defining their culture and way of life and preserving a folkloric texture here that had echoed perhaps through millennia.

To the north-east, rising beyond Llyn Gwynen and misleadingly dull in profile from this angle, was Moel Siabod – best ascended by its eastern ridge of Daear Ddu, which leads directly to the top – another of the great outlier-viewpoints among these hills of Eryri, from which the sight of Yr Wyddfa against the sunset is one of the perfect moments the region can give. Straight below me to the south-east as I rested on top of Yr Aran was Cwm y Bleiddiaid, and I could see another cwm of that name below the summit cliffs of Moel Hebog westerly.

'Valley of wolves' is the meaning of the name, as though to lend credence to the spurious legend of the faithful, wolf-killing hound Gelert which a profiteering innkeeper at the turn of the eighteenth century attached to his home village of Beddgelert – even going so far as to provide the fictitious dog with a grave for tourists' delectation. This in its turn gave the habitually robust George Borrow another pretext for the use of a delicate irony that permeates his writing and is so seldom perceived as such: 'Such is the legend, which, whether it is true or not, is singularly beautiful and affecting.'

Cwm y Bleiddiaid below me as I looked south-east from Yr Aran is – though the National Trust's recent acquisition of Craflwyn Hall has resulted in more visitors being urged in this direction, and despite its ease of accessibility along the old mine-track from Hafod y Porth farm – one of the loneliest and most affecting valleys on Snowdon. Just as with the cwm on Moel Hebog opposite, imagine that chance and a summer's evening were to find you here alone? It would feel then like a right re-assertion of the elemental landscape if the dusk howl of a wolf were to raise the echoes as well as the hairs on the back of your neck; or if you were to glimpse one like a flicker of grey ash drifting through the boulders and the heather. Perhaps, with sheep-farming in Wales now in such terminal decline, we should urge their reintroduction here, as has been achieved with some success in Wyoming's Yellowstone National Park. The goat population would then be 'managed' by natural means and even the conservationists might make common cause and be appeased, whilst the tourist potential would be immense and (obviously a good thing) the Health & Safety Executive driven to terminal apoplexy. Though it would only take the demise of some favoured pug or King Charles spaniel belonging to one of those aforementioned Nant Gwynen Surrey retirees for the culling, of a different species this time, to begin all over again.

Such wayward fancies occupied my mind as I skittered back by the ridge to collect my rucksack at Bwlch Cwm Llan and saunter down the quarry track. Afternoon light was illuminating Cwm Garegog between the Allt Maenderyn and Llechog ridges, ruddying its blanched grasses and inflaming the hillside rocks. This cwm might be entirely circumscribed within popular paths, but it remains a square mountain mile of secret fascination and discreet splendour, in character quite unlike any of the other hollows of the mountain. I had intended continuing down the easy way to Rhyd Ddu, paying my respects there to the old schoolhouse, which was the birthplace of the great modern Welsh-language poet of Snowdon, Sir T. H. Parry-Williams (about whom more in the chapter dealing with the literature of the mountain), and stopping for a quick pint in the Cwellyn Arms before threading my way along more quarry pathways around Clogwyn y Gwin – the son of which farm was notable as having fired the last shot at the Battle of

Waterloo. (The story runs that after the battle was over, he had been lying among the heaps of dead and dying soldiers with a musket-ball in his kneecap when he saw an old woman moving about nearby, robbing the corpses of their valuables, and despatching those who still groaned and breathed with a hammer she carried. She glanced across at him and nodded as though to say 'I'll deal with you presently', so he raised himself on an elbow, took careful aim with his musket, loosed off a round and she went head-over-heels dead – 'and that was the last shot to be fired at Waterloo'.)

In remembering the tale and wondering about its provenance,[19] I'd arrived at Pen-ar-lôn, where the path from Ffridd Uchaf crosses the one I was following, so I sat down for a rest, drank water and ate chocolate, and on impulse, seduced by the light, decided to follow the Rhyd Ddu path towards Snowdon from here as far as the spur above Llyn Nadroedd, then drop down past the steep little rocky bluffs on the north-western gable of the Llechog ridge into Cwm Clogwyn, a place very few visit even today. Its trio of shallow tarns – Llynnau Nadroedd, Coch and Glas – snakes' lake, red lake and green lake – are perfect swimming places, and beneath the ridge the fine and unjustly neglected cliff of Llechog curves round the back of the cwm as if to give them privacy.

I'd long had an interest in this cliff, and it was poignant to revisit it. In 1970, when I was working on the climbing guidebook to *Cwm Silyn and Cwellyn*, writing up the rock-

---

19 It was first collected by the folklorist William Jones (his bardic name was Bleddyn – 'wolf cub' – which makes a neat connection back to the previous theme) and published in an article in *Y Brython*, the notable literary and antiquarian journal which was responsible for the preservation of a great deal of the material I'll be drawing on particularly in the next chapter, in 1861. So William Jones had it from the protagonist in his old age as first-hand recollection.

climbs here had been part of my remit. The cliff's best buttress – a slabby red tower 400 feet high that J. M. Archer Thomson, the pioneer of climbing here before the Great War, had referred to as 'the gaunt, red crag' and described as 'quite impossible', was then still unclimbed. I came here with Nick Estcourt, who was one of my frequent and favourite climbing partners, endlessly enthusiastic and fiercely disputatious, in those years before his death in an avalanche on K2 in 1978. We had lazed around, swum in the lake and climbed two pitches up the 'red crag' before a torrential cloudburst turned the rock into something like a vertical skating rink set under a waterfall and sent us scurrying for the valley. Next day we returned with a professor of mathematical logic in tow in case the problems we might face required a different perspective, and in damp conditions we finished the line – 'climbing days, happy, more or less!'

Round from the cliffs of Llechog, the back wall of the cwm, which is the huge and broken west face of Snowdon, under hard snow in the best of winter conditions and the shadowy blue chill of morning can give long, straightforward and characterful climbs where you choose your own line and never see another climber. (Better to come here than to queue for the popular lines on the Trinity face of Clogwyn yr Wyddfa, where everyone goes and that will invariably be hacked to pieces under these conditions, your ascent nothing more than a plod up other people's pick-marks). The lines on the west face lead straight to the summit from a surprising direction. I'd been here several times in those rare years when good winter-climbing conditions prevailed, and had all this texture of memory from Cwm Clogwyn to sustain me over the long, rough mile from Llyn y Nadroedd to my next objective, Bwlch Cwm Brwynog. By the time I arrived there, aching and bemired in the fading light, I was beginning to regret the choice of route. But once I'd skirted the margins of Llyn Ffynnon y Gwas, crossed the Snowdon Ranger Path, which follows the west ridge of the mountain to the summit from here, and gone through the *bwlch* under Moel Cynghorion to drop down on the far side, Maen Du'r Arddu dominating the view in front, the terrain eased. The east-facing crags of Clogwyn Llechwedd Llo that so impressed George Borrow when he climbed Snowdon in 1854 were deep in shadow, which was stretching too across the rushy bed of Cwm Brwynog and surging up the farther slope to reach the mountain railway as I contoured round to reach Afon Arddu, feeling distinctly better now about route and terrain. I boulder-hopped across the outflow from Llyn Du'r Arddu and strolled across the springy turf on its northern shore.

This was to arrive at my day's journey's end, and come to a place where I'd often slept out over the years. I looked around for a comfortable stretch of grass to spread out my mat and sleeping bag, found one with a convenient boulder nearby as backrest, and set the stove to boil a kettle in the most dramatic and powerfully beautiful mountain setting not just on Snowdon, but perhaps in Wales or even (and if you have not been here yet, then rest assured that this is not simply hyperbole) in the whole of Britain. There is a pseudo-legend frequently recounted about Cwm Cau on Cader Idris, forty miles to the south: that to sleep there alone is to wake either as poet or madman, so sublime are the surroundings. It was applied to that location by the pious, and to a modern ear quite excruciating, early nineteenth-century poet Felicia Hemans, who had appropriated or purloined it from its original setting – here, beneath Clogwyn Du'r Arddu, the finest cliff in Britain. Delectable mountain though Cader Idris undoubtedly is, it is here by Llyn Du'r Arddu that the story feels as though it properly belongs.

There are few places I know where the affective power of landscape is more concentrated. To come to rest in the quiet hours by the shore of Llyn Du'r Arddu, the last clacking and huffing trains having run, the late few stragglers down from the ridges, the low sun streaming through the *bwlch*, the magnificent cliff seeming almost to absorb its suffused light until the rock begins to glow, is to experience the best that our British hills can offer – 'the lost traveller's dream under the hill'.[20] I made tea, prepared food, and ate as the detail of the rock walls across the water faded and the milky shadow crept stealthily around the cwm. I remembered blue-skied, vigorous days of my long climbing years on those sheer and intricate walls and slabs and arêtes, and the challenge of doing them in better style and with less aid than the more gifted but less technologically advantaged climbers who were my predecessors, and who became in many cases my older friends. I relived the climbs I'd done here with my son Will in his teenage years, before he went on to become one of the pre-eminent climbers of his own day, and recalled too his account of coming up here in the mist, alone with no one else on the crag, and ascending unroped and alone the most notable of the routes of my generation.

Beyond his loss, there was the other grief, too, at friends' deaths here, the agonising moments when their consciousnesses were snuffed out and they were absorbed into the great stillness this place holds. By the time I'd pulled my sleeping bag up to my chin and settled to sleep among all these silent echoes, a bright half-moon had sailed above the eastern ridge and was silvering the sheer walls and sheaves of overlapping

---

20 The phrase is the concluding line from Blake's eerie last poem, 'Truly, my Satan, thou art but a dunce'.

slabs opposite, setting a mercury sheen across the rippling surface of the lake, and transmuting the scene to something still of this world, yet apart and grand and perfectly magical.

I woke neither poet nor madman to a sky of pale azure and a harsh dawn chorus. Close at hand, a wren was chittering away loudly from a rock, flicking its tail in agitation at my intrusion on its habitual spider-hunting ground. High above, meanwhile, the high squealing cries of a pair of choughs were punctuated by a raven's deep guttural notes. Over on Clogwyn Coch – the broken, mine-riddled cliff below the railway track – battle had been joined, the ravens playful and opportunistic as they swooped and dived around the entrance to an old adit in the crags where the choughs had their nest. To and fro went the tumbling aerial skirmish, fierce protective instinct of the smaller birds eventually winning the day as the ravens sauntered away, honking as though in sardonic laughter, to search for easier prey. And I make no apologies for anthropomorphizing. Anyone who has studied ravens for long will come away with the impression of intelligence, calculation and a sense of malicious fun manifest in their behaviour.

The ravens having soared away over the ridge, soon one of the choughs was feeding on the slope to the left of my bivouac, probing the turf intently with its curved red bill. Across the lake, from the opposite direction to last night and with a clearer light, the sun was again illuminating the cliff, every feature of it standing out with such clarity that I could see actual handholds and remember the feel of them in some cases from over forty years before. There was the quartz seam, glistening, that Ray Evans and I had used to bypass the old lasso-move in making the first free ascent of Troach, one of the most delectable sections of steep wall-climbing in Wales. There were the dimplings in the pale surface of the first long pitch of White Slab, that many have argued to be the most exquisite and classic of all rock-climbs in Britain.

For a period of sixty years, from 1926 to 1986, this was the stage where every advance in rock-climbing history was enacted. That's material for the chapter on rock-climbing, but seeing the great cliff afresh in the first light, I could feel again the magnetic appeal that made this place the lodestone. It has an extraordinary, architectonic balance to it. It's not the biggest cliff in Wales by any means – the vertical height is only 500 feet or so – but the exposures of rock on it are so clean and continuous, and the structure so aesthetically satisfying. The great bulk of the West Buttress is cradled within the bold diagonals of Eastern and Western Terraces (the former of which, in 1798 by the Reverends Bayley Williams and Bingley, is generally accepted as the first recorded rock-climb in Wales), and its mass is scored by slant-wise overlapping slabs, so that the whole weight of it seems in imminent danger of toppling leftwards, against which eventuality it is supported by the solid, triangular bastion of the East Buttress. Right and left, more exposures of bare rock act as balance to the impeccable centrepiece. This is the masterpiece of natural rock-architecture in Britain.

It is also an astonishingly clear illustration of the evolution of Snowdon, the succession of all the major systems on the mountain apparent in its plan-like faulted synclinal structure. A detailed exposition of the mountain's geology is beyond both my expertise and this book's purpose – you would, after all, hardly begin a biography with a lengthy exposition of its subject's DNA, and if any reader wants a more detailed explanation of the geology of Snowdon, then the bibliography offers relevant guidance.

Having said that, a brief and summary digression on this

theme is perhaps appropriate here, at Clogwyn Du'r Arddu, where the evidence of geological process is most startling. It's worth remembering too that for the founding fathers of the science of geology, Snowdonia was the main attraction. Here all the pioneers, from Darwin and Sedgwick to Ramsay and Murchison, sharpened their eyes, wielded their hammers, attuned their intelligence and came to the conclusions on which our understanding of mountain formation is based to this day. The basic concepts relevant to Snowdon, and the key to knowing how the mountains of Eryri were formed, lie in what are known as the Snowdon Syncline and the Harlech-Rhinog Anticline (or more usually the Harlech Dome), of which present-day Snowdon, having formed the bottom of the syncline which carries its name, is a resistant remnant left at the foot of the northern slope of this latter feature after the erosion over aeons of the capping Ordovician rocks. The geologist F. J. North explained this paradox of 'what was formerly at the bottom now being at the top' with his customary clarity in the following manner in his essay from the first *New Naturalist* volume on the region:

> It may at first seem a matter for surprise that high mountains should be part of trough-like folds or that their summits should, as in the case of Snowdon, possess a basin-like or … synclinal structure. An arch-like (or anticlinal) structure would seem more appropriate to a mountain and a synclinal structure to a valley or other area of low ground. There are, of course, anticlinal hills and mountains and synclinal valleys or belts of lower ground, but quite often – and our area provides excellent examples – it is the reverse that applies. The reason is that when the rocks are folded (due … to the operation of

compressional forces), those at the crests of the folds tend to be stretched and to find relief from the strain by cracking, so that they are weakened and more easily worn away. The rocks in the trough, on the other hand, are squeezed and rendered harder and more compact; they are, in consequence, better able to resist erosion and so tend to remain as high ground when the rocks of the anticlines have been worn to lower levels. The longer an area of folded rocks has been subject to erosion the more likely are synclinal structures to be characteristic of its elevated regions.[21]

As an even simpler reiteration of North's point, when Joseph Cradock toured Wales in 1776, his guide remarked to him, 'Aye, master, this must have been an ancient country indeed, for you see, it is worn down to the very stones.' In essence, that's the fact of the matter. The geologist, by widespread, careful and laborious measurement of the dip of strata and analysis of rock types, can explain the story of the mountains' formation. Thereafter, the tale is one of the forces of weathering acting upon these products of the earth's beginnings, its heavings and jostlings, strainings and settlings. And in the case of Snowdon, the defining and concluding factor in the present appearance of the mountain – human activity aside, which is our principal concern in this book – has been the Great Ice Age of the Pleistocene era, which began a million or more years ago in the yesterday of geological time, and through the agents of ice and snow carved the mountain into its present form, created its cirques and arêtes, its cliffs and moraines. Crib Goch and Glaslyn, Cwm Brwynog and the Llanberis Pass, Llyn Du'r Arddu and the story-haunted mounds of Cwm Tregalan all

<hr />

21   F. J. North, Bruce Campbell, Richenda Scott, *Snowdonia: The National Park of North Wales* (Collins, 1949), pp. 15–16.

owe their existence to the action of the glaciers throughout the Pleistocene.

So, too, have successive ice ages bequeathed us the relict arctic-alpine flora which is one of the subtle glories of Snowdon and which, having breakfasted and packed up my rucksack, I now went in search of, for Clogwyn Du'r Arddu is one of the best places to find the rarities. Not that a cold May was the perfect time to find the plant that bears the mountain's name. The Snowdon Lily is a delicate, lilac-veined white flower, difficult to distinguish when not in flower from the sparse grasses and fescues of the few ledges on which it grows. When I reached the ledge for which I was heading – a steep scramble of twenty feet or so up from the path, and invisible from it – the plants were there, but weeks away from flowering.

So too was the roseroot on wet rocks a little way along the cliff, and the alpine cinquefoil, and chickweed across the silted shallows of the lake. But on wet slabs right by the path starry saxifrage was blooming in profusion, and on a favourite dark boulder near the entrance to an old mine adit that Bill Condry – who was one of Britain's finest field naturalists and the best of all writers on the natural history of Wales – had shown me years ago, the big, bold flowers of purple saxifrage, startlingly vibrant in this drab setting, entirely covered one side whilst the other was bedecked with lavish clumps of moss campion. Delighted by them, and by the memory of Bill's friendship and his presence here, I zigzagged up the grass slope to reach the railway track at Clogwyn Station and followed the Llanberis Track as it diverged from the rails towards the rim of Cwm Glas.

This is often heavily corniced in winter, and potentially dangerous – but less so than the innocent-looking railway track, which can be lethal when banked out with snow. One particularly terrible accident here in the 1960s saw a group of schoolboys slide one after another down the convex, steepening slope to plunge over the 400-foot-high cliffs of Clogwyn Coch beneath. There have been other fatalities more recently at the same place. Warily, therefore, I kept to the rim of Cwm Glas and negotiated a descent of the shallow-angled slabs that lead down from the rim to arrive at tiny, rock-bound Llyn Bach beneath Clogwyn y Ddysgl.

These complex northern slopes and cliffs of Snowdon that fall away into Cwm Glas and the Pass of Llanberis are a hazardous place where precise knowledge and good route-finding are essential. The truth of that came back to me as I sat by the little lake remembering the story of Colette Fleetwood, a mature student who was brought up here by the leader of a group of students from the University of the West of England in Bristol one January day in 1994. Conditions were bad, with snow on the hills, low cloud and a high, gusting wind. From Llyn Bach, the leader took a compass bearing to the summit of Garnedd Ugain – an incomprehensible decision in a place like this – and then walked his group of complete novices blindly along it into the mist.

The bearing led them into the steep, broken, snow-covered ground to the left of the classic winter climb of Parsley Fern Gully – terrain fit and proper only for competent, well-equipped and experienced winter-mountaineers. Soon two of the students slipped and fell, one of them disappearing away down into the mist. Offers of help from nearby climbers who were carrying the right equipment of ice-axe, rope and crampons, and who were heading for Parsley Fern Gully, were incomprehensibly rejected by the leader.

The party pressed on, their terror and the drop increasing. On the slope approaching the summit, Colette Fleetwood

– an intelligent, beautiful, adventurous young woman in her mid twenties with her life ahead of her – was plucked from her kicked steps in the hard snow by a gale-force, gusting wind. She went hurtling back down into the cwm below. Her body was found by a mountain rescue party later that night beneath the cliffs. She had died of multiple injuries. I appeared for the family as an expert witness at her inquest in Llandudno. The coroner, faced with repeated objections from a phalanx of solicitors representing the university, which itself might have been open to charges of neglect, allowed little discussion and only the barest testimony. The family, bereft and uncomprehending, were left with the stark verdict of 'death by misadventure'.

It was, to my mind, something other than that, its circumstances thrusting a vexed salient into the whole notion of group and individual responsibility in the hills. I have seldom felt with greater force either the moral complexities that can weigh even in the supposedly simple contexts of the outdoors, or the moral bankruptcy of legal process and many of its practitioners. Mountains do not bear signs that say, 'Whatever your leaders say, you travel here at your own risk.' Perhaps, in a world grown litigious, they should (though litigation would never compensate a parent for the loss of a child in circumstances like these). This, if you like, is the moral counterpart to the physical landscape of the hills, and one we do well always to bear in mind when we venture there. Your responsibility here is to yourself. If you take upon yourself the welfare of others in this environment, then look continually and with your full attention to the consequences ...

I shouldered my rucksack and traversed round and down beneath the Parson's Nose into upper Cwm Glas, with its little lake, Llyn Glas, on the island in which grow stunted pines, shiny and fertilised from the herring gulls which, although they throng the summit in search of tourist scraps, choose to nest and roost here. Beyond it, above the glacier-smoothed ribs and hummocks of Cwm Glas a path traversing across a stretch of scree slope, neither very loose nor very long, led me to the start of Crib Goch's North Ridge. But I was going to leave that for today, so instead I slipped round the corner, with Cwm Beudy Mawr opening up below me, and followed what was once a sheep-trod but is increasingly a thoroughfare beloved of Mountain Leader training and assessment groups across the mountain's east face to Bwlch Moch.

As I sat by the latter mustering the resolve to face the crowds at Gorffwysfa, two or three parties engrossed in map and compass seemed to be intent on heading in the direction from which I'd come. I wished them good luck and a safe passage and sped off down the Pig Track,[22] the Llanberis Pass stretching away to the north-west beneath me and the huge boulders by Pont Cromlech diminutive from this height, to Gorffwysfa, passing on my way the bluff through which the National Park Authority blasted an easier way a couple of decades ago to facilitate access to the mountain – raising a furore in the outdoor and local press by doing so and raising an interesting line of speculation as to how far this reasoning

---

22 Often rendered as the Pyg or P.y.G. Track, from some supposed connection to the Pen-y-Gwryd Hotel, from which it does not start and which it predates. The name – the origin of which is slightly mysterious – seems most likely to have derived from Bwlch Moch – the pass of the pigs, through which it passes. However, this too may be a misapprehension – Bwlch Moch could also, appropriately in this case, mean the first or soonest pass, rather than being a reference to the Twrch Trwyth, or other matter from Welsh legendry. Whatever the truth (or *trwyth*) of the matter, Pyg Track is clearly wrong, so for the purposes of this book the name is Pig Track – all of which confusion is an endearingly frequent trait in Welsh toponymy.

can be taken. Wheelchair access to all points on Snowdon? Jonathan Swift could give you an apt view on that.

A few minutes more along the 'improved' path and I'd completed this eccentric fifteen-mile and two-day circuit of our hill, which will I hope have engraved a sense of its layout into your imagination for you to consult in chapters to come, as well as hinting at its richness and variety of interest and association. To quote T. H. Parry-Williams, the poet from the school-house of Rhyd Ddu, '*Mae lleisiau a drychiolaethau ar hyd y lle*' – there are voices and phantoms throughout the place. So now let's move on and listen to these, in the proper detail they deserve.

2

Faeries, Giants, Wizards and Sleeping Knights

Everything is older than we think. — W. G. HOSKINS

After geology and geomorphology, which we touched on in the previous chapter with perhaps as much detail as a non-specialist account requires, comes prehistory, the disciplines for the exploration of which include paleontology, archaeology and perhaps even Jungian psychology. Trailing at some chronological distance behind these are the beginnings of history itself, and its looser associates of the oral tradition and folklore. There was an idea prevalent at one time in the study of history (I hardly need point out that this was long ago, and even by the mid twentieth century the notion had been thoroughly and deservedly discredited), that it was ultimately dependent on 'written sources', in which could be found, to quote R. G. Collingwood, 'ready-made statements asserting or implying alleged facts belonging to the subject in which the historian was interested'.[23]

If we were to apply this outdated formula to our consideration of Snowdon's story, it would force us to a conclusion that

---

23   R. G. Collingwood, *The Idea of History* (Oxford University Press, 1961), p. 277. A case could be made for the popular television series, with its incessant appetite for the sound-bite and inability to cope with reasoned and protracted argument, providing a Trojan Horse for the return of this approach, but that's best left for the historians to argue out among themselves.

the history of the mountain proper only begins some time in the late twelfth or early thirteenth centuries, and even then in the most fragmentary fashion through the grants of land within defined boundaries, the names of which are archaic but recognizable versions of ones still in currency – 'Grib Goch' (Crib Goch), for example, or 'Crombroinok Hir' (Cwm Brwynog).

It is fortunate that we have those aforementioned parallel disciplines and associated areas of study to give us some sense of what took place before recorded history. Though it may be the case that they leave us with a remarkably misty atmosphere, at the same time they provide us with source material that is richly suggestive and evocative. Like the glimpses down through rifts in the cloud from the summit on one of those late-autumn or spring days when temperature inversions leave Yr Wyddfa islanded in a cloud-sea, the details thus isolated, the forms half-perceived or barely suggested, the dissociated epic scraps that have survived time's scatterings, seem to resonate the more truly with the landscape. However apparently meagre, these fragments and glimmers are the sole surviving expression of the earliest phases in the human dimensions of its story.

The fact remains that physical evidence for human activity on Snowdon – not just before the Christian era but even up to the late Middle Ages – is, relative to more seaward landscapes in quite close proximity, distinctly slight. By comparison with the proliferation of signs pointing to early agricultural settlement along the western flanks of the Eifionydd hills, for example, or the extraordinary concentrations of stone circles, hut circles, burial chambers, field systems, pathways, axe factories and copper mines on the northern foothills of the Carneddau and around Conwy Bay, Snowdon itself in the

Neolithic, Bronze and Iron Ages would seem to have been far less densely populated.

It has to be said that this is not a particularly surprising conclusion. The seaward hills of Eryri were, it is true, the scene of considerable human activity beginning perhaps 5,000 years ago. But even given the much more favourable climate[24] of that epoch compared either to our contemporary one or that which prevailed for perhaps five millennia in the wake of the Late Glacial Period of 12,000-8,000 BCE, then as now the ice-scoured cirques and rocky crests of Snowdon would not have appeared as a particularly hospitable domestic and agrarian landscape. Nor would it have been one easily accessible through the densely wooded valleys of the period, at a time when the treeline lay at between six and seven hundred metres – an altitude sufficient to reach into most of the high *cymoedd* on the mountain.

To set the stage on which the human drama of Snowdon can commence its enactment, we need now to provide some of the evidence uncovered by the minute and arduous labour and intelligent conjecture of the archaeologists,[25] which has served to paint a vivid backcloth of human migration, tradition, ritual practice, industry and settlement (all of which earnest practical and scholarly endeavour will bring us in due course to the land of the fairies).

---

24   This balmy and temperate weather is estimated to have lasted from 7000 to 2000 BCE, from the Mesolithic through to a time of deteriorating conditions in the Late Bronze and Early Iron Ages.

25   Foremost among those working in our geographical area of interest for the last thirty years has been the important pioneering rock-climber from the 1960s, Peter Crew, who we will meet in that context in the appropriate later chapter. He was, until his retirement in 2007, the Archaeology Officer for the Snowdonia National Park Authority, and his work particularly on early metalworking techniques has been of international importance.

It used to be thought that the prehistory of Wales consisted of successive invasions of incoming peoples from Europe and particularly from the Danube Basin, where Celtic culture appears to have taken root at Hallstatt and developed and spread throughout the Iron Age to its full flowering in the exquisite metalwork of the craftsmen of La Tène. It was thence disseminated throughout Gaul, eventually reaching Wales in the centuries immediately preceding the Christian era and leaving its significant mark there. However, the interpretation now generally held, and derived from assessments of the archaeological discoveries of the last several decades, scales down the tidal nature of that model, and rather than mass invasions posits successive waves of migration along established trading routes of the Atlantic seaboard by relatively small numbers of people into a landscape already settled and socially developed before the Roman conquest,[26] which was completed around AD 79. This may give a more accurate representation of a process which had been continuous at least from Neolithic times, and significantly, in view of the content to come in this chapter, argues a high degree of overlap and a landscape peopled simultaneously by different tribal or even racial groupings. It postulates coexistence, mutually beneficial trading links, possible absorption and intermarriage, along with the importation of technical innovations in metalwork, agriculture and animal husbandry.

All this bears on the life story of our mountain in the following way. The tensions and conflicting demands of increasing numbers and different 'tribal' groupings, ultimately inhabiting a landscape at a time when climate change towards

---

26   An excellent popular account of this process is given by Barry Cunliffe, *Facing the Ocean: The Atlantic and its Peoples* (Oxford University Press, 2001).

the end of the Medieval Warm Period was diminishing its potential as agricultural resource, formed a complex matrix. Out of these there developed the recurrent, stylised and intensely mysterious expressions in those repositories of folk-memory which are folk-tale, myth and legend. In their turn, the matter of these became not only indissociable from Snowdon in the local imagination, but also to an exceptional degree at a much later period through literature. The literary efforts of such as Nennius and Geoffrey of Monmouth (the latter our first historical novelist, in the view of many) were crucial to the flowering of imaginative literature throughout Europe in the centuries immediately preceding the Renaissance. But all this is highly conceptual, and we need to embroider it more specifically now into the fabric and design of our mountain.

This is where our problems begin, because early evidence of human activity on Snowdon, as has been implied above, is marked by its relative paucity compared even to immediately surrounding areas. Moel Hebog, for example, which lies just across the Nant Colwyn to the west of Snowdon, has, on its shoulder of Braich y Gornel above Cwm Ystradllyn, what amounts virtually to a Bronze Age townland (in the western Irish or Hebridean usage of that term). There is no comparable extant residue of past human occupation and dwelling on Snowdon itself. True, there are a few cairns,[27] hut circles and mounds of burnt stone – used, it is generally assumed, by family groups of the late Bronze Age for cooking meat – around the northernmost spur of the long ridge running down from Yr Wyddfa over Moel Cynghorion to Moel Eilio and Cefn Du. Also, there are a couple of small defensive enclosures at

---

27   Among these were Carnedd Arthur on Bwlch y Saethau and Carnedd Rhita on Yr Wyddfa, for both of which there is documentary but no surviving physical evidence for their existence.

Caer Carreg y Frân above Cwm-y-glo and Dinas Tŷ Du just outside Llanberis. These date from the Iron Age and a time in which the trend was towards living in fortified communities, of which there are several notable examples along the coastal strip – Dinas Dinorwig near Bethel and Tre'r Ceiri ('the town of giants') above Trefor prominent among them, both being clearly visible from Snowdon. And here and there, particularly in the northern and western lower *cymoedd*, can be found groups of hut circles or the remains of long huts, unexcavated and of indeterminate date, possibly medieval but which – if we bear Hoskins' motto to this chapter in mind – may also be of Iron Age or even late Bronze Age origin (the Llanberis Track up Snowdon actually cuts right through a long hut at an altitude of about 300 metres above Hebron Station in Cwm Brwynog).[28]

Even when we get to the period of the Roman occupation, and history begins to enlist the support of documentation, we hear nothing of Snowdon, and see only the marcher camp built of piled turves which encompasses within its north-eastern boundary the present-day Pen-y-Gwryd Hotel. Probability suggests this would have been used by the new governor of Britain, Agricola, in the subjugation of the dangerous and rebellious Snowdonian tribe of the Ordovices[29] in AD 77.

28 The same track, it might be noted, as it climbs higher takes you on a remarkable journey through geological time, from the light-coloured slates and sandstones near the start through darker slates and massive, fractured rocks of volcanic origin around Clogwyn station through the lavas of the last mile or so to the final slate and ash fossiliferous beds around the summit itself.
29 'Agricola decided to meet the crisis head on. After he had assembled detachments of the legions and a small band of the auxiliaries, since the Ordovices did not dare to descend to the level plain, he led his troops up the hill, himself at the head of the column, so that the rest might have equal courage to face similar danger. And, when he had destroyed almost the entire tribe, realizing full well that he must follow up his reputation . . . he decided to reduce to his power the island of Mona.' (Tacitus, *Agricola*, Chapter 18)

The lower proximity to this Roman marcher camp of the settlement of Muriau'r Dre (close to the present-day Cwm Dyli power station), with its associated folklore, is tantalising. However, stone artefacts found at Muriau'r Dre suggest for it a much earlier date than that of the Roman invasion, and the Irish element in tales from the oral tradition which also locate here may possibly signify continuing occupation after the withdrawal of the legions.

If all this scantness of material is inclining you to despair at an authenticated story ever beginning, then have patience or effect a paradigm shift, because here in Nant Gwynen is one of the most evocative and truly marvellous historical sites in the British Isles. But before we visit it, we must return to the western and northern aspects of the mountain to consider a clue which may well be a vital one to the earliest, unwritten chapters of the mountain's human story; which is also, in the sense that it transmits some kind of interaction between cultures, the only one of its kind that we have; and such reality as it may possess takes us straight into the realm of faery.[30]

---

30 I've deliberately used the version 'faery' here and in the chapter heading in order to stress the derivation from the Old French *faerie*. The usual Welsh name for the fairies – *Y Tylwyth Teg*, which translates as 'the fair people' – had no recorded use before its appearance in a *cywydd* dating from the first quarter of the fifteenth century and formerly attributed to the great lyric poet Dafydd ap Gwilym. The consensus among scholars is that the term is a misapprehended late translation of 'fairie' or 'feiri' – a Middle English borrowing from Old French – rather than a propitiatory phrase, as the Welsh one has sometimes been thought to be. Fairy scholars (and they do exist) and interpreters such as W. Y. Evans-Wentz, Marie von Frantz and C. G. Jung are apt to approach this matter rather differently, but their readings, though interesting and suggestive, are not germane to my purposes here. Which is simply to record the proliferation of 'fairy stories' that locate in the Snowdon region, and to put forward a view held by some Welsh scholars who have sought to explain recurrent themes and motifs in them. I should record here the debt I owe in trying to make sense of these stories to the pioneering work in Welsh folklore studies of W. J. Gruffydd, a quarryman's son born at Bethel,

In my time living in Cwm Pennant, which is a raven's flight of four miles to the west of Yr Wyddfa, I was befriended by a neighbour, Gwilym Morus – then an old man in his seventies, monoglot Welsh-speaking, who farmed with his brother by the most traditional means near the head of the valley. As I understood the genealogy he gave me (and you might remember Shakespeare's gentle teasing of this Welsh obsession through the person of 'Owen Glendower' in *Henry IV, Part One*), he was a relative newcomer there, his family only having lived in the valley for a matter of a century or so.[31] The farmer at the topmost holding in the cwm, Wil Braich Dinas, was, Mr Morus gave me to believe, descended from the fairies. When I asked around, everyone in the valley of Mr Morus' generation knew this – it was an accepted fact that he was one of the *Belisiaid*. And by her fireside on a winter's afternoon old Mrs Owen of Cwrt Isaf told me the story of their origins, though the name she had for them was 'Pellings'.

It was not unfamiliar to me. There are versions of it recounted from locations all along the western and northern flanks of Snowdon from Llyn y Dywarchen and Rhyd Ddu through Nant y Betws to Betws Garmon and round into Cwm Brwynog. The most famous of them in this area takes

within sight of Yr Wyddfa – particularly to his seminal edition of *Math vab Mathonwy* (University of Wales Press Board, 1928) – the Fourth Branch of the Mabinogi and a text uniquely located in the hills of Eryri; and also to his lecture delivered to the National Museum of Wales in 1950 on *Folklore and Myth in the Mabinogion* (University of Wales Press 1958).

31 Not so unusual, this, in the Welsh hills forty or more years ago. The poet Nesta Wyn Jones, who farms at Abergeirw near Trawsfynydd, told me once not entirely in jest that her family were still regarded as incomers, having arrived there 300 years before from Y Bala, fifteen miles away to the east. Now that the hills echo to the sporadic rumble of Chelsea Tractors and '*Bratiaith Saeson y De*' (see Gwenallt's '*Rhydcymerau*'), and even the loneliest farmhouses are decorated with satellite dishes, this closeness of identification with a landscape has almost entirely gone.

place at Llyn Du'r Arddu,[32] where we spent the night in Chapter One. All the classic studies of Welsh folklore cite at least some of them, and the concentration of them around Snowdon is perhaps more marked than anywhere else in this wonderful and superstition-haunted little country of Wales. The version that follows is quite typical, and though it has been subject to frequent later recension, as given here it comes from William Williams of Llandygái's *Observations on the Snowdon Mountains*, and is well worth quoting at length. The farm where it takes place lies under the western shoulder of Moel Eilio, and it is worth mentioning also that in his book Williams claims that 'the best blood in my own veins is this Fairy's':[33]

> In a meadow belonging to Ystrad, bounded by the river which falls from Cwellyn Lake, they say the Fairies used to assemble, and dance on fair moon-light-nights. One evening a young man, who was the heir and occupier of this farm, hid himself in a thicket close to the spot where they used to gambol; presently they appeared, and when in their merry mood he bounced from his covert and seized one of their females; the rest of the company dispersed themselves, and disappeared in an instant. Disregarding her struggles and screams he hauled her to his home, where he treated her so very kindly that she became content to live with him as his maid-servant; but he could not prevail upon her to tell him her name. Some time after, happening again to see the Fairies upon the same

---

32 . . . and closely parallels, of course, the very well-known South Walian story of the fairy lady of Llyn y Fan Fach.
33 If genetic material were available, that statement might be viewed with interest by modern researchers, particularly in view of widely-reported results from studies of long-established populations in Wales and Ireland in recent years.

spot, he heard one of them saying, 'The last time we met here, our sister Penelope was snatched away from us by one of the mortals.' Rejoiced at knowing the name of his Incognita, he returned home; and as she was very beautiful and extremely active, he proposed to marry her, which she would not for a long time consent to; at last, however, she complied, but on this condition, 'That if ever he should strike her with iron, she would leave him, and never return to him again.' They lived happily for many years together, and he had by her a son, and a daughter; and by her industry and prudent management as a house-wife he became one of the richest men in the country. He farmed, besides his own freehold, all the lands on the north side of Nant-y-Bettws to the top of Snowdon, and all Cwmbrwynog in Llanberis; an extent of about five thousand acres or upwards.

Unfortunately, one day Penelope followed her husband into a field to catch a horse; and he, being in a rage at the animal as he ran away from him, threw at him the bridle that was in his hand, which unluckily fell on poor Penelope. She disappeared in an instant, and he never saw her afterwards, but heard her voice in the window of his room one night after, requesting him to take care of the children in these words:

> Rhag bod anwyd ar fy mab,
> Yn rhodd rhowch arno gob ei dad,
> Rhag bod anwyd ar liw'r cann.
> Rhoddwch arni bais ei mam.

That is:

> Oh! Lest my son should suffer cold,
> Him in his father's coat infold,
> Lest cold should seize my darling fair,
> For her, her mother's robe prepare.

These children and their descendants, they say, were called Pellings; a word corrupted from their mother's name, Penelope.[34]

'Pellings? Belisiaid? They say . . .'! In Cwm Pennant forty years ago, I heard applied by a septuagenarian Welsh bachelor-farmer and an octogenarian monoglot-Welsh farmer's widow to their near-neighbour the same genealogy and versions of the original surname that William Williams reported over two hundred years ago about those from the next valley over the pass at Cwm Pennant's head. The story was old even in his time. For how many generations had it been descending down through the oral tradition, and where did its roots lie?

I want to add in at this point material from other versions of this fairy tale. At Llyn y Dywarchen above Rhyd Ddu the lady disappears back into the lake, but is afterwards able to meet her husband on a floating islet. Her name is Bela, whence derives *Belisiaid*.[35] The fairy wife of Cwellyn likewise vanishes into the lake; and the famous ones of Llyn y Fan Fach and Llyn Du'r Arddu do so too. In some of the versions of the story much is made of the manner of baking bread *(Llaith dy fara,| Ti ni fynna* retorts the lady of Llyn y Fan Fach to her suitor – 'moist is your bread, I'll not have you'); of objections to the ploughing of greensward; of the ways the fairies have of counting; of the appearance of their cattle; of the skill of the woman in animal husbandry. The constants in each are: their small stature, the terrifying effect of iron, the way in which the use of the horse is alien to them.

Is there then, as W. J. Gruffydd suggests, some 'folk recollection of an aboriginal people living in inaccessible parts

---

34   William Williams, *Observations on the Snowdon Mountains* (1802).
35   T. Gwynn Jones, *Welsh Folklore and Folk Custom* (Methuen, 1930), p. 65.

of the countryside, having no contact with the dominant race, and living in fear and suspicion of them'[36] behind this repetitive rehearsal of motifs? And what of the connection with water? Remember the Bronze Age canoe mentioned in Chapter One as having been recovered from Llyn Llydaw?[37]

Is it possible that there was a culture similar to that of the Mesolithic crannog-dwellers (whose habitations were discovered in the lakes of County Sligo and also of Connemara in the 1950s) still extant around the foot of Snowdon at the time of the arrival here of the first bearers of iron tools and weapons, the evidence for which may yet present itself to the archaeologists of the future? Would the newcomers, as they settled here and became the dominant race, have enshrined in their folk memory the following qualities of their predecessors here:

> . . . the sallowness of their skins and the smallness of their
> stature, their dwelling underground, *their* dislike of iron,
> and the comparative poverty of their homes in the matter
> of useful articles of furniture, their deep-rooted objection to
> the green sward being broken up by the plough, the success
> of the fairy wife in attending to the domestic animals and
> to the dairy, the limited range generally of the fairies' ability
> to count; and lastly, one may perhaps mention their using a

---

36 W. J. Gruffydd, *Folklore and Myth in the Mabinogion* (University of Wales Press, 1958), p. 8

37 In fact there were two of them: '. . . some thirty years ago Mr Colliver, a Cornish gentleman, told the writer that whilst engaged in mining operations near Llyn Llydaw he had occasion to lower the water level of that lake, when he discovered embedded in the mud a canoe formed out of the trunk of a single tree. He saw another in the lake, but this he did not disturb, and it is there at the present day.' Rev. Elias Owen, *Welsh Folklore* (Oswestry, 1896), p. 28.

Thomas Colliver was mine-captain at the Cwm Dyli mine from 1852 to 1856, and would have been responsible for commissioning David Jones of Beddgelert to lower the lake level.

language of their own ... which would imply a time when the
little people understood no other?[38]

If you think it far-fetched that a folk-memory can filter down
through the oral tradition in some recognizable form, however
distorted or vague, even over two or three millennia, consider
this example – as unsatisfying as they mostly are in terms of
precise and logical recall, but undeniably possessed of a frisson
of flickering remembrance – from the writing of the Welsh
and East Anglian folklorist George Ewart Evans:

> One of the best known examples of the [oral] tradition relating
> to a site, which later revealed an outstanding archaeological
> find, comes from Wales. This is the well-known Bryn-yr-
> Ellyllon ['hill of the ghosts'] discovery near the town of Mold.
> A mound near the side of the road ... was broken into at the
> beginning of last [i.e. nineteenth] century ... for stone to
> mend the roads; towards the lower part they found some very
> large bones – a skull of greater than the usual size of man – a
> bright corslet with 200 to 300 amber beads; the bones became
> dust on being exposed to the air.
>
> 'The bright corslet' – now in the British Museum – turned
> out to be pure gold but later examination has established
> that it was not a corslet but a tippet or cape that fitted over
> the shoulders of a Bronze Age chieftain whose burial place
> the mound is assumed to be. Numerous stories were told
> at the time of the discovery of how local people had been
> frightened on different occasions by a Golden Spectre or the
> ghost of a Man in Golden Armour which appeared on or
> near the mound while they were passing to or from Mold.

---

38 Sir John Rhys, *Celtic Folklore: Welsh and Manx* (Clarendon Press, 1901),
p. 660.

Many of the stories can be discounted as vague memories that had been stiffened by the discovery itself. But Dr. H. N. Savory of the National Museum of Wales has looked at the evidence critically and has written: 'I think it is fair to say that it seems to be established that the local people believed in a ghost at Bryn-yr-Ellyllon long before the gold 'corslet' was discovered'[39]

The dismissive rejoinder here would be to point out that the name alone tells us that. Which begs the question of how the feature originally came by it. But then, story telling comes naturally to humankind, and as we leave this conjecture on the matter of unions with the fairies and return now to Nant Gwynen, we are perhaps arriving at the heartland and source for one of the greatest story-cycles of them all – that of Arthur, Merlin and the Knights of the Round Table.

(It might be useful at this point to stress Arthur's total lack of historicity. Marc Morris, in a persuasive and thrilling biography of Edward I, makes the point succinctly:

> ... as all sane historians will nowadays readily attest (whatever the assertions of lamentable Hollywood films to the contrary), Arthur himself never existed. Beyond any reasonable doubt, the legendary 'king' began life as an elemental figure or demi-god – a sort of low-grade Thor or Wodin.)[40]

Dinas Emrys is, to quote D. E. Jenkins, author of the invaluable work of local history entitled *Beddgelert: Its Facts, Fairies and Folklore,*[41] 'the prettiest little hill in Nant Gwynant'. It is also

39 George Ewart Evans, *Where Beards Wag All: The Relevance of the Oral Tradition* (Faber, 1970), pp. 227–228.
40 Marc Morris, *A Great and Terrible King: Edward I and the Forging of Britain* (Hutchinson, 2008) p. 162.
41 D. E. Jenkins, *Beddgelert: Its Facts, Fairies and Folklore* (Porthmadog, 1899).

reasonable to consider it as the site richest in story in the whole of Wales, and it is only with the most famous of these – that of the wizard and enchanter best known from Arthurian literature as Merlin – that I'm concerned here.[42]

As given by Nennius (see note 42), the story runs thus. Vortigern – an historical figure[43] prominent in north-east

---

42 Things here could become horribly complicated – or not – as we choose. We had better look briefly at the way in which Arthur and Merlin became historicised from the ninth century onwards. The name Merlin for the figure of the wizard in Arthurian literature derives from Merlinus Ambrosius, which was bestowed on this character by Geoffrey of Monmouth in his *Historia Regum Britanniae* of 1136 (in the historian Marc Morris' words, 'the startlingly inventive book that set the whole Arthurian avalanche in motion') and in the *Vita Merlini* – a playful and fanciful poem of about 1500 lines which followed it in about 1148–1150.

Geoffrey took the story in which his original, there called Ambrosius, occurs directly out of the *Historia Brittonum* of the ninth-century monk Nennius – the earliest source of Arthurian material. It is from Nennius that the connection with Dinas Emrys (Emrys = Ambrosius in Welsh) derives. Geoffrey's imaginative writings –bestsellers of their day, as the large number of extant manuscripts testify – quickly crossed over to France where, by 1155, they had been translated into verse by Wace under the title of the *Roman de Brut*. This, and much of the rest of the 'Matter of Britain', particularly as incorporated into the Old French prose romances of the Vulgate Cycle of the early thirteenth century, eventually made its way back across the Channel where, leavened with contemporary chivalric ideals, it was incorporated by Sir Thomas Malory into his *Morte Darthur*, completed in about 1469 and printed by William Caxton in 1485.

This was the crucial text that fixed the stories in the – by then English – cultural imagination (Edward's late-thirteenth century annexation of the Arthurian material is a fascinating political sub-text here). As to Merlin, here too are complex antecedents, the best short account of which can be found in A. O. H. Jarman's *The Legend of Merlin* (University of Wales Press, 1960). For those who wish to pursue the matter more fully, Count Nikolai Tolstoy's *The Quest for Merlin* (Hamish Hamilton, 1985) is quirky, entertaining and at times persuasive.

43 Vortigern was much reviled by the sixth-century monk Gildas in his *De Excidio et Conquestu Britanniae*, perhaps on account of his Pelagianism. The origins of this 'heresy' – a very sympathetic one to the modern mind since, in despite of the teachings of Augustine of Hippo and notwithstanding its magical rebuttal by Dewi Sant at the Convocation of Llanddewibrefi in

Wales in the first half of the fifth century, possibly a Pelagian heretic and probably a war leader who fought against Hengist and Horsa in Kent in AD 455 – sought alliance with the Saxons against his fellow British princes. Having lost control of these mercenary forces, after the 'Night of the Long Knives' he was forced to flee to Wales and build a stronghold there. The site chosen by his wizards was Dinas Emrys – probably an existing Iron Age defensive site – and building work began there, but every morning the work of the previous day would be discovered thrown down. The wizards declared that a spell was upon the project, which could only be broken by sacrificing a fatherless child and sprinkling his blood upon the walls.

The whole country was searched, and the child Ambrosius – conceived by an incubus upon a nun (or so the nun must have testified) – was found and brought to Vortigern's court. Not surprisingly, he argued against his fate, questioned the wizards' interpretation, and told them that beneath where Vortigern wished to build his tower was a lake, in which would be found two vessels, one inside the other, and a white cloth between them. The objects were found, Ambrosius ordered them to be opened, and wrapped within the cloth were two dragons, one red and one white. On being awakened, they fought over the cloth, the red one finally chasing the white one across the lake and the cloth vanishing – which Ambrosius

---

AD 545, it disputed the doctrine of original sin, believed unbaptised infants to be safe from damnation and animals to have souls, and thought good works in themselves meritorious – can be traced to the monastery of Bangor-is-y-Coed on Vortigern's home ground in what is now the Maelor Saesneg.

Vortigern does appear to have fallen foul of the 'spin-doctors' of the early Church, from whom his later evil reputation mostly derives. The monks of Bangor were, of course, slaughtered by the Saxons not long after Gildas' time, in AD 613 – at the behest of Augustine of Canterbury according to Bede of Jarrow. All very *august* and Christian . . .

interpreted as being a sign that the Saxon invaders would be ousted and the British people would prevail. But he added that Vortigern himself would never succeed in building his fortress here. Vortigern duly ceded possession of Dinas Emrys to Ambrosius, killed his useless wizards – who traditionally lie buried by the side of the present-day track leading to the farm of Hafod y Porth (the site is under the barn marked on the current map as Beudy Bedd Owen – the cowshed of the grave of Owen) – and, according to one source, went on his way either to Nant Gwrtheyrn near Llithfaen, now the home to the Welsh Language Centre, or to Craig Gwrtheyrn near Llandysul in Ceredigion from another.

We could now throw into this heady mix the character of another Ambrosius – Ambrosius Aurelianus – a Romano-British war leader, who is said in one legend to have persuaded our Ambrosius, later to be transmuted into Merlin, to go away with him, having buried his treasure at Dinas Emrys. The transmutations of oral history and the alchemical power of legend will deliver the pair up in due course – the process being a complex one, as you will have gathered from this incomplete account and the footnotes to it – to our modern consciousness as Arthur and Merlin, and allow them thoroughly to claim the locality in their names. As a coda to this process, it is interesting to quote the entry from the *Cadw/HMSO guide to Ancient and Historic Wales'* volume on Gwynedd by the archaeologist Frances Lynch on Dinas Emrys:[44]

> The archaeological features of the hilltop appear, in an astonishing way, to correspond to the situation described in the ancient story. It is certainly a most precipitous rock, which might be judged the strongest natural fortress in Gwynedd,

44   Frances Lynch, *Gwynedd* (HMSO, 1995), p. 128.

but the most notable coincidence is the discovery of evidence for 5th–6th century occupation around the pool at the centre of the site.

Some vague historicity having been established – in that we can assert with a degree of certainty that something of significance was going on around here a very long time ago, and nothing more definite than that – we could now jump a gap of a mere fourteen centuries and bring into play in order to enrich the story of our mountain the account from a book I've already had occasion to mention several times in this narrative – D. E. Jenkins' *Beddgelert: Its Facts, Fairies and Folklore* – of Arthur's death on Snowdon:

> When King Arthur was pursuing his enemies among the mountains of Eryri, he heard in Dinas Emrys that they were encamped in strong force within the walls of Tregalan, and that all the passes were under defence. He summoned all his forces to meet on the flat ground opposite Craflwyn, called 'Y Waen Wen', and there selected a strong regiment from the pick of his men. He then directed his march to Cwm Llan, over the mountain of Hafod y Porth, and through Bwlch Castell y Wawch. After a tremendous struggle, Arthur drove the enemy from the town in the direction of Cwm Dylif, and then followed them in pursuit. But when the leading portion of the army had reached the top of the pass, the ranks of the enemy let fly a shower of arrows, and Arthur received a fatal wound. His soldiers buried him in the pass, so as to prevent a single man of the foe from returning that way while Arthur's body rested there. To this day there remains in the middle of this pass a large heap of stones, which is called 'Carnedd Arthur'... [45]

---

45   op cit p. 255.

The pass is, of course, Bwlch y Saethau – 'the pass of the arrows' between Yr Wyddfa and Y Lliwedd – and we would be perfectly justified in feeling the presence here of an habitual onomastic element in the early stories, by which existing names were given explanations (Thomas Pennant, himself a considerable collector of tales, has quite a different and perhaps more prosaic take on this name, as we shall hear in a later chapter). In a continuation to the story, after Arthur's death his men ascend the ridge of Y Lliwedd, then climb down into a vast cave in the face of the cliff, Ogof Llanciau Eryri ('the cave of the lads of Eryri'), which they seal up behind them, there to sleep in their armour and await the second coming of Arthur, when the governance of Britain shall be restored to the Welsh. On the whole, their sleep is undisturbed, though as John Rhys relates:

> As the local shepherds were one day long ago collecting their sheep on the Lliwedd, one sheep fell down to a shelf in this precipice, and when the Cwm Dyli shepherd made his way to the spot he perceived that the ledge of rock on which he stood led to the hidden cave of Llanciau Eryri. There was light within: he looked in and beheld a host of warriors without number all asleep, resting on their arms and equipped for battle. Seeing that they were all asleep , he felt a strong desire to explore the whole place; but as he was squeezing in he struck his head against the bell hanging in the entrance. It rang so that every corner of the immense cave rang again, and all the warriors woke uttering a terrible shout, which so frightened the shepherd that he never more enjoyed a day's health; nor has anybody since dared as much as to approach the mouth of the cave.[46]

---

46 Sir John Rhys, *Celtic Folklore: Welsh and Manx* op. cit. pp. 473–474.

Whether the last statement is true or not is a matter we shall examine in a later chapter. As to the cairn, it was clearly visible in the mid nineteenth century and the poet Glaslyn at that time could write:

Gerllaw Carnedd Arthur ar ysgwydd y Wyddfa
Y gorwedd gweddillion y cawr enwog Ricca.
(Near Arthur's cairn on the shoulder of Yr Wyddfa
Rest the remains of the famous giant Ricca.)

These days there is no apparent trace of any ancient and substantial cairn on the pass of the arrows − one rather unlikely supposition being that it was dismantled and the stone carried up to be used in the building of Victorian refreshment huts at the summit. As for the giant Ricca (or Rhita), you can make his closer acquaintance in the earliest Welsh folk tale *Culhwch ac Olwen*.[47]

I want to conclude this chapter with introductions for you to three charming former residents of the slopes of Snowdon whose existence here was quite as likely as those of Arthur and Merlin. The first of them was known as *Canthrig Bwt*, and she lived under the boulders by Pont y Gromlech.[48]

---

47 See Bibliography, p. 234.
48 This name and that of the cliff above − Dinas Cromlech − may refer simply to the boulders themselves resembling a cromlech − not a likeness ever apparent to my eyes − or they may suggest the former presence hereabouts of a prehistoric monument. In Welsh a *cromlech* is generally a burial chamber consisting of a capstone supported on three or more uprights − though in Breton, interestingly, it signifies a circle of standing stones. The *Canthrig Bwt* story has close parallels to others associated with stone circles in Denbighshire, farther to the east. The point of this is to isolate the echo of the story's possible association with a ritual site. Though there is no trace of a monument here now, there are prehistoric settlements very close at hand, and many clearly important prehistoric sites in Wales were destroyed even as late as the eighteenth and nineteenth centuries, by road-building and farming operations.

She was known to the inhabitants, and the children feared her, but nobody thought that she did them any harm. It happened that several children were lost and no trace could be found of them. One day a workman noticed his dog devouring something near the cromlech and found it was a child's hand. One finger was wanting, not through any recent accident, and the hand was thus recognized as that of a missing boy. The hag was observed. A man went to the place and heard a child crying. He called to the hag, telling her he had children for her. She replied she would come out after dressing the head of her child. When she came, the man struck off her head.[49]

The second member of this triad of grotesques we may (but probably won't) have the misfortune to encounter lives in the depths of Llyn y Ffynnon Las, or Glaslyn as it is better known nowadays, which Sir John Lloyd tells us

has a most sinister reputation in folklore, answering well to its uncanny aspect. It is the abode of demons and, needless to say, it is bottomless, harbours no ordinary fish, and never freezes. Any living creature venturing into it comes to a speedy end and no bird will fly over its eerie waters.[50]

'Wild swimmers' beware, then, if ever you feel tempted to take a bracing dip after descending from the summit on a hot day. Fishermen have pulled strange creatures from this pool on the end of their lines, and been forced to flee in dread – or so the stories go.

What lives most notably in the lake is the *Afanc*,[51] a monster

---

49   T. Gwynn Jones, *Welsh Folklore and Folk Custom* op. cit. p. 82.

50   *The Mountains of Snowdonia in history*, eds. H. R. C. Carr & G. A Lister, (2nd edition, Crosby Lockwood, 1948), p. 16.

51   Not to be confused with the humble beaver, which also once lived here-abouts and for which *afanc* is also the Welsh name.

which had caused grievous losses to the people living near its former lair, and which seemed invulnerable. Until one day, lured by a maiden's trickery out of the Beaver Pool below the confluence of the Conwy and the Lledr near Betws-y-coed, and bound in iron chains, it was dragged away by the oxen of Hu Gadarn, which were the strongest in the world, across the shoulder of Moel Siabod. In the field now known as Gwaun Llygad yr Ych, on the mountain-land of Gwastad Annas farm, so great were one of the oxen's exertions that an eye started out of its socket and fell on the ground, forming a pool, Pwll Llygad yr Ych, which never dries though no water runs into or out from it. Eventually, at Llyn y Ffynnon Las, the chains binding the *Afanc* were loosed and it jumped headlong into the lake, and the local people did not mind its dwelling there, for they knew what terrible company it kept in so doing, and many stories are told about these other creatures as well.

So much for the *Afanc* and his friends – enormous toads, terrible water-horses and the like. For our last new acquaintance, we need to descend back into Nant Gwynen, and make our way up the Afon Merch, which we came down alongside in the journey described in Chapter One. There is a story located here, mentioned in a letter of Edward Lhuyd's and told again by D. E. Jenkins, about Ogof y Gŵr Blewog – the cave of the hairy man.

The version Jenkins relates in order to explain the name is a garbled mix of folk tale motifs familiar from other Welsh, Scottish and Irish sources: stolen food, mischief-making, red greyhounds, chases over the mountains, disappearances, severed hands. In brief, it runs thus: a very long time ago the people of Nant Gwynen were troubled by an unknown and audacious robber, who used to break into their houses during the night, robbing them of their food and other items without ever being seen or heard. The cows and goats were frequently milked dry before morning and often the fattest sheep were stolen from the folds in spite of every watchfulness. One day a shepherd on his way down from the mountain spotted a man covered all over with red hair sitting on a hill above his farmhouse, and concluded that this was the robber. The hairy man sprang to his feet, a chase ensued, but he leapt like a roe deer over the rocks and disappeared from sight.

On a subsequent occasion when he was spotted basking in the sun, dogs were set after him but he fled like a hare and the dogs lost him so completely they did not know in which direction to go. A magician was consulted, and he advised the people to seek a greyhound, uniformly red, and this would surely catch him. One was found and brought to Nant Gwynen, but just at the point of its snatching at the hairy man's heel, he jumped clean over a cliff and was seen at its foot speeding away unharmed. The people came to believe that he must be a demon, and would never be caught. One day, however, when the people of the house had taken a newborn child to the church to be baptized and its woman was still confined, she heard a sound, saw the hairy man stretching his hand through the door to open it, and picking up a hatchet she struck and severed his hand from his wrist. When her family returned from church they could follow the trail of blood to the cave where he lived, in the inaccessible depths of which he was presumed to have perished from loss of blood, for he was never seen again.

On a drenching December day of the present time, when all the southern flanks of Snowdon were braided with white threads of rushing streams and the water spirits were garrulous in every cwm, I set off up the Afon Merch, Jenkins' description of the whereabouts of the cave committed to memory. A rocky scramble past a sidelong, broken fall brought me to a long, narrow pool between steep walls that exactly matched it. Down to its swift green water hung a veil of ivy, leaves glistening, to conceal the farthest dark recesses into which a waterspout thundered.

All the old mystery gathered about the place. To arrive here alone on a winter's afternoon is to find yourself in the presence of the *Uruisg*, the water-sprite, stories of whom recur throughout the Celtic countries; who 'haunts lonely places and waterfalls and, according to his mood, helps or harms the wayfarer. His appearance is that of a man with shaggy hair and beard . . .'[52]

With *Canthrig Bwt*, the *Afanc* and the Hairy Man, what you are encountering may well be aspects of an old, religious response to the land (the presence of water in the cases of the latter two is suggestive), embodied in story and grotesque character, the original significance corrupted and obscure. Some of the detail is obviously later accretion and comment: some of it starts out at you in repeated familiarity; some of it seems to be included from a necessity of the original reason for which the storyteller is not entirely aware. All three have parallels with tales from other countries than Wales (a fact which might suggest to you a relevance in the Jungian view of the archetypes and the collective unconscious).

With the tales from the realm of faery, it may be legitimate, and is certainly fascinating, to ponder their provenance in terms of ancient and aboriginal encounters. The hero sagas alchemically transmuted through generations of imaginative elaboration around the memory of troubled and distant

---

52 J. A. MacCulloch, *The Religion of the Ancient Celts* (T & T Clark, 1911), pp. 189–190.

events are endlessly enthralling. The truth or basis or degree of historicity of any of them will remain very tenuously approachable, ultimately and essentially undiscoverable. The enabling factor for the survival and increase of all, I would suggest, is the interplay between landscape and affect. It seems appropriate to me that so grand a peak as Snowdon, impacting as powerfully as it does upon imagination and mood, should have such continuing texture of story and belief gathered around it, enabling us still to meet the characters, demons and demigods created from human response to landscape down the long ages, bringing us closer in understanding to what we were and – under the veneers of so-called civilization – perhaps still essentially are.

3

The Natural Fortress

To travel further west or south than Caernarfon was to show considerable courage bordering on folly. Here lay what even Gerald had no hesitation in calling 'the wildest and most terrifying region in all Wales' (and he was bolstered by the ecclesiastical security of his mission). Should anyone be tempted to go by horseback he would probably be well advised to follow the general steps of Gerald's itinerary – south-westwards from Caernarfon towards Nefyn (anything was preferable to the mountain passes of Snowdonia . . .)

— REES DAVIES [53]

The first chapter surveyed Snowdon in terms of the mountain's physical structure; the second gave a brief overview focused on what might be termed its subliminal, folkloric dimension. We need now to explore the historical hinterland, as the shimmering, graceful form of Yr Wyddfa rises out of what are habitually, and to a historian's mind misleadingly, referred to as 'The Dark Ages' in Britain, and gradually registers on the medieval human consciousness.

There is a clear element of geographical determinism to be taken into account in this phase of our mountain's story.

---

53 R. R. Davies, *The Revolt of Owain Glyn Dŵr* (Oxford University Press, 1995), p. 11.

A good analogy in considering Snowdon's slow surfacing into British topographical awareness is perhaps to think of the explorations up the Rishi Gorge and into the Nanda Devi sanctuary in the Garhwal Himalaya of India by mountaineers in the early decades of the twentieth century. The terrain in Garhwal is certainly higher and more rugged than the approaches to Snowdon. It was more problematical and physically challenging to its first explorers than the geographical hinterland of Snowdon, even to the visitors to and invaders of Wales in the medieval period. But this comparison should not lead us to underestimate equally real problems – quite apart from the physical barriers of trackless forests, wild moors, foul weather and perilous tidal crossings – that would periodically have been faced by travellers who desired to make their way to the Snowdon region before the so-called Act of Union[54] of 1536. This brought a degree of political and administrative stability to relations between England and Wales, and a final dismantling of the *cordon sanitaire* which was the Welsh March, with all its warring baronies.

Before that date, throughout early medieval times and down to the failure of Owain Glyndŵr's great uprising at the beginning of the second decade of the fifteenth century, if travel to the mountain was not a physical impossibility, it was certainly fraught with political and tribal dangers. Not

---

54 The term 'Act of Union' for this statute, *27 Henry VIII c. 26*, was not coined until 1901, when it was tentatively put forward by the eminent Welsh historian and educator O. M. Edwards. Anachronistic though it may be, it is nonetheless useful and descriptive, and I hope any more serious students of Welsh history reading this book will excuse its generalized application here. Contemporary sources, of course, claimed that a state of union already existed through Edward I's Statute of Rhuddlan of 1284. Though true in strict legal terms, for a quarter of a millennium thereafter it would scarcely have felt thus on the ground.

only that, but the very notion of interest in a mountain for its own sake rather than for any strategic or economic advantage it might represent or provide would have been antipathetic until the latter half of the eighteenth century. Only then did the rise of Romanticism and an increasing enthusiasm for natural scenery that conformed to ideas of the Burkean Sublime finally give justification to the appreciation of mountain scenery per se.

We need a different paradigm, then, to the modern one predicated on recreational pleasure and ease of access, to comprehend the slow emergence of the mountain through long centuries into cultural consciousness. A perspective on the history of the region is invaluable here, and fascinating in its own right. The crucial context is that of political history. Wales is not, nor ever has been, culturally a part of the peculiarly amorphous and deracinated entity which has, if not forever then at least for the larger part of the last millennium, been called England. This very name 'Wales' that the English have bestowed on the land west of the Mercian king Offa's late eighth century territorial marker-dyke – one of the most impressive, and certainly the longest, of British historical constructions, the scale of which correlates with that of the problem which caused it to be built – gives us a clue. Wales is not the name that the Welsh themselves use for their own country. That is *Cymru* – the country of the *Cymry*, which derives from the Brittonic word *Combrogi*, meaning 'fellow-countryman'. The name Wales, conversely, derives from the Saxon word *weallas*, meaning 'foreigners'. The Welsh word for an Englishman is *Saeson* – a Saxon. You might pick up from all this the notion of degrees of historical enmity, and you would be right to do so. Wales was always a land apart. It took even the invincible armies of Imperial Rome at least thirteen campaigns between AD 48 and 79 to subdue its native tribes, and thereafter form reasonably stable alliances to maintain a version of peace that lasted for three centuries.

By AD 390 however, no Imperial troops in Wales were recorded in the Roman military register, the *Notitia Dignitatum*. There is some archaeological evidence to suggest that the great hilltop fortifications and upland settlements from the Iron Age or even the late Bronze Age – Tre'r Ceiri, Dinas Dinorwig, Braich y Gornel – all of them clearly visible in the immediate foreground north and west of Yr Wyddfa – were resettled at the time of the Legions' departure, which argues an instability in the region and an insecurity in its population. This period has often been identified as the time of the towering mythico-syncretic figure of Arthur, whose long, diffuse and restless shadow, as we have seen, haunts so much of Snowdon's texture of story. His role in history – if indeed he had one, or existed at all, and we need to take close heed here of Marc Morris' statement quoted in the previous chapter – might have been as war leader, resister of Saxon incursion, and upholder of an idealized tradition (qualities desired and replicated in the *mythos* of any nation oppressed by a more powerful neighbour – the traits and even the adapted tales of Arthur were to be re-invested many centuries later in the figure of Owain Glyndŵr.[55] Perhaps even now the Welsh mythopoeic imagination is working the same alchemy with the equally shadowy leaders and anonymous foot-soldiers in the late-twentieth-century campaign of the significantly-

---

55   Also, of course, in other Welsh heroes – Owain Lawgoch for example – as well as heroic resistance leaders from other nations: El Cid, Frederick Barbarossa *et al*. For those interested, the parallels can be pursued through the various indices – Stith Thompson, Balys etc. – of folk-tale motifs. Elyssa R. Henken gives a lucid and entertaining account of these recurrences and confusions in her *National Redeemer: Owain Glyndŵr in Welsh Tradition* (University of Wales Press, 1996)

named *Meibion Glyndŵr*, which was waged against English material appropriation in *Y Fro Gymraeg*,[56] and its consequent attenuation of modern Welsh culture and community.)

The process of transmutation by which shadowy war lords from the centuries after the withdrawal of the Roman legions were invested with characteristics of, and incorporated into mythical tales about, even more shadowy demigods found fertile ground for growth in the Welsh fictive imagination. Arthur's first appearance is in a mention by the monk Nennius nearly 300 years after his supposed death at the battle of Camlann. This took place – according to the *Annales Cambriae*, a composite Victorian redaction from early manuscript sources,[57] which is perhaps the most reliable of the relevant texts, though Arthur is not mentioned in this connection – in AD 537 at any one of a dozen supposed locations from Somerset to Yr Ystog.

Arthur's reputed crucial earlier victory at Mons Badonicus over the colonizing Saxons, who themselves first came to Britain as legionaries recruited into the service of Imperial Rome, can be cross-referenced in the monk Gildas' ferocious polemic *De Excidio et Conquestu Britanniae*, written before AD 547. It seems, therefore, that some event that came to be known as the 'Battle of Mount Badon' possesses a reasonable likelihood of historicity, was most likely to have been a stand taken under a unifying leader by Romano-British forces against Saxon incursion, and historians now favour a probable date for it of around AD 496, though the early texts suggest a date some twenty years later. As to Arthur's presence among

---

56 The Welsh-speaking areas, chiefly in the north and west of the country.
57 Some of them obviously available to the earlier compiler of the *Brut y Tywysogion*, of which more below.

all this confusion, Marc Morris laconically notes[58] that, 'the deity was . . . demoted into a warrior who successfully battled for the Britons around the year AD 500.'

So much for the uncertain and at times contradictory possibilities of embryonic historiography. From that date to the so-called Act of Union there were a thousand years, more or less, in which this mountainous, densely-forested land of Wales was a dangerous, factional, bloodthirsty one, of warring tribes and conquering princes and kings, speaking its own language, practising and refining its own arts, and with the region around Snowdon itself an enduring stronghold of its national identity. Travel to these parts in the course of those centuries, as the epigraph to this chapter makes clear, would not have been a matter to be taken lightly. One authoritative modern biographer of Edward I remarks of the period of which he writes that 'much of North Wales was remarkably remote'.[59] To walk the length of Afghanistan alone in the early twenty-first century would be about as safe and sensible an undertaking as for an Englishman to travel thus through Eryri in the thirteenth century.

John Davies, in what has become the standard and indispensable one-volume work on Welsh history, gives a telling insight into the temper of the times when he comments as follows on the *Brut y Tywysogion* ('The Chronicle of the Princes'), an important early source-text for Welsh history probably written at the Ceredigion monastery of Strata Florida in the fourteenth century and covering the period from the death of Cadwaladr Fendigaid in 682 to that of Llywelyn ap Gruffydd ('Llew Olaf'), unwittingly slain by a Shropshire

58 Marc Morris, *A Great and Terrible King*, op. cit. p. 162.
59 Michael Prestwich, *Edward I* (Methuen, 1988), p. 171.

soldier at a ford on the River Ithon by Cilmeri in November 1282:

> The contents of the *Brut* in the years 950 to 1150 are harrowing; it records twenty-eight murders and four blindings. As it contains little beyond these horrors, historians have been mesmerized by the heinousness of the chronicler's account and have thus portrayed the decades around the year 1000 as the most savage and fruitless in the history of Wales.[60]

These were atrocities committed against the most powerful and best-connected people in Wales – its ruling dynasties. The fate of those from lower orders was beneath the scribe's notice. To say that you journeyed through Wales at your own risk would have been the understatement of long and perilous centuries. Here's Marc Morris, extrapolating from Chapter Eight of Giraldus Cambrensis' twelfth-century *Description of Wales* to give a portrait of the Taliban-like Welsh warriors and the nature of the Wales in defence of which they fought even as late as the second half of the thirteenth century:[61]

> Everything west of Chester was hostile terrain that afforded neither shelter nor safe haven. In this environment, unforgiving and inhospitable, even the greatest armies might become entangled and bogged down, and once that happened the eerie silence might suddenly be broken by the noise of a surprise attack. The Welsh might have lacked the latest military hardware, but they were famously fierce and fearsome. Dressed in leather, armed with bows, arrows and spears, they would sweep down on their enemies, catching

---

60 John Davies, *A History of Wales* (Penguin, 1994), p. 99.
61 Gerald of Wales, *The Journey Through Wales / A Description of Wales*, tr. Lewis Thorpe (Penguin, 1978), pp. 233–234.

them unawares and wreaking havoc, before retreating with equal swiftness into the woods and hills. Such guerrilla tactics had served them well against would-be invaders for centuries. They were precisely the tactics by which a small nation might defeat a superpower.[62]

Our peak, Snowdon, was in the most vexed territory of them all, a Helmand province of its day, the stronghold of the house of Aberffraw. By the time matters with England – an increasingly powerful and dominant neighbour from the time of the Norman invasion onwards – were coming to a head in the late thirteenth century, a succession of influential Welsh kings and princes, from Maelgwn Gwynedd and Rhodri the Great to Hywel the Good (the supreme legal mind of his age), Owain Gwynedd, Llywelyn ap Iorwerth ('Llywelyn the Great') and – arguably the slipperiest and most skilful political operator, and in English eyes the most dangerous of them all – Llywelyn ap Iorwerth's grandson Llywelyn ap Gruffydd, had established a power base in Snowdonia, provisioned from the grain, stock and dairies of Anglesey, which came to be perceived by the new Norman succession to the English throne as one of the major threats to its stability. The subjugation of this dynasty of Aberffraw, where Llywelyn ap Gruffydd had his chief court, became therefore one of the decisive chapters in Welsh history.

Prior to that, a policy of containment had been operative for two centuries or more, implemented chiefly by the gift of annexed lands throughout the March of Wales to powerful Norman barons and seasoned fighting men, the first of whom had come over with William the Conqueror's victorious

---

62   Marc Morris, *A Great and Terrible King*, op. cit. p. 151.

expeditionary force of 1066. The March, stretching from Chester to Chepstow, was essentially a strongly-garrisoned buffer zone between the fractious independence of Wales and the conquered state of England.

So here was yet another barrier debarring access – assuming anyone at the time had wanted it – to Snowdon. The reputation of what lay beyond the March to the west had long been acutely forbidding. As one of the classic commentators has it, 'the Welsh of Snowdonia and the Four Cantreds were anti-English throughout from prince to peasant.'[63] Even relatively pacific expeditions through Wales by such as the Norman-Welsh chronicler Giraldus, who accompanied Archbishop Baldwin on his 1188 quasi-military ecclesiastical mission to raise men and funds for the Third Crusade, returned with stories of a demon-haunted, guerrilla-patrolled, warlike nation which any sensible Saxon or Anglo-Norman would be well advised to avoid. This point of view the Archbishop endorsed with a smile in his comment that 'if it never comes to Wales the nightingale is a very sensible bird. We are not quite so wise, for not only have we come here but we have traversed the whole country.'[64]

The people of the northern part of Wales in particular lived by Giraldus' account (he himself came from Manorbier on the south-western coast – internal Welsh rivalry between north and south is long-established) in flimsy dwellings that could be razed to the ground at the first threat of invasion; their crops, if they could not be harvested, would be ploughed in, their corn-mills destroyed, their cattle driven off into mountain fastnesses

---

63 John E. Morris, *The Welsh Wars of Edward I* (Clarendon Press, 1901), p. 150. 'The Four Cantreds' were the administrative departments of medieval Wales along the north-eastern coastal strip.
64 Gerald of Wales, *The Journey Through Wales*, ibid. p. 185

where no heavily-armoured Saxon or Norman soldiery would dare follow. If they tried to do so, they moved into the terrain of an unseen and deadly foe whose presence was only revealed in ambush; in great rocks crashing down from slopes above at the narrowest point of a pass; in chimeras glimpsed in the mist, shadows flitting through the forest. Such travellers as dared venture into Wales were accompanied by the constant sense of being observed: and observed by those who moved over the most difficult slopes with the ease of animals; those whose skill with the longbow in the south or the spear in the north was such that at any moment a wuthering hail of goose-feathered shafts might descend to pierce a rider's neck, or his thigh be spear-riveted to the flank of his mount, sending both to a terrorized, agonized, fearful death. Time and again the English forces were turned back from the margins of the stronghold, from the boundaries of Eryri[65] itself. John Morris, in his classic work on the period, explains it thus:

> these royal expeditions utterly failed. The armies were either composed of the feudal vassals of the crown, or mercenaries. In any case they were clumsy and unfitted for an invasion of mountainous districts in the face of an active race of patriots. Time after time they penetrated far west. The Welsh retreated upon their natural fortress of Snowdon, restricted themselves to guerilla warfare, and relied upon the rains and

---

65   The term 'Eryri', first recorded in 1191 as Ereri, and still in common modern usage, as in Parc Cenedlaethol Eryri, refers to the hill-region surrounding Snowdon itself. It has generally and popularly been assumed to have a connection with 'Eryr' – an eagle – and is often translated as 'place of eagles'. There is little, other than romanticism, to recommend this derivation, and the more likely root-meaning is eryr as a ridge, rise or mount. 'Snowdonia' is a Latinization that first occurs in documents of Edward I's from 1284. It disappeared thereafter for centuries, to re-emerge in Victorian times as a term for touristic convenience.

the difficulties presented by the geography of their country ...
Sooner or later the heavy columns of the invaders, wearied out
by the bad weather and profitless tramping through pathless
forests, had to fall back.[66]

In the *Brut y Tywysogion* the anonymous redactor from the
early fourteenth century exemplifies Morris' point as he tells
in vivid language of how, in 1164, Henry the Second, king
from the Scottish borders to the Pyrenees, unwilling to accept
impudence from the little country of Wales, marched with
an army of English, Norman, Gascon, Flemish and Angevin
warriors on the Welsh heartland. The warriors of Gwynedd, as
ever, were ready for him, their forces massed along the banks
of the Dyfrdwy, harrying his flanks, cutting off his lines of
supply, forcing his army to camp at Foel y Gwynt – hill of the
wind – above Carrog, 'where he remained a few days. Then a
tremendous storm of wind and foul weather and driving rain
broke on them, and they lacked food. He withdrew his camping
place back to England, and in his fury he caused to be taken out
the eyes of his [Welsh] hostages whom he had long held.'

Half a century later, in 1212, with the blessing of the Pope,
Llywelyn ap Iorwerth ('The Great') rose against the English
King John, to whom he had been obliged to yield authority
the previous year. Llywelyn sacked John's new castle at
Aberystwyth and regained power in Gwynedd – a power still
retained by his grandson Llywelyn ap Gruffydd at the time of
Edward I's accession in 1272 to the kingship of England.[67]

Once established on the throne of England, this most
formidable of English warrior kings was to find plenty to

---

66 Marc Morris, *A Great and Terrible King*, op. cit. pp. 8–9.
67 Edward's coronation was not until 1274, he having been crusading and
campaigning through Italy and France when his father Henry III died.

occupy his attention among his own strife-torn home nations, and one troublesome neighbour in particular would bear the brunt of his wrath. This neighbour had been invited to, but did not attend, Edward's coronation; this neighbour's wife Elinor had been captured and imprisoned by Edward in 1275; this neighbour had five times by April 1276 disregarded summonses to pay homage to the king. Inevitably, that king lost patience. So that finally, in the last quarter of the thirteenth century, the ruling dynasty of the heartland of Gwynedd was faced by a calculating and tactically astute adversary who had heeded the lessons of history.

In August 1277 an army of 800 knights and 15,000 foot soldiers had been assembled by Edward. The Anglesey grain harvest, in an aggressive logistical masterstroke, was gathered in by 360 English reapers who had crossed over to the island from Aberconwy. The adherents to the house of Aberffraw were driven back into hills that could not provide forage and provender for their horses, herds and flocks through the coming winter. With ruthless efficiency and careful preparation, Edward had brought Llywelyn to bay:

> Edward I's first campaign against Llywelyn ap Gruffydd lasted in its entirety just under one year. Llywelyn was proclaimed a rebel on 12 November 1276; he submitted to the king's terms on 9 November 1277. The campaign was carefully planned, well co-ordinated and, above all, well paced, so that it reached its climax effortlessly.[68]

The penultimate chapter in Gwynedd's independent history was about to be written, though the liberation of our mountain

---

68   R. R. Davies, *The Age of Conquest: Wales 1063–1415* (Oxford University Press, 1991), p. 333.

to the independent traveller was still two-and-a-half centuries away.

The final subjugation didn't take long – it was over within little more than five years from the arrival of those reapers on Anglesey – though it was bought at enormous financial expense to the English exchequer, and a consequent burden of taxation upon the Welsh. By the closing months of 1282 Edward had effectively conquered north Wales.

Not content with the Welsh nation's mere physical subjection, he had also appropriated to himself the stuff of the region's legends. In the aftermath of his Welsh campaign of 1277, the monks of Glastonbury fortuitously produced the coffins of Arthur and Guinevere, the thought of increased royal benefice no doubt driving their archaeological zeal. Their self-interested prompt worked upon Edward in an interesting manner, though it brought the monks themselves little advantage from this notoriously mean monarch. In 1284 celebrations were held at Cwm Dulyn, a significant legendary site in Dyffryn Nantlle, and on top of Snowdon.[69] These were followed by a Round Table feast and a tournament at Nefyn, ostensibly to celebrate the Statute of Rhuddlan, at which the subjugated Welsh presented to their conqueror, along with a supposed fragment of the True Cross,[70] and a curious relic known as Arthur's Crown, which the King's goldsmiths immediately enlarged and enhanced. Over in Powys Gwenwynwyn meanwhile, in the court of the last independent Welsh princes, an anonymous storyteller was

---

69 'No sooner had Edward effected his conquest, than he held a triumphal fair upon this our chief of mountains', declares Thomas Pennant.
70 To distinguish it, of course, though by what means is unclear, from the plethora of false ones. Unsubstantiated assertion then as now was a potent political tool.

gleefully encoding the first British political satire, *Breudwyt Rhonabwy.*[71] Once a dynasty attracts satire, it can truly be said

---

71   This extraordinary text, set in the uplands of Arwystli, survived in the medieval collection *Llyfr Coch Hergest* (*c.*1382–1410), where it was sandwiched between a version of the *Brut y Tywysogion* and the tales now known as *The Mabinogion*. It has long been a puzzle to Welsh scholars, most of whom traditionally describe it as a mnemonic exercise for the *cyfarwyddion* – the itinerant storytellers of medieval Wales, who were so important during this period in upholding the country's cultural traditions.

The crucial piece of research in unlocking the code of the extremely detailed descriptions that characterize *Breudwyt Rhonabwy* came in the form of a brief paper given by Mary Giffin to the fifth International Arthurian Congress at Bangor in August 1957, and subsequently published under the predictable title of 'The Date of the Dream of Rhonabwy' in the *Transactions of the Honourable Society of Cymmrodorion* for 1958. The implications of this paper have so far largely and bewilderingly been ignored by Welsh scholars. Even a younger generation – Helen Fulton, Edgar Slotkin and Dafydd Glyn Jones prominent among them – has been influenced by the preoccupation of the late Professor Melville Richards, in his introduction to the standard edition of *Breudwyt Rhonabwy*, with the matter of date rather than textual content and tenor, and the latest translator of *The Mabinogion* into English, Professor Sioned Davies of Cardiff, is remarkably vague in her reading of this text.

What Sister Giffin's painstaking and original research into sources from the dawn of heraldry established, however, were 'striking resemblances' between descriptions in *Breudwyt Rhonabwy* and the Roll of Horse drawn up for Edward at the Battle of Falkirk against William Wallace (properly William de Walles, incidentally) in 1298. She makes richly suggestive remarks on the so-called 'Arwystli Question' of 1277–8 – crucial in Welsh resistance to the imposition of English law – and most importantly, she provides convincing heraldic evidence to identify within the tale the characters of Arthur with Edward, and the early Welsh hero Owain ap Urien with the House of Powys in the late thirteenth century.

When Edward's annexation of the Arthurian matter, the distinctly mocking tone of the text towards this erstwhile hero, and the morally triumphant role of Owain are taken into account, it becomes perfectly clear that this is the first British political satire, written from within the court of the last independent princes of Powys against Edward at the height of his powers, and setting up an alternative heroic tradition to the one that was in the process of being appropriated by the English king. Lucky for the storyteller in question that Edward couldn't read Welsh! But then, nor, avowedly, could Ms Giffin – an American nun – which may explain her neglect by the notoriously incestuous community of medieval Welsh scholars. At which point I had better let the matter rest, before I get into even more trouble.

to have arrived. Even today, from the summit of Snowdon on a clear day, the evidence of Edward's power and planning stands plain. Right at the toe of the mountain's northern ridge is Caernarfon Castle; to the west Cricieth, to the south Harlech. Beaumaris is a dark smudge to the north-east above the Menai shore. Out of sight behind the Carneddau is Conwy, and beyond that are Rhuddlan and Fflint. These astonishing fortifications are stark proof of the difficulty Edward faced in subduing Wales, and the calculated determination he brought to the task. As with Offa's Dyke five centuries before, they testify to the character of the foe against whom they were built.

That foe rose again briefly in 1294–5, in protest at the punitive taxes that were a joint result of the Statute of Rhuddlan and the fiscal need of a ruler whose exchequer was not only depleted by the castle-building, but also by the necessities of an army overextended by successive campaigns in Scotland, Flanders and Gascony. Caernarfon Castle was taken and sacked, the Sheriff of Anglesey hanged, drawn and quartered before it in a way brutally mimetic of the death of Llywelyn ap Gruffydd's brother Dafydd in Shrewsbury a dozen years before. Edward put the rising down, with habitual savagery and scores of executions. The Marcher barons, too, had been brought to heel by this most martial and bloody of kings. Another century was to pass – one in which the Black Death changed the structures of British society forever – before Wales would rebel once more against English rule.

That revolt, led by Owain Glyndŵr, is one of the great romantic stories from British history. Even Shakespeare regards Owain with humorous and kindly fascination as a 'worthy gentleman, | Exceedingly well read, and profited | In strange concealments, valiant as a lion | And wondrous affable, and as bountiful | as mines of India'.[72] The successes he achieved through the fifteen years in which his rebellion ran its course can certainly be explained, as Professor Rees Davies does in his authoritative study of the uprising, as the result of 'exploiting the fissures of English domestic politics and England's foreign entanglements'[73]. For a decade and a half, Owain rendered Wales once again a forbidden land to travellers from England. Not that it had been entirely accessible in the century leading up to 1400, the year in which Owain took to arms, as Professor Davies' summing-up of the perils of contemporary travel to Caernarfon – the town at Snowdon's foot – used as epigraph to this chapter makes plain.

According to folk tradition, it was to the region around Snowdon that Owain fled after the first phase of his uprising, which took place in 1400. This had been precipitated by machinations against him at the court of the new king, Henry IV, by his territorial neighbour and mortal foe, Reginald Grey the Marcher lord of Rhuthun. Realizing that he would come by no redress within the English legal system for land seizures by Grey, and having gathered a powerful group of supporters, Owain – a linear descendant[74] of the house of Aberffraw – was proclaimed Prince of Wales on the 16th September. On the Eve of St. Matthew's Day (21st September in the Western Calendar), when Rhuthun was thronging with people attending the

---

72 *Henry IV, Part One*, III, i. 164–8. This whole scene gives a fascinating insight into views of Wales current in late-Elizabethan London. The stage directions even call for some of the dialogue to be in Welsh. Unfortunately, Shakespeare didn't provide the text for this, but the opportunity has been freely exercised by Welsh-speaking actors, to the amusement of bilingual members in the audiences ever since.

73 R. R. Davies, *The Revolt of Owain Glyn Dŵr*, op. cit. p. 117

74 Even Shakespeare mockingly acknowledges the importance of genealogy at this stage of Welsh history.

annual fair, Owain attacked and burned the town, following up his devastating assault with further onslaughts on Dinbych, Rhuddlan, Fflint, Holt, Croesoswallt and Y Trallwng. News of the revolt spread quickly throughout England, disaffected Welsh students at Oxford joining countrymen who had been pressed into villeinage to flock to the cause.

The surprise and precipitous offensive against the ring of fortifications by which the English had kept the Welsh hemmed in and cowed for a century drew an immediate response from the English crown. Owain was outlawed and his estates in Glyndyfrdwy and Dyffryn Tanat declared forfeit. In the face of draconian threats and hasty new laws, and as yet lacking an efficient organizing principle, his support for the moment evaporated and Owain himself, pursued by the English soldiery, according to folk tradition made his way to the time-honoured geographical stronghold of the Welsh, to the vicinity of Snowdon itself. Here in Hafod Garegog, Nantmor, just south of Snowdon, he took refuge with his loyal supporter Rhys Goch. D. E. Jenkins summarizes the stories of Glyndŵr's sojourn around Snowdon thus:

> The enemy caught sight of Owen, and seeing that he was secretly making his escape, they pursued him. When he saw that they were after him, he threw himself headlong into the water [of the Afon Glaslyn, tidal at this point and time], and though the tide was then high, swam safely to the shore by Dinas Ddu. He made his way up Cwm Oerddwr, fixing his eye on Moel Hebog, being closely pressed by his pursuers. When he had ascended the hillside until close by Moel Hebog, he found himself in the greatest straits. Before him stood the Simnai [a prominent gully in the eastern flank of the south buttress of Hebog], close behind him panted his

pursuers, and only the common ascent on the left was clear. To climb that would be like courting capture, as his pursuers would be sure to overtake him. What could he do? He looked up the steep rock, and thought that if he could only climb it he would get the lead of them; but it was steep, bare, and stepless, and should he once miss his hold, there was nothing but instantaneous death before him. Like the hero that he was, he made a dash for the rock and immediately began to climb the Chimney; his daring and determination conquered his difficulty, and soon his enemies could see him mounting his peak in safety. Not one of them would follow in this venture, so they had to go round the easier path.

In the meantime Owen made his way, unperceived by them, along the ridge of Diffwys, and descended over the brow of that appalling precipice to a large, cave-like cleft, where he remained concealed for six months. His pursuers pressed onto Pennant, thinking that he had taken that direction, and thus completely lost every trace of him. During his concealment in this cleft, called ever since 'Ogof Owain Glyndŵr',[75] the Prior of Bedd Gelert provided for all his immediate wants.[76]

The subsequent history of Glyndŵr's great rising has very little to do with our region. His victories at Hyddgen below Pumlumon in the summer of 1401, and Bryn Glas, south-west of Trefyclawdd, in 1402, where he captured Edmund Mortimer (who then voluntarily married Glyndŵr's daughter Catherine before having a ransom of 10,000 marks paid by

75 The 'Ogof Owain Glyndŵr' marked on modern OS maps on Moel yr Ogof, just north of Moel Hebog, is thus by a more recent tradition. A sloping, nettle-infested ledge under a huge overhang, approached by a very narrow terrace above a 300-foot drop, is assuredly not the place Jenkins has in mind in this description.
76 D. E. Jenkins, loc. cit. p. 132.

93

Henry), all happened well to the south of Snowdon. So too did the parliaments in Machynlleth, Harlech and Pennal, the formulation of the Tripartite Indenture and the proposed transfer of obedience to the Avignonese Pope Benedict VIII, which would have forged a strong French alliance. In Rees Davies' overview:

> the Welsh showed remarkable stamina; but it has to be recognized that the achievement and duration of their revolt probably owed most to the domestic preoccupations of Henry IV. Until 1408 Henry was never free from plots and rumours of plots against himself and his dynasty. The plotters, almost without exception, made use of the Welsh revolt to try to destabilize Henry's regime.[77]

The date of 1408 is significant. The tide was then turning against Owain. By 1415, after a series of defeats, he had retreated into his home region of Powys. The new king, Henry V, seeking stability for his realm from the brink of another French campaign, offered Owain and his remaining supporters a pardon if they would submit. Owain did not do so, but nor was he hunted down. The offer was repeated, but he had by now faded from the pages of history.

A potent tradition holds that his last years were spent with his daughter Alice, at her husband John Scudamore's seat of Kentchurch Court in the Golden Valley of western Herefordshire, and many believe that the remarkable small portrait of 'Siôn Cent' still displayed in the corner of a landing at Kentchurch Court is of Glyndŵr himself in extreme old age. If this is the case – and it's an argument that enlists my sympathies – that ferocious and ravaged countenance gives

---

77   R. R. Davies, *The Age of Conquest*, op. cit. p. 454.

remarkable expression to the times through which Glyndŵr lived. And beyond that, it embodies something of the wild essence of the Welsh hills among which Owain made his grand protest of independence. Of the probable location in which Glyndŵr spent his last years, Sir John Lloyd wrote that 'it has around it the immemorial peace of the western countryside. At last the flame had flickered out which had once blazed fiercely and wildly throughout the length and breadth of Wales.'[78] That flame – of the independent and martial Welsh spirit – had ensured the remoteness and isolation of the Snowdon region over long centuries.

> By 1415 Wales had been conquered, finally and irreversibly. The story of that conquest dominated the history of the country for ... 350 years. What was surprising was that conquest had taken so long. Already by 1093 the odds against the survival of Wales's political independence seemed hopeless. But the Welsh showed remarkable resourcefulness and resilience. For almost two centuries they survived and even, periodically, flourished. They took full advantage of their own terrain, climate and hardiness; they exploited the lack of stamina and frequent diversions of the Anglo-Norman invaders.[79]

So these were, and perhaps are still, the abiding qualities of the native people of the Snowdon region. We do well to remember them as we turn to the accounts of English visitors to Eryri. A few score years on from Owain Glyndŵr's passing, and for the next 463 years the separate political existence of Wales from England was ended by the statute of 1536. Snowdon, from being remote political fastness, was shape-shifting towards

---

78   Sir J. E. Lloyd, *Owen Glendower (Owain Glyndŵr)* (Clarendon Press, 1931) p. 145.
79   R. R. Davies, *The Age of Conquest*, op. cit. p. 461.

what it is today as common property of the people of Britain. Within a few more decades from that 'Act of Union', travellers for purposes other than conquest and commerce, crusading recruitment or government accounting would begin to make their way to Snowdon, and to take back with them descriptions of its character and wonder that would bring others in their wake, in a surge of interest that has continued exponentially to the present day.

Even in the face of that new onslaught, just as Montcalm's defeat by General Wolf brought no change to the essential Frenchness of Quebec, so too did Snowdon remain Welsh, enduringly and unchangingly so in all the most important considerations of language, culture and community right down to the present day. The conqueror is so seldom the victor in these matters, the human spirit upholding what is most appropriate to its home place, and most dear. As writers from Hesiod and Rousseau to Geoffrey Winthrop Young have observed, the character of a landscape is invariably reflected in the people who inhabit there. The great Welsh educator O. M. Edwards states the case for Wales in this respect succinctly, summing up all the historical turmoil related in this chapter:

Wales is a land of mountains. Its mountains explain its isolation and its love of independence; they explain its internal divisions; they have determined, throughout its history, what the direction and method of its progress were to be ... if the mountains of Wales made political union difficult, they gave their inhabitants the same characteristics, and gave them a community of ideas and of aims centuries before combined action became possible ... A land of mountains which forms the character of those who come to it, giving them a vague similarity of ideas which makes most unity possible in history and literature – that is the abiding fact in the history of Wales. The inhabitants of the mountains feel, amid all their differences, that they are one nation, because their land is unlike any other land . . . This belief in a unity of race, and in a continuity of language, has this much truth in it – the mountains absorb all races that come and give them their character. A land of mountains naturally becomes the early home of patriotism and legend.[80]

The openness and intelligence, the refusal of easy options and the challenges to incipient racism here, deserve applause and are worthy of the landscape itself. Yet the passage is far from precluding defence of cultural identity. With Snowdon, the manifestations of these human truths down the long centuries constitute an indefinable and wonderful aspect to the mountain's appeal. It is a fortress still in defence of all that has become most Welsh.

---

80 From *Wales* (1901), quoted in Ioan Bowen Rees, *The Mountains of Wales* (2nd Edition, University of Wales Press, 1992), p. 17.

4

Antiquaries, Cartographers, Simples Gatherers and Fern Collectors

> Having heard and read the aforesaid authors, tourists, higher philatelists, and lovers of the Celt, I need hardly say, firstly, that I have come under their influence; secondly, that I have tried to avoid it; and thirdly, that I am not equal to the task of apportioning the blame between them and myself for what I write.[81] — EDWARD THOMAS

Jean-Luc Godard's response when asked for the meaning of his film *Weekend* – '*Le moral? C'est le travelling.*' – might be an apt philosophy for gap-year students, but it would surely have perplexed the earliest travellers to leave written records of their journeys to Snowdon. They came with clearly avowed purposes to which ends travel was only the undesirable and difficult means. The first of them to arrive after the statute of 1536 was Henry VIII's King's Antiquary – an unprecedented appointment that required its first and only holder, John Leland, to investigate the records of abbeys, cathedrals, colleges, priories and the like at the time of the dissolution of the monasteries in order to establish what riches might

---

81   Edward Thomas, *Wales*, loc. cit. p. 15.

accrue from them to his patron Henry's exchequer. The task ultimately and literally drove him insane, though at a time long after the three years he spent in Wales between 1536 and 1539. He did visit Snowdonia, but his impressions to a later generation of readers are disappointingly sparse. We learn from him, for example, of the distinguishing characteristic of 'Cregeryri Mountaines . . . horrible with the sighte of bare stones; that 'Caernarvonshire about the shore hath reasonable good corne . . . Then more upward be Eryri hilles, and in them ys very little corne, except otes in some places, and a little barle, but scantly rye.'

This lack of corn turns out to be no great matter because 'if there were the deer wolde destroye it.' (The number of red deer in Snowdonia is commented on by most early visitors but, according to Thomas Pennant, 'they were extirpated before the year 1626'. Pennant goes on to suggest that Bwlch y Saethau – 'The Pass of the Arrows' – between Yr Wyddfa and Y Lliwedd, was so-called because it had been 'probably a station for hunters, to watch the wanderings of the deer'.) Leland also informs us that the keep of Dolbadarn Castle, on a rocky knoll above where the alluvium washed down from Cwm Brwynog has separated the two lakes at Llanberis, was the fortress in which Llywelyn ap Gruffydd imprisoned his elder brother Owain Goch for twenty years, and where, a century and a half later, Owain Glyndŵr incarcerated Reginald Grey of Rhuthun.

If Leland left us little by way of impressions of our mountain, not much more was added by other visitors in his century. The greatest of the sixteenth-century antiquaries, William Camden, who did at least take the trouble to learn Welsh, in his *Britannia*[82] of 1586 noted only of the Welsh

---

82   Michael Drayton, in his *Poly-Olbion* of 1612/1622, essentially set

hills that 'on the interior parts nature has reared groupes of mountains as if she meant here to bind the island fast to the bowels of the earth' – rather a difficult concept for the modern mind to grasp, though oddly satisfying in its notion of the mountain as organically rooted entity. The map-maker John Speed, in the course of an unattributed *Description of Wales* (1599) intended to accompany his series of maps published from 1610 onwards and now in the National Library of Wales' collection of early travel-accounts, is at least comprehensible, if a little exaggerated:

> These Mountaines may not unfitly be termed the British Alpes, as being the most vaste of all Britaine, and for their steepnesse and cragginesse not unlike to those of Italy, all of them towring up into the Aire, and round encompassing one far higher than all the rest, peculiarly called Snowdon-Hill, though the other likewise in the same sense, are by the Welsh termed Craig-Eriry, as much as Snowy Mountaines . . . For all the yeare long these lye mantelled over with Snow hard crusted together, though otherwise for their height they are open and liable both to the Sunne to dissolve them, and the windes to over-sweepe them.

What was to temper this early subjectivity and impressionism with a more rigorously scientific discipline found its earliest Welsh expression through a native of the eastern margins of Eryri. William Salesbury, who lived from about 1520 to about

---

the rough prosings of *Britannia* to poetic metre and varnished them with Spenserian patriotism and pastoralism. But he added little that was new or directly informed, and it is to be doubted whether he ever actually visited the region, so the traditional inclusion of his name among considerations of early travellers is perhaps to be regarded as suspect. The precedent he set still frequently obtains among metropolitan writers, of course, who consider themselves authorities on the region after a weekend's visit.

1584, and spent most of his life at Llanrwst, was one of the most learned Welshmen of his day. He translated the *Book of Common Prayer* and the *New Testament* into a beautiful and idiosyncratic Welsh to which the later translator of the whole of the Welsh Bible, William Morgan, was indebted. Salesbury also wrote, between 1568 and 1574, his *Llysieulyfr*, as it was later entitled. Transcripts of this 'plant-book' or herbal found their way into important collections and libraries, and despite its being in Welsh, albeit heavily Latinized in Salesbury's characteristic style, it was to act as significant incentive and lure to visitors to Snowdonia throughout the seventeenth century. So between the cartographer and the early botanist, by the fourth decade of that century a certain light of knowledge was dissipating the earlier dread. In addition, the first explorations of Snowdon itself by other than native dwellers in the region was about to begin.

According to Anthony Wood – one of those delightful gossipy anecdotalists with whom the seventeenth century abounds – Thomas Johnson was 'the best herbalist of his age, and no less eminent in the garrison for his valour and conduct as a soldier'. So it's perhaps fitting that the earliest non-mythical account that we have of an ascent on Snowdon should have been written by so sterling a character. Johnson was an apothecary with a practice on Snow Hill in London, and one whose distinction is evident from his having, in 1633, published a revised and augmented edition of John Gerard's great *Herball* of 1597. The herbalists were the doctors of their age (Johnson in fact had the degree of MD conferred on him by Oxford in 1643). They tapped into an extensive fund of local knowledge about plant attributes and habitats for collection of the raw materials for their 'simples' – the herbal medicinal remedies which are even now the basis of the pharmaceutical industry.

One of the beliefs widespread among 'simples collectors' was in the transference of properties between habitat and plant. Hence where the latter grew in a 'strong' environment like that of the rocks and crags of Snowdon, its potency would be all the more marked. Thus were the promptings for the arrival of Thomas Johnson in August 1639 at Glynllifon, the house of his fellow botanist and correspondent Thomas Glynne. In his *Mercurii Bot. pars altera* of 1641 Johnson gives his account of the expedition of 3rd August 1639 to Snowdon, with Glynne, a farm boy as guide, and an interpreter to explain anything the latter might have to say:

> we betook ourselves to our British Alps. The highest of all these is called Snowdon by the English, and Widhfa by the Britons . . . The whole mass of the mountain was veiled in cloud . . . Leaving our horses and outer garments, we began to climb the mountain. The ascent at first is difficult, but after a bit a broad open space is found, but equally sloping, great precipices on the left, and a difficult climb on the right. Having climbed three miles, we at last gained the highest ridge of the mountain, which was shrouded in thick cloud. Here the way was very narrow, and climbers are horror-stricken by the rough rocky precipices on either hand and the Stygian marshes, both on this side and on that.

The party pressed on to the summit, where they 'sat down in the midst of the clouds, and first of all we arranged in order the plants we had, at our peril, collected among the rocks and precipices, and then we ate the food we had brought with us.'[83] The eminent modern botanist Dewi Jones of Pen-y-groes, in

---

83   The translation from Johnson's Latin is by William Jenkyn Thomas, *The Itinerary of a Botanist through North Wales in the year 1639 A.D.* (Evan Thomas, 1908).

a definitive study, comments that 'This is the first published record of a guide being hired in Snowdonia', and adds that:

> These early mountaineers were ordinary hill farmers whose forefathers had tended their flocks, dug for peat and hunted on the same wild mountain terrain for generations. History and folklore had been passed down among them from father to son in the customary oral tradition and with it, in some instances, came the specialized knowledge needed to prepare herbal medicine. It would therefore have been essential for certain members of these isolated communities to know the habitats of the plants used for medicinal purposes. The mountain plants were believed to contain healing qualities equal to, if not stronger than, those of the lowland species ... Localities such as Clogwyn Du'r Arddu, Cwmglas Mawr and Cwmglas Bach on Snowdon ... were noted for their variety of flowers from the earliest times. It must also be remembered that these early herbalists and apothecaries could identify plants from foliage alone, a necessary skill during out of season botanical excursions.[84]

The route by which Johnson and his party climbed Snowdon is rather obscure – a feature common to many early accounts – though the topography described suggests that they climbed by way of what is now the Snowdon Ranger Path from Cwellyn, the likelihood of this being enhanced by its reasonable proximity to Glynllifon. This would have taken them along the ridge above the cliffs of Clogwyn Du'r Arddu

---

84 Dewi Jones, *The Botanists and Mountain Guides of Snowdonia* (2nd edition, Gwasg Carreg Gwalch, 2007), pp. 20–21. I am indebted to Dewi, an extraordinary contemporary personification of the tradition he describes, for much in the way of perspectives and direction to source materials in this and other chapters.

('great precipices on the left'), and on to the summit ridge after a steep climb up to the right. This probability is further enhanced by the plant list for the excursion, which includes northern rock cress, mountain sorrel, roseroot, moss campion and thrift as well as purple, starry and mossy saxifrage, all of which are still to be found growing in the vicinity of Clogwyn Du'r Arddu (many of them in the back of the wide ramp at the top of the Eastern Terrace, which is easily accessible from the path along the ridge above).[85]

---

85 The great twentieth century field-naturalist William Condry, in one of the incomparable 'Country Diaries' he contributed to the *Guardian* newspaper fortnightly for forty years, makes the following point, which is crucially relevant here: 'Although it was high summer when Johnson climbed Snowdon, the whole mountain remained buried in cloud all day and he and his friends would surely have got lost in the mists if they had not "obtained the services of a country boy as guide" There has always been something of a mystery about Johnson's visit. Snowdon is a big, sprawling mountain whose botanically exciting localities are so few that a stranger could easily spend a day up there and miss all the choicest spots. But we know from his list that Johnson did really well and must have got to the most rewarding places. So how did he manage it? I can't help thinking that although the credit for the discovery of these alpines is given to Johnson and other English visitors, they had probably been known to the local Welsh herbalists for ages but had never been placed on record. I wish we knew more about that "country boy" who acted as Johnson's guide. Perhaps he had already learned more about mountain plants than Johnson ever was to know?' Reprinted in William Condry, *A Welsh Country Diary* (Gomer, 1993), pp. 104–105.
    I would certainly applaud Bill's demotic instincts here, especially as we'll encounter similarly colonialist impulses at play in the chapter on climbing history; but the element of chance perhaps also needs to be taken into account. The likeliest route by which Johnson made his ascent would have taken him straight across the top of Clogwyn Du'r Arddu's Eastern Terrace, which is one of the arctic-alpine *loci classici*. It was also, as we shall see in the next chapter, the first recorded rock-climb in Snowdonia (if you exclude Owain Glyndŵr's eponymous chimney on Moel Hebog, that is), and perhaps that fact is not entirely attributable to chance? The interplay between the probable, the possible, and the speculative in this area of study is entirely fascinating. Finally, an absorbing modern slant on this traditional indigenous knowledge is given in the memoir *Llyfr Rhedyn ei Daid* (Gwasg Dwyfor, 1987) of the pre-eminent expert on Snowdonia's arctic-alpine flora, the late Evan Roberts of Capel Curig.

What is certain is that their recorded finds acted as a keen enticement to the botanists who, assisted and enthused by his account, came after him. By the time of their coming, though, Johnson himself was dead. A lieutenant-colonel in the Royalist army, at the siege of Basing Castle in September 1644 his shoulder was shattered by a musket-ball and he died of a fever a fortnight later. George Lister hails his Snowdon account as 'the first chapter in British mountaineering literature', and comments further that the 'narrative possesses all the essential features of the countless descriptive essays' which have subsequently been published, 'from the start at dawn to the inevitable finale of food on the summit.'[86]

After the turmoil of the English Revolution, which had claimed Johnson's life,[87] and the Restoration of the House of Stuart in 1660, the visitors began to arrive in the region 'thick as autumnall leaves that strow the brooks in Vallombrosa'. The vanguard arrived even before the Restoration. Just under fourteen years after Thomas Johnson's death, another of the great early botanists, John Ray, arrived in Caernarfon, where he hired a Snowdon guide, set off for the peak, was rained off, rode on to Beddgelert and took lodgings there, from which, on the 2nd September and with a fresh guide, he climbed to the cloud-wreathed summit of Snowdon, which provided him with the consolation of 'Divers rare plants . . . found on the top and sides of the hill which were then strangers to me'.

---

86 G. A. Lister, 'The Coming of the Mountaineer, 1750–1850', in H. R. C. Carr & G. A. Lister, eds., *The Mountains of Snowdonia* (2nd edition, Crosby, Lockwood, 1948), p. 45.

87 His death, according to Bill Condry, was a loss to mountain literature as well as to botany, for he was the first Snowdon traveller to entertain his readers with accounts of scrambling above horrifying chasms amid tempests and floods of rain. W. M. Condry, *The Snowdonia National Park* (Collins, New Naturalist, 1966), p. 6.

Undeterred by the weather, though thinking to try a season other than autumn, he returned in 1662 with two more botanists, Francis Willughby and Phillip Skippon, once more climbing Snowdon from Beddgelert, having walked round the mountain from Llanberis. They confirmed many of Johnson's discoveries from twenty-three years before, and added several species of their own, including that ubiquitous and vivid plant of Welsh screes and stony places, the parsley fern, as well as Welsh poppies and the now very rare small-white orchid.

John Ray connects directly with one of the most significant figures in Snowdon's history, and the man whose name was to be given to a beautiful rarity of the region. This was Edward Lhuyd,[88] a native of Llanforda near Croesoswallt, with whom Ray took up a correspondence in the summer of 1689. The younger man, Lhuyd, initially displayed an endearing admiration for the established scientist, calling him 'a man of the most agreeable temper imaginable ... doubtless the best acquainted with Natural History of any now living', though he himself was soon to surpass his mentor in knowledge and achievement and by 1706 had become, in the words of Sir Hans Sloane, a distinguished London physician and future President of the Royal Society, 'the best naturalist now in Europe'.

Lhuyd, who worked under the auspices of Oxford's Ashmolean Museum from 1684, firstly as under-keeper and from 1690 to his death in 1709 as its keeper, perhaps knew the mountains of Eryri better than anyone had done before his time or for several centuries after. He sensibly dispelled Speed's notion of them as a realm of perpetual snow: 'Generally speaking there's no snow here from the end of April to the

---

88 'Lhuyd' is simply an archaic variant of the modern Welsh word 'Llwyd' ('grey'), and is pronounced in exactly the same way.

midst of September . . . It often snows on the tops of these mountains in May and June, but that snow, or rather sleet, melts as fast as it falls'. Here is the authoritative voice of first-hand experience!

Lhuyd made extensive revisions and augmentations to Camden's *Britannia*, his revised edition of which appeared in 1695. He toured relentlessly through the Welsh hills and other British regions, assisting Ray with his British plant *Synopsis Methodica Stirpium Britannicorum* of 1690, studying archaeology, philology and geology as well as natural history wherever he went. When he died of pleurisy at the early age of 49, he left an archive of detailed observations in more than 150 manuscript volumes which was offered to Jesus College, Oxford, and which would have been, judging by what little remained after its dispersal, a national record without equal. But 'Honest' Lhuyd, as he was known to his contemporaries, had quarrelled with an influential fellow of Jesus College and future Bishop of St. Asaph over the significance of fossil records from Snowdon summit – ascribed by the bishop-to-be, of course, on the authority of Holy Writ to The Deluge, and God help the poor heretic who cared to gainsay and put forward a more scientific argument for their presence.

So neither Jesus College nor Oxford University were minded to accept the bequest, and it was thus sold at auction, broken up, and the greater part of it was lost in fires at a London bookbinders and at Thomas Johnes' mansion of Hafod Uchdryd. If his archive were still extant, Lhuyd would surely be recognized as one of the great polymathic figures of his age. Instead, his lasting memorial came years after his death in the decision to name in his honour the delicate and singularly lovely little plant of Snowdon cliff-ledges that he had first described as *Bulbosa Alpina juncifolia, pericarpio unico erecto in summo cauliculo dodrantali.* Nowadays it is celebrated as the region's special and identifying rarity under the Latin name of *Lloydia Serotina* – the Snowdon Lily. It is gratifying that, though the institution through individual pique rejected his life's labours, the mountain's name is now inseparably conjoined with that of Edward Lhuyd.

By comparison with the breadth and intelligence of Lhuyd's work, the first half of the eighteenth century is an arid intellectual tract in terms of visitor accounts. It doesn't much improve with the first book to include the name of the mountain in its title – Joseph Cradock's *Letters from Snowdon* of 1770. A brief extract will give you the tone, and it's one which repeats incessantly and in little-differentiated form through the work of succeeding travellers for two centuries.[89] Cradock and his companions have found shelter from the Snowdon rain in 'a small thatched hut at the foot of the mountain near the lake they call Llyn Cychwhechlyn which I leave you to pronounce as well as you are able'.

Required jibe at the Welsh language duly worked in, Cradock calls on the tradition of Thomas Gray's 'The Bard'[90]

---

89 If you disbelieve this assertion, I would recommend close study of the text by the American environmentalist Amory Lovins to the sumptuous Sierra Club volume, *Eryri: The Mountains of Longing* (1972), in which you'll find the solitary wanderer bending his ear once more to the sound of a harp emanating from the open window of some picturesque lonely cottage.

90 Gray's poem was written after hearing a Cambridge performance by the blind Welsh harpist John Parry in 1757 – the same year in which Edmund Burke's seminal essay on the sublime, of which more in the next chapter, was published. The poem imagines a bard among the ruins of Conwy Castle reviling and cursing Edward Longshanks for his treatment of Wales – a nation transmuted after five centuries from guerrilla threat to romantic archetype. 'The Bard' became an oddly influential text, and not only in its own time and culture. A famous Hungarian poem, János Arany's 'A Walesi Bárdok' ('The Welsh Bards') of 1863, written against the Habsburg occupation, reworks its theme of cultural resistance for that context.

and moves on to his quasi-naturalistic description: 'We were determined to amuse ourselves as well as we could in this dreary situation. For this purpose we sent for a poor blind harper and procured a number of blooming country girls to divert us with their music and dancing. Thus, no doubt, have a thousand subsequent wet days in Snowdon's shadow been spent (mostly in the hotels of large chains whilst on Saga Holidays coach tours). We must move on hurriedly to far better things.

The quality of Snowdon's ascensionists certainly improved after Cradock had taken his leave of the mountain (though the pall of his prose style took longer to clear away – the sheer number of later borrowers and imitators is wholly inexplicable except as ultimate confirmation of our obsession with cliché). In 1773 Joseph Banks, future President of the Royal Society and a co-founder of the Botanical Gardens at Kew, fresh from his circumnavigation of the globe in the *Endeavour* with James Cook, thought the mountain of sufficient interest to make the climb, though he left no published record of his impressions. This same year of 1773 saw the arrival in Snowdonia of Thomas Pennant, whose monumental and best-selling *A Tour in Wales* (two volumes, 1778 and 1781), lavishly illustrated by the delightful and remarkably accurate engravings of Moses Griffith. (The one of Pennant standing on the very end of the cantilever stone near the summit of Glyder Fach has probably, down the ages, been responsible for more ascents of this mountain – and more facsimile photographs – than any other factor in its history.) This was the first substantial literary treatment of its subject, and contributed significantly to a contemporary movement towards appreciation of Celtic landscapes and cultures, which also found expression in the Hebridean tours of Johnson and Boswell and the fabrications of blind Ossian's inventor, James Macpherson.

Already famous for his *British Zoology*, which began publication in 1761, and soon to publish his account of a 1769 *A Tour in Scotland* (it appeared in 1776, and was extremely influential in its views of that nation), Pennant was chiefly an antiquary and zoologist. Gilbert White's *The Natural History and Antiquities of Selborne* of 1789 – arguably the first classic of nature-writing in English – is in the form of letters written to Pennant and to Daines Barrington. To Dr. Johnson, in the course of a comic, heated exchange with Dr. Percy, whose Northumbrian feathers had been ruffled by some imagined slights in the Scottish book, Pennant was 'the best traveller I ever read; he observes more things than any one else does'.[91] That Pennant was also an indefatigable walker will be abundantly clear to anyone who reads his accounts of ascents on Snowdon.

He arrived at the mountain by way of a novel route from Llanrwst over Nant Bwlch yr Haiarn to Capel Curig, and thence past Llynnau Mymbyr into the Nant y Gwryd: 'Snowdon and all his sons, Crib Coch, Crib y Distyll, Lliwedd yr Aran, and many others, here burst at once full in view, and make this far the finest approach to our boasted Alps'.[92]

Pennant's account of his climb up Snowdon – a composite account really, and at times potentially confusing, since it frequently refers back to an earlier ascent in the same year – begins with observations on the deforestation around Llanberis since the time of Leland; with mention of the divinatory trout in Ffynnon Peris at Nant Peris (the well is still there in the garden of Tyn-y-Ffynnon, though the trout are long gone); with the history, much repeated by subsequent writers, of the

91 James Boswell, *Life of Johnson* (Oxford Standard Authors, 1976), p. 993.
92 Thomas Pennant, *A Tour in Wales*, vol. II (Henry Hughes, London, 1781), p. 159.

ANTIQUARIES, CARTOGRAPHERS, SIMPLES GATHERERS

Amazonian Margaret uch Evan of Penllyn, 'last specimen of
the strength and spirit of the antient British fair', by whose
rowing prowess visitors approaching from Caernarfon were
conveyed to Llanberis throughout several decades of the
eighteenth century (Pennant records with obvious amusement
that 'At length she gave her hand to the most effeminate of
her admirers, as if predetermined to maintain the superiority
which nature had bestowed upon her').[93] He mentions the
antiquities around Llanberis and Cwm-y-glo, and takes up
lodgings at the Nant Peris inn with the Closs family, agents
to the Llanberis copper-mines. Guided by the 'most able
conductor' Hugh Shone, the two men out early in the morning
to 'begin our ascent to the highest peak of Snowdon', passing
the waterfall of Ceunant Mawr and discoursing as he goes on
the practice of transhumance in Cwm Brwynog, the use of
lichens, and the diet of the men and women tending sheep and
goats on the summer pastures. All of this perfectly substantiate
Johnson's view of him, especially by comparison with any of
his predecessors and contemporaries, as a man who 'observes
more things than any one else does'.

His account of the climb itself is worth giving in substantial
extracts, being a classic of its kind, written in exact descriptive
prose mercifully economical with the rhetorical flourishes that
bedevil most of his contemporaries. Hugh Shone, the guide,
took him along the right-hand side of Maesgwm and through
the *bwlch* at its head to join the route (now the Snowdon
Ranger Path) by which Thomas Johnson had almost certainly
made his ascent over a century before:

> . . . we reach Bwlch y Cwm Brwynog, where the ascent
> becomes very difficult, by reason of its vast steepness. People

---

93   ibid. p. 167.

here usually quit their horses. We began a toilsome march, clambering among the rocks. On the left were the precipices over Cwm Brwynog, with Llyn du yr Ardwy at their foot. On our right were those over the small lakes Llyn Glas, Llyn y Nadroedd, and Llyn Coch. The last is the highest on this side of the mountain; and on whose margins, we were told, that, in fairy days, those diminutive gentry kept their revels.

Interesting again, the extent to which the vicinity of Cwellyn was an epicentre of fairy lore. Pennant continues:

This space between precipice and precipice, forms a short, and no very agreeable isthmus, till we reached a verdant expanse, which gave us some respite, before we labored up another series of broken crags: after these is a second smooth tract, which reaches almost to the summit, which, by way of pre-eminence, is styled Y WYDDFA, or The Conspicuous.[94] It rises almost to a point, or, at best, there is but room for a circular wall of loose stones, within which travellers usually take their repast.[95]

---

94 It is probably worth quoting the definitive authority, to put to rest any lingering confusion around the names of 'Snowdon' and 'Yr Wyddfa'. Hence, from Hywel Wyn Owen's and Richard Morgan's *Dictionary of the Place-Names of Wales* (Gomer Press, 2007), p. 443: 'Both names characterize the mountain as being visible from considerable distances and likely to be snow-covered . . . *gwyddfa* here is 'height, eminence, promontory' (from *gwydd* 'presence, sight' and thus 'prominent', *–ma* 'place') . . . It occurs in several hill-names, leading to this, the highest mountain in Wales, being described occasionally as Yr Wyddfa Fawr . . . *gwydd* and *gwyddfa* also developed the meaning 'burial mound, memorial cairn, tumulus' (probably from the location of such cairns on prominent hills) and this meaning has been attributed to Yr Wyddfa, with popular association with a legendary giant R(h)ita Gawr . . . reputedly buried under the large cairn at the summit.'

95 Thomas Pennant, *A Tour in Wales*, vol. II, ibid. pp. 170–171.

This is both perfectly recognizable hence trustworthy and useful in the first detailed picture it gives of Snowdon summit at this or indeed any period, its summit cairn hollowed out (doubtless after having been robbed by those in quest of R[h]ita's jewellery), to make the kind of shelter that you still find built from rearranged stones of the cairns on most Welsh hill-tops. Pennant also gives us an extraordinarily precise description of the immediate and the far views, merged with a marvellous account – the first extant – of sunrise from the top of the mountain, the viewing of which very soon became a tradition for which Pennant, through this surprisingly influential book,[96] is surely the one to thank or blame:

> The mountain from hence seems propped by four vast buttresses; between which are four deep Cwms, or hollows: each, excepting one, had one or more lakes, lodged in its distant bottom. The nearest was Ffynnon Llas, or The Green Well, lying immediately below us. One of the company had the curiosity to descend a very bad way to a jutting rock, that impended over the monstrous precipice; and he seemed like Mercury ready to take his flight from the summit of Atlas. The waters of Ffynnon Las, from this height, appeared black and unfathomable, and the edges quite green. From thence is a succession of bottoms, surrounded by the most lofty and rugged hills, the greatest part of the whole sides are quite

---

96   Resistance to Welsh-themed topographical books has been an acknowledged fact in British publishing certainly since the time of George Borrow. The extraordinary glut of them which succeeded Pennant's tour and lasted until well into the nineteenth century is surely a factor here, as also is an English Cymrophobia, the origins of which were touched on in the previous chapter. On the whole, latter-day Saxons have preferred to take their outdoor recreation in the English Lake District (formerly, of course, the Brittonic kingdom of Rheged). We can blame Wordsworth here, but as Robert Graves had it in his poem 'Welsh Incident' – 'I was coming to that'.

mural, and form the most magnificent amphitheatre in nature. The Wyddfa is on one side; Crib y Distill, with its serrated tops, on another; Crib Coch, a ridge of fiery redness, appears beneath the preceding; and opposite to it is the boundary called the Lliwedd. Another singular support to this mountain is Y Clawdd Coch, rising into a sharp ridge, so narrow, as not to afford breadth even for a path.[97]

This is an exemplary topographical description of the eastwards view from the summit, and all the more remarkable by contrast with the fashion for nebulous exaggeration current at Pennant's time. In the conclusion to his account, he takes us back to a previous visit:

The view from this exalted situation is unbounded. In a former tour, I saw from it the county of Chester, the high hills of Yorkshire, part of the north of England, Scotland and Ireland: a plain view of the Isle of Man; and that of Anglesea lay extended like a map beneath us, with every rill visible.[98]

All this is entirely feasible. I've frequently seen the Wicklow Hills of Ireland, the Isle of Man, Pen-y-ghent in Yorkshire and the unmistakable outline of Criffell above Dumfries on those crystal days when every stream on Anglesey glints in the sun. The problem with this clarity in the misty west, as Shakespeare's Sonnet 33, 'Full many a glorious morning have I seen | Flatter the mountain tops with sovereign eye' points out, is that it generally presages rain. But back to Pennant, and his innovative way of experiencing the full atmosphere of Snowdon:

---

97   Thomas Pennant, *A Tour in Wales*, vol. II, ibid. p. 171. 'Y Clawdd Coch' is the ridge from Bwlch Main to Yr Wyddfa, its narrowness a little over-stated here.

98   ibid. p. 172.

I took much pains to see this prospect to advantage: sat up at a farm on the west till about twelve, and walked up the whole way. The night was remarkably fine and starry: towards morn, the stars faded away, and left a short interval of darkness, which was soon dispersed by the dawn of day. The body of the sun appeared most distinct, with the rotundity of the moon, before it rose high enough to render its beams too brilliant for our sight. The sea which bounded the western part was gilt by its beams, first in slender streaks, at length glowed with redness. The prospect was disclosed to us like the gradual drawing up of a curtain in a theatre. We saw more and more, till the heat became so powerful, as to attract the mists from the various lakes, which in a slight degree obscured the prospect. The shadow of the mountain was flung many miles, and shewed its bicapitated form; the Wyddfa making one, Crib y Distill the other head.[99]

What happened next will be familiar to many who have witnessed mornings like this from a mountain-top:

. . . the sky was obscured very soon after I got up. A vast mist enveloped the whole circuit of the mountain. The prospect down was horrible. It gave an idea of numbers of abysses, concealed by a thick smoke, furiously circulating around us. Very often a gust of wind formed an opening in the clouds, which gave a fine and distinct visto of lake and valley. Sometimes they opened only in one place; at others, in many at once, exhibiting a most strange and perplexing sight of water, fields, rocks, or chasms, in fifty different places. They then closed at once, and left us involved in darkness; in a small space they would separate again, and fly in wild eddies

---

99   ibid.

round the middle of the mountains, and expose, in parts, both tops and bases clear to our view.[100]

I do not know of a better description of the disorientations and dramatic shifts of scene and perspective that mist produces among the hills. This to my mind is the first significant passage in mountain literature, and Wordsworth bases his celebrated later Snowdon passage from *The Prelude* heavily upon it. It takes Johnson's description of almost exactly the same spot from the previous century and dramatizes it, explores the affective dimension of being on a mountain in adverse conditions:

we descended from this various scene with great reluctance; but before we reached our horses, a thunderstorm overtook us. Its rolling among the mountains was inexpressibly awful: the rain uncommonly heavy. We remounted our horses and gained the bottom with great hazard. The little rills, which on our ascent trickled along the gullies on the sides of the mountain, were now swelled into torrents; and we and our steeds passed with the utmost risque of being swept away by these sudden waters. At length we arrived safe, yet sufficiently wet and weary, to our former quarters.

He caps this masterful conflation of two separate accounts with a summary paragraph that will gain the assent of everyone who knows well these western, seaward hills of Britain:

It is very rare that the traveller gets a proper day to ascend the hill; for it often appears clear, but by the evident attraction of the clouds by this lofty mountain, it becomes suddenly and unexpectedly enveloped in mist, when the clouds have just before appeared very remote, and at great heights. At

---

100   ibid. pp. 172–173.

times, I have observed them lower to half their height, and
notwithstanding they have been dispersed to the right and
to the left, yet they have met from both sides, and united to
involve the summit in one great obscurity.

The absolute authenticity of this directly and simply stated
experience of the mountain environment is an entirely new
note in the Snowdon story, and establishes Pennant as pre-
eminent among the hill-travellers of his time. In his book he
records the height of Yr Wyddfa, as being 'one thousand one
hundred and eighty-nine yards and one foot, reckoning from
the quay at Caernarvon to the highest peak' – not at all a bad
estimate at 3,568 feet, and one that compares very favourably
with the mean of Ordnance Survey triangulations since the
first edition of the map in 1839. He is also eminently sensible
about the name, citing 'Snawdune's' first appearance in the
Anglo-Saxon Chronicle and pointing out that Snowdonia is 'a
literal translation of the ancient appellation, Creigie'r Eryri,
The Snowy mountains, from the frequency of snow on them,
and nothing to do with eagles, that bird [appearing] very
seldom among them'. On the question of the snow too he
retains his good sense:

not that it is to be imagined that they are covered in snow
in some part or other the whole year, as has been idly fabled;
there being frequently whole weeks, even in winter, in which
they are totally free.

His elaboration around this last point is still entirely valid:

The earliest appearance of snow, is commonly between the
middle of October, and the beginning of November: the falls
which happen then, are usually washed away with the rains,
and the hills remain clear till Christmas. Between that time

and the end of January, the greatest falls happen; which are
succeeded by others, about the latter end of April, or beginning
of May, which remain in certain places till the middle of June,
in which month has been seen a depth of some feet. It has
even happened, that the greatest fall has been in April, or
beginning of May;[101] and that never fails happening, when
the preceding winter has had the smallest falls. But the fable
of Giraldus, concerning the continuance of snow the whole
year, is totally to be exploded.[102]

From personal acquaintance stretching over more than
fifty years, even given our current preoccupation with 'climate
change' (as if climate were ever a static entity), this seems to me
sensible and exact. Pennant also leaves us with the impression,
in a delightful last excursion before he quits the subject of
Snowdon, of a man who was by no means solely bent on
achieving the summit – or to use that offensive and spurious
modern term, on 'conquering' the mountain. His last section
on the mountain we touched upon in the first chapter and it's
fitting to revisit his descriptions at this point. He recounts a
walk into Cwm Dyli, where he dines on curds and whey with
a farmer and his family resident in their *hafoty* for the summer
season. At Llyn Llydaw he comes across the black-backed
gulls that then nested on an islet in the lake and, disturbed by
the rare intrusion of humans, took to the air and 'set the place
echoing with their raucous screams'. Passing beneath the 'vast
mural steeps of Lliwedd' he arrives at Ffynnon Las (Glaslyn),

---

101   When I was living in Cwm Pennant, just to the west of the mountain,
in the 1970s, there was a name still current among the shepherds of the valley
for this phenomenon: *Eira bach yr wyn ieuainc* – the small snow of the young
lambs. It would occur reliably every year, as the name suggests, during the
April lambing time of the upland flocks.
102   Thomas Pennant, *A Tour in Wales*, vol. II, ibid. pp. 178–179.

where he describes how the deep coppery-green colouring of the lake water and the reflection on its surface of the strata above, 'varied with stripes of the richest colors, like the most beautiful lute-strings; and changed almost to infinity'.

On the grassy slopes by the outflow of the lake, where the ascent to Y Gribin begins, is where he notices the 'wheat-ear, a small and seemingly tender bird'. It is still one of the surest places on the mountain to observe this exquisite little long-distance migrant and summer visitor to the Welsh hills – see Chapter One for verification! Whenever I see it on these slopes of Snowdon, it reminds me again of the honesty, the precise observation, the scrupulous exactitude that are the defining characteristics of Snowdon's first great literary celebrant.[103] For those who came after him and aspired to record the mountain scene, Thomas Pennant had set a very high mark indeed. Perhaps if we still possessed the work of Edward Lhuyd in sufficient quantity, this would have been of equal or greater value. But of all that remains extant in writings about Snowdon up to the end of the eighteenth century, it is Pennant's work – clear-sighted, truth-seeking, encyclopedically informed, uncluttered by alternative discourses or ideals – that is avowedly modern in its uncompromising adherence to a representation of the world as we actually see it, and as we can still see it today.

---

103 An interesting point here is that the name 'wheatear' is generally accepted as having been thus bowdlerized in Victorian times from the old folk name of 'white-arse' – a very apt description. Pennant's use of 'Wheat-ear' suggests that this was not the case – unless, as a gentleman, he didn't use the coarser folk version and the change pre-dated Victorian times.

5

The Starting of the Wild Idea

The passion caused by the great and sublime in nature, when those causes operate most powerfully, is astonishment; and astonishment is that state of the soul, in which all its motions are suspended, with some degree of horror. In this case the mind is so entirely filled with its object, that it cannot entertain any other, nor by consequence reason on that object which employs it. Hence arises the great power of the sublime, that, far from being produced by them, it anticipates our reasonings, and hurries us on by an irresistible force. Astonishment, as I have said, is the effect of the sublime in its highest degree; the inferior effects are admiration, reverence, and respect . . .[104] — EDMUND BURKE

Just as the contemporary 'X-treme Sports' enthusiast clamours for the momentary suspensions of the adrenaline rush, so too did the late-eighteenth-century traveller seek assiduously after the affective transports of encounters with the 'sublime in nature'. To a modern reader, it is almost comical, the extent to which the language and concepts of Burke's Longinus-based 1757 'canonical text in the history of aesthetic theory', quoted from above, for half a century and more are repeated either

---

104   Edmund Burke, 'A Philosophical Inquiry into the Sublime and the Beautiful', in *The Portable Edmund Burke*, ed. Isaac Kramnick (Penguin, 1999), p. 64.

directly or through the filtering echo-phraseology of poets such as Gray and Wordsworth.

They permeate the visual arts, too. The contribution made by Moses Griffith's engravings to Pennant's seminal tours has already been mentioned in the preceding chapter. The eighteenth-century near-contemporaries and co-founders in 1768 of the Royal Academy, Richard Wilson and Paul Sandby (the latter, according to Gainsborough, 'the only man of genius to paint real views from Nature in this country'), became gently obsessed with the Welsh hills. The formal classicism of Wilson's innumerable paintings of Snowdon, illuminated by a Claudean light, grace many major British landscape collections, with particularly fine examples of *Snowdon from Llyn Nantlle* – a design-from-Nature so good it could bear, and indeed received, frequent repetitions from the artist – hanging in Birmingham and, my own particular favourite, in Liverpool's Walker Art Gallery. The appeal that the cultural conservatism and iconography worked in to these canvases held for Wilson's wealthy patrons no doubt explains the proliferation of his studies on the theme. By contemporary accounts, Sandby's masterpiece – a considerable departure from his usual themes and style – was a vast canvas, now lost, illustrating Gray's Bard within a ruggedly typological Welsh landscape. As romantically-informed neoclassicism gave way to its full-blown Romantic successor, the great names of that period (the Grand Tour for long periods throughout these years being rendered impossible) also made their way to the Welsh mountains. Turner was one of the foremost among them, the range of styles in the work of our greatest British painter being well illustrated by the contrast between an exquisite little watercolour of Snowdon from across Llyn Padarn of 1798 (now in the British Museum), and a startling, overbearing oilon-canvas from 1800 of a gothically-transfigured Dolbadarn Castle – sublimely horrible indeed! – that hangs at the Royal Academy.

Every visitor of the time who leaves a literary account of a journey to Snowdon provides conclusive evidence that the pervasively derivative nature of English culture's writing project is by no means a solely modern invention, and has been a constant at least since the time of the Enlightenment. Pennant is imbued with Burke's philosophy.[105] Wordsworth is steeped in the vocabulary of the sublime from both influences. Burke's essay is the foundation stone of the Romantic response to landscape in Britain; and at a time when the true horrors of war in Europe were occluding the possibility of Britons' experiencing those sublimely affective horrors of alpine mountain scenery about which Gray had written with such influential and tempting afflatus a few decades before, it was fortunate indeed that a generation's philosophically-directed cravings after mind-expanding encounters with the beautiful and the sublime could find a satisfying object rather closer to home, in that strange and unknown landscape of potential horror called Wales.

Snowdon was the psychedelic trip of its Romantic day; philosophy had thrust cultural significance upon its cloudy brow, and as with a later generation of 'X-perimenters' and sensation-seekers, the artistic minds of the time wanted to sample, however superficially, something of what it was all about.

---

105   Not always a bad thing, of course, as the example of Shakespeare, who was entirely promiscuous in his use of sources, demonstrates. Having said that, he did tend to leave the acknowledgements to later scholars, which nowadays would rightly be thought shabby behaviour.

From the time of Pennant onwards, they came by the score. That description of mist on the mountain from his *A Journey to Snowdon* of 1781 quoted in Chapter Four is as perfect an illustration as you will find of the Burkean aesthetic in all its horrible sublimity, nature in it grandly mysterious, animated, threatening: 'And lo!' We find it again, Pennant's book having been used by the poet both as guide and literary model, in an extract from the 1805–6 version of Wordsworth's auto-biographical poem[106] *The Prelude, or The Growth of a Poet's Mind*.

The account is of a night ascent on the mountain that took place in the summer of 1793 in the company of a local guide and of Robert Jones of Plas-yn-Llan near Rhuthun, who Wordsworth had met whilst they were fellow-students at Cambridge and whose home he had been revisiting in a time when he was grieving over the abandonment in revolutionary France of his mistress Annette Vallon and their

---

106 My personal preference with Wordsworth's poetry – and this is a widespread one which runs counter to the received wisdom that the authoritative texts are the last ones to have been revised in a writer's lifetime – is generally for earlier versions. His later emendations, imposed at a time long after his poetic moment had passed and its former fine instincts grown attenuated, all too often rob the verse of its appealing honesty, fresh insight, delicately nuanced resonance and immediacy. Compare, for example, the 'Matthew' poems from the *Lyrical Ballads* text of 1798 with their revised versions in the *Standard Edition* (the last one Wordsworth himself saw through to publication) of 1849–1850. I frankly do not like the older Wordsworth, with all his snobbery, vainglory, misrepresentation, minor treacheries to former friends, apostasy from youthful principle, vicious social attitudes and incessant craving for public recognition. There is an excellent parallel-text edition of *The Prelude* in the Penguin English Poets series (ed. J. C. Maxwell, Penguin, 1972), where the 1805–6 manuscript version and the 1850 published one are printed on opposite pages for purposes of comparison. The later version has interesting added recollections (for example, that the 'shepherd's cur' of 1805–6 was a lurcher), but in it, somehow, as he writes in one of the saddest and truest confessional poems in the language, 'there hath past away a glory from the earth'.

daughter Caroline (born at Orleans in December 1792 whilst Wordsworth was in Paris and about to return to Britain).

This, and another tragedy that occurred in 1805 – the death of his brother John in the *Earl of Abergavenny*[107] disaster – whilst he was struggling with 'emotion recollected in tranquility' and composing the putative philosophical epic, colour the mood of a narrative worth quoting at length for the insights it provides not only into the usual physical approach to the mountain of those days,[108] but also into the way in which Wordsworth, in a very modern way, at this stage of his work was subtly transmuting landscape into emotional representation. What T. S. Eliot was later to define as the 'objective correlative' is markedly present here:

> In one of these excursions, travelling then
> Through Wales on foot, and with a youthful friend,
> I left Bethgelert's huts at couching time,
> And westward took my way, to see the sun
> Rise from the top of Snowdon. Having reached
> The cottage at the mountain's foot, we there

---

107 *The Earl of Abergavenny* – one of the largest merchant vessels of the East India Company's fleet and captained by John Wordsworth – sank on the 5th of February 1805 after hitting the dangerous Shambles reef south of Portland Bill. The ship was carrying a valuable trading cargo in which John had a large sum invested, hoping to make the fortune that might aid his brother's poetic career. Impatient to set sail from Portsmouth in stormy weather, the tide turned whilst the ship waited for the pilot, whose duty it was to navigate the course. A strong ebb drove the ship on to the Shambles and of the 400 people on board, 250 were lost. John was reported as having clung to the ropes of his ship until he drowned with it, rather than attempting to save himself. The effect on his brother William was profound, echoing all through the conclusion to these extracts.

108 From the Beddgelert side, by way of some combination of what later became known as the Snowdon Ranger, Rhyd Ddu or Beddgelert paths. Wordsworth's route was the latter leading on to Clawdd Coch ('the Bwlch Main ridge'), of which more below when we come to the admirable Mr Bingley.

Roused up the shepherd who by ancient right
Of office is the stranger's usual guide;
And after short refreshment sallied forth.[109]

So the night ascent begins, and it quickly runs into the kind of conditions that have on occasion (not infrequent occasion, it has to be admitted) dispirited would-be ascensionists from Wordsworth's time to our own:

It was a summer's night, a close warm night,
Wan, dull and glaring, with a dripping mist
Low-hung and thick that covered all the sky,
Half threatening storm and rain; but on we went
Unchecked, being full of heart and having faith
In our tried pilot. Little could we see
Hemmed round on every side with fog and damp,
And after ordinary travellers' chat
With our conductor, silently we sank
Each into commerce with his private thoughts:
Thus did we breast the ascent, and by myself
Was nothing either seen or heard the while
Which took me from my musings, save that once
The shepherd's cur did to his own great joy
Unearth a hedgehog in the mountain crags
Round which he made a barking turbulent.[110]

As low-key preparatory work, establishing a prosaic, downbeat, reflective mood (apart from the delicious little comic, everyday incident of dog and hedgehog) before the revelations to come, this is masterfully supple and relaxed use of blank verse.

---

109 *The Prelude*, Book Thirteenth, ibid. p. 510.
110 ibid.

This small adventure, for even such it seemed
In that wild place and at the dead of night,
Being over and forgotten, on we wound
In silence as before. With foreheads bent
Earthward, as if in opposition set
Against an enemy, I panted up
With eager pace, and no less eager thoughts.
Thus might we wear perhaps an hour away,
Ascending at loose distance each from each,
And I, as chanced, the foremost of the band;[111]

Thus the egotistical; and now it is time for a visitation from the eagerly-sought sublime:

... at my feet the ground appeared to brighten,
And with a step or two seemed brighter still;
Nor had I time to ask the cause of this,
For instantly a light upon the turf
Fell like a flash: I looked about, and lo!
The moon stood naked in the heavens, at height
Immense above my head, and on the shore
I found myself of a huge sea of mist,
Which, meek and silent, rested at my feet.

These cloud-inversion moments, whether they be by sunlight or moonlight (a similar one is described in the introduction, seen at dawn from Bwlch Coch) are some of the most moving and transfiguring that you can experience on mountains. They seem more frequently encountered on sea-proximous Snowdon, or Brandon Mountain on the Dingle Peninsula in the far west of Ireland, or The Black Cuillin of Skye than on

---

111   ibid. pp. 510–512.

any other hills I know, the mist-islanded peaks at these times taking on a new form and presence in your awareness:

A hundred hills their dusky backs upheaved
All over this still ocean; and beyond,
Far, far beyond, the vapours shot themselves,
In headlands, tongues, and promontory shapes,
Into the sea, the real sea, that seemed
To dwindle, and give up its majesty,
Usurped upon as far as sight could reach.
Meanwhile, the Moon looked down upon this show
In single glory, and we stood, the mist
Touching our very feet; and from the shore
At distance not the third part of a mile
Was a blue chasm; a fracture in the vapour,
A deep and gloomy breathing-place through which
Mounted the roar of waters, torrents, streams
Innumerable, roaring with one voice![112]

It is from this point that Wordsworth shapes and redirects the account of an almost exactly similar experience to the one described by Pennant in his habitually and admirably precise prose into a crucial poetic statement about landscape and psychological affect:

The universal spectacle throughout
Was shaped for admiration and delight,
Grand in itself alone, but in that breach
Through which the homeless voice of waters rose,
That dark deep thoroughfare, had Nature lodged
The soul, the imagination of the whole.[113]

---

112   ibid. p. 512.
113   ibid. p. 512

The substance of Pennant's two descriptions can clearly be seen as the underlying structural principle here. Through poetic sleight of hand Wordsworth has transmuted those wonderfully evocative and thrilling visions of mountain strangeness and confusion into a sonorous epiphany of his own torn and tortured human condition, and the need for mental mastery over it. It is a setting to verse of the religious implications in the succession of canvases representing solitary figures and objects in wild landscapes by Wordsworth's near-contemporary, the Dresden Romantic painter Caspar David Friedrich, and the nexus of relationships between the work in the two genres is very striking.[114]

In a sense, what we are witnessing here is also a creative expression of something very similar to the belief of the old apothecaries and simples collectors of a century or so before, that plants derived stronger virtues from their growing within the potency of the mountain environment. For Wordsworth, as with plants so too for the human mind and imagination – contact with this place rendering them both all the more virile, and thereby initiating a process of psychological healing.[115] This in essence and in simple terms is the baited hook of Romanticism's connection with landscape, and after Wordsworth, how the people thronged to the place of his mountain epiphanies in order to take the lure! How often in political and cultural history does one human being's psychological and emotional ruin become the agency sought

---

114 This point obviously merits far more detailed discussion, but that would belong more properly in a volume on the history of ideas than in one recounting the simple story of a mountain. So I leave the hint to the reader to follow up.
115 The belief has not gone away, merely remained dormant within our culture, re-emerging from time to time to re-assert itself, as the recent publishing fad for books – most of which are anything but – with the word 'wild' in their titles amply demonstrates.

out by the many in quest of their own forms of salvation. That Snowdon should have been the focusing mechanism here, following on from Pennant's hints, seems somehow in keeping with the extraordinary character of the mountain.

Wordsworth was followed to Wales within little more than a year of this 1793 ascent by that remarkable, honourable and excitingly original figure, Samuel Taylor Coleridge, who arrived with Joseph Hucks and two other former Cambridge contemporaries – the tradition of outdoor dilettantes at England's second university is of long provenance – John Brooke and Thomas Berdmore, at Beddgelert in July of 1794. Hucks recounts what happened:

> As this is the usual place from which travellers make the ascent of Snowdon, we determined to do the same, and in pursuance of this resolution set off at eleven in the evening, though it was quite dark, and a very rainy and stormy night; however, there was a probability that it would be fine in the morning; and that hope was sufficient to make us undergo a few inconveniences; but in attempting to find the guide's house, which was five miles from our inn, and situated quite out of the road at the foot of the mountain, we became completely bewildered: in this perplexity we were directed by the glimmering of a light to an habitation, which, with extreme difficulty and danger, we contrived to reach.[116]

Put yourself in the situation here, and ask yourself if you would have left the comfort and safety of that inn for a dark and unknown drenching landscape in a pre-Goretex age? And it gets worse.

---

116 Joseph Hucks, *A Pedestrian Tour Through North Wales, in a Series of Letters* (1795), eds. A. R. Jones and W. Tydeman (University of Wales Press, 1979), p. 44.

It was a small hut, and its inhabitants, if we might judge from the impenetrable silence that reined within, were all asleep. It was some time before we could prevail upon them to open the door, and answer our entreaties for a proper direction; at length an elderly man appeared, to whom we endeavoured to make known our grievances; but alas! he only spoke his native language, and did not understand a word that we said.[117]

Eventually, through exercise of the universal languages of pointing, reiteration of the single name with which they had been armed, raised voices and the proffering of money, they are led for what Hucks claims to have been a further half-hour, which is surely a subjective truth rather than a measurement in real time, along rough paths through the deluge to the door of another small cottage, which proves to be the one where the guide lives. There they talk themselves or are talked out of the ascent that night, and settle down to spend the hours of darkness on benches or the cold ground, whilst 'without doors nought but the "pelting of the pitiless storm" was heard, and the loud roar of the mountain torrents.'[118]

The name of this second house in which they had taken shelter was Bron y Fedw Uchaf, very close to the start of what is now the Snowdon Ranger Path above the south-eastern end of Llyn Cwellyn and generally known at the time as 'the guide's house' – the guide being a young man by the name of Ellis Griffith, who through personal recommendations and the hospitality of his roof and hearth was becoming much in demand. Given the lateness of the hour and the inclemency of the weather, Cradocks' poor blind harpist and comely dancing maidens for once were unavailable. Hucks continues:

---

117   ibid. p. 45.
118   ibid.

At four in the morning I thought it prudent to waken the whole party, which I effected with some difficulty; we then sallied from our habitation, and made our observations upon the weather, which gave us no encouragement to proceed; however, they [i.e. Coleridge and the guide] determined to venture upon their aerial excursion, more from hope of finding the plants, for which this mountain is remarkable, than of seeing any thing when at the top; at their persuasions, added to my own inclination, I declined the enterprise, as my cold increased considerably during the night, and went back again to the inn, where I impatiently expected their return, which did not happen till four in the afternoon. It turned out, as might have been foreseen, a fruitless and fatiguing expedition; for when they arrived at the top, they could see nothing but the impenetrable clouds, that almost constantly envelope these huge mountains.[119]

Here was one of the great lost opportunities in Snowdon's story, one of the mountain's most-to-be-regretted might-have -beens, a marvellous possibility now forever occluded. The notion of a Coleridgean account in prose or verse of botanizing for a day where Thomas Johnson and others had been before him is so thrilling, so tantalising – and it was not to be. The mountain rains of Wales, then as now, have much to answer for, and so, probably, did the presence of garrulous companions who were, with the exception of the guide, perhaps not wholly congenial if we pick up on certain hints in Hucks' account.

When I think of the description from Coleridge's journals of what was probably the first descent of Scafell's Broad Stand in the summer of 1802,[120] the sense of loss at how writing

---

119 ibid. pp. 46–47.
120 'My Limbs were all in a tremble – I lay upon my Back to rest myself,

of this audacious, swirling and bizarre quality, originality and psychological veracity – a few paragraphs of which might have outweighed whole books of poetical pontificating by the older Wordsworth – could so easily have been, and yet was not, produced about Snowdon is palpable. Coleridge and his companions went on their unrecorded way. To add to the sense of desolation with which the Romantics leave us in their association with the peak, though Hazlitt and Southey,[121] Shelley and De Quincey all came here, they left us little other than a few brief and scattered general references. De Quincey does, however, vouchsafe to us in the best Thomas Gray and Joseph Cradock tradition, that 'a luxury of another class, and quite peculiar to Wales, was in those days (I hope in these) the Welsh harp, in attendance at every inn'.

Romanticism's early literary prospectors and poets may not, for the most part, have produced much of substance by way of recounting their experience of Snowdon, but hard on their heels in the summer of 1798 the coach from Chester conveyed along the 'great Irish road' and deposited at Caernarfon a plump and indefatigable Cambridge student, at 24 quite old to be counted thus, who was an enthusiastic botanist and a reversion

---

& was beginning according to my Custom to laugh at myself for a Madman, when the sight of the Crags above me on each side, & the impetuous Clouds just over them, posting so luridly & so rapidly northward, overawed me. I lay in a state of almost prophetic Trance & Delight – & blessed God aloud, for the powers of Reason & the Will, which remaining no Danger can overpower us! O God, I exclaimed aloud – how calm, how blessed I am now; I know not how to proceed, how to return; but I am calm & fearless & confident; if this Reality were a Dream, if I were asleep, what agonies had I suffered! What screams! – When the Reason & the Will are away, what remains to us but Darkness & Dimness & a bewildering Shame, and the Pain that is utterly Lord over us, or fantastic Pleasure, that draws the Soul along swimming through the air in many shapes, even as a Flight of Starlings in a Wind.'

121   This point is perhaps not entirely true in the case of Southey, though on the whole one wishes it were.

in many ways to the earlier exploratory and scientific tradition of Johnson, Ray and Lhuyd. This was Mister (soon to be the Reverend) William Bingley, and in his *North Wales Delineated from Two Excursions; including its Scenery, Antiquities, Customs, and some sketches of its Natural History*[122] of 1804, which included an appendix termed by its author a 'Flora Cambrica', he provided one of the indispensable records in the history of our mountain. It is also, along with that of Pennant and the later one by George Borrow, one of the most abidingly useful, sympathetic, and certainly the most impressively energetic of all the classic Welsh tours. The passage that is always – and quite rightly and necessarily – quoted in books about Snowdon runs thus:

> In my first journey I went from [Dolbadarn] castle to Cwm Brwynog, but instead of following the above route, I wandered to Clogwyn du'r Arddu, to search that rock for some plants which Lhwyd and Ray have described as growing there. The Reverend Mr Williams accompanied me, and he started the wild idea of attempting to climb up the precipice. I was too eager in my pursuit to object to the adventure, and we began our laborious task without once reflecting on the dangers that might attend it. For a while we got on without much difficulty, but we were soon obliged to have recourse both to our hands and knees, in clambering from one crag to another. Every step now required the utmost caution, and it was necessary to try that every stone was firm in its place before the weight of the body was trusted upon it. I had once lain hold of a piece of rock, and was in the act of raising myself upon it, when it

---

122   William Bingley, *North Wales Delineated from Two Excursions* (Longman and Rees, 1804). An earlier edition had appeared in 1800, but the greatly expanded one of 1804, written after a second tour undertaken in the summer of 1801, is much the more useful and comprehensive.

loosened from its bed, and I should have been precipitated headlong, had I not in a moment snatched hold of a tuft of rushes, and saved myself. When we had ascended somewhat more than halfway, there seemed no chance of our being able to proceed much farther, on account of the increasing size of the masses of rock above us. We rested a moment from our labour to consider what was to be done. The danger of again descending was much too great, for us to think of attempting it, unless we found it absolutely impossible to proceed. On looking down, the precipice, for at least three hundred feet, seemed almost perpendicular. We were eager in our botanical pursuit, and extremely desirous to be at the top, but I believe it was the prospect downwards that determined us to brave every difficulty.[123]

So far, so extraordinary. That the two botanists were seeking to ascend a line right up the centre of the most impressive and forbidding cliff on Snowdon flew in the face of contemporary prudence. They were venturing into the darkest heart of horrible sublimity, though being rationalists and botanists on a quest, this inflated language probably registered very little with them. What they were tackling is known as the Eastern Terrace. Nowadays it is most usually employed as a descent route by climbers who have completed one of the courses of extreme severity pioneered on the steepest faces hereabouts in modern times; but that should not be allowed to detract from the scale and atmosphere of this magnificent cliff feature. A presiding principle of the cliff's unique geological structure, it slants up at a steep diagonal from right to left below the huge, leaning mass of the slabby West Buttress and above the steeply angular East Buttress.

---

123   ibid. vol. I. pp. 248–249.

The lower part of it runs over a subsidiary 200-foot buttress known as the Middle Rock, with steep ground beneath it (Bingley is scarcely exaggerated in his estimates – looked at from above, from the steepness of the slope beneath this would certainly seem to be 300 feet or more). It is, I think, altogether improbable that Williams and Bingley followed this first section, and much more likely that they traversed in along ledges below the great central wall of the East Buttress to join the terrace above and left of the Middle Rock, by way of an open gully with steep, wet, rock-steps of loose material where Bingley's grabbing for the tuft of rushes most likely took place – the rushes still grow there, the gully taking all the drainage from the terrace above, and its rock is notably fissile. All of this lends authenticity to Bingley's account.

At the top of the gully, which is the first easy and natural line of ascent after traversing under the East Buttress (and no doubt having collected the roseroot, Snowdon Lilies, several varieties of saxifrage and other rare examples of relict arctic-alpine flora that grow thereabouts), they would have landed on a slabby, ascending ramp where 'the increasing size of the masses of rock above' must have become very obvious as the ramp narrowed and slipped beneath a huge, bulging buttress, which is known to climbers as 'The Boulder'. A belt of smooth slabs comes in here from the left and abuts this, making a short rock-pitch, not steep – twelve or fifteen feet high at most – and cutting off access to the easier scree-slopes of the basin-like upper terrace (down which, incidentally, it is most likely that Thomas Johnson descended some distance to secure specimens that still grow across the base-rich rocks at the back of the terrace). We take up Bingley's narrative again at this point:

It happened fortunately that the steep immediately above us was the only one that presented any material danger. Mr Williams having on a pair of strong shoes with nails in them, which would hold their footing better than mine, requested to make the first attempt, and after some difficulty he succeeded. We had along with us a small basket to contain our provisions, and hold the roots of such plants as we wished to transfer to his garden; this he carried behind him by means of a leathern belt fastened round his waist. When, therefore, he had fixed himself securely to a part of the rock, he took off his belt, and holding firmly to one end, gave the other to me: I laid hold, and, with a little aid from the stones, fairly pulled myself up by it. After this we got on pretty well, and in about an hour and a quarter from the commencement of our labour, found ourselves on the brow of this dreadful precipice, and in possession of all the plants we expected to find.[124]

This is all admirably sensible, uninflated and sharply observed – yet it was one of the most remarkable departures from precedent in the entire history of the mountain. People at this time just did not choose to ascend places of such grim and terrifying aspect. It has gone down in history as the first recorded rock-climb in Wales, and though it is little more than an atmospheric scramble (a very similar Cumbrian parallel would be Jack's Rake on Pavey Ark), the claim seems to me a reasonable one, given the appearance of the line of ascent, the two or more sections where it is necessary to use both hands and feet, the exposure at several points above sheer and considerable drops, problems of route-finding, and the ground through which it leads. It's a feat that grows in stature the more consideration you give to it, and it certainly makes me

---

124   ibid. p. 249.

want to know more about the two characters who achieved it.

Bingley's companion, Peter Bailey Williams, was a Carmarthenshire man who, after study at Edward Lhuyd's old and neglectful Oxford college of Jesus, had been Rector of Llanberis and Llanrug since 1792 and was to remain thus until his death in 1836. His prowess among the mountains can be judged from Bingley's account of him in his hobnailed boots casually making the fearsomely exposed leap between the two natural obelisks known as Adam and Eve that form the summit of Tryfan, the rockiest of Eryri's hills. A prickly conservative and an anti-Jacobin, he became through the long years of his ministry under Snowdon an eminent botanist in correspondence with many leading figures of his day, a very worthy and invaluable local educator and historian, and a crucial figure in a renaissance of the Welsh cultural life in the region. He was one of a group of clergyman-scholars, known as *yr offeiriaid llengar* or the learned priests, who did much to preserve the poetry, traditions and purity of the Welsh language in the region around Snowdon.

Peter Bailey Williams was also the first communicator since Edward Lhuyd really to have known his home hills, and it was this knowledge, imparted to his young friend Bingley that makes the latter's tour-accounts so distinguished and remarkable. It also makes them invaluable as a source of information about the physical aspect of the mountain and its botanical riches before later generations of visitors and collectors came and, with the profiteering collusion of local botanical guides, decimated these.[125]

---

125 For all his other admirable qualities, Peter Bailey Williams' own writings in either language, mostly published in the periodicals and journals of the time, are undistinguished, and his *Tourist's Guide to the County of Caernarvon* of 1821, though useful for contemporary material unavailable

It is well worth recounting Bingley's other explorations on Snowdon after the Eastern Terrace ascent. On the same day, he and Williams went on to seek for plants on the gully-seamed and decaying cliff of Clogwyn y Garnedd right under the summit itself, where there 'is at all times some difficulty in searching . . . but when the rocks are rendered slippery from heavy mists or rain, this becomes, from the insecurity of the footing, greatly increased.'[126] The information imparted here assuredly came straight from Williams. Bingley then made a vigorously promiscuous circuit of the botanical sites across the north-eastern face of the mountain around what are now known as Cwm Glas and Cwm Glas Mawr. He crossed into them by way of Bwlch Coch, between Crib Goch and Crib y Ddysgl, and finishing his day by descending an arduous route, the embarking on which he came much to regret directly down to Nant Peris through the broken crags of Clogwyn Llwyd.

Nothing daunted, the next day he rode round to Bron y Fedw Uchaf (which we previously visited in Coleridge's company), hired Ellis Griffith as his guide, stayed on horseback as far as Llyn Ffynnon-y-gwas, and from there traversed the ridge above the cliff he and Williams had ascended the previous day and climbed back towards the summit. As with Pennant twenty-odd years before, the clear morning was not to last, and gave way to rough weather. There was a brief spat between Bingley and Griffiths when the latter urged the necessity of immediate descent, but the severity of the storm that arrived, the battering by huge hailstones and the soaking they received on the way down convinced Bingley, on reflection, of Griffith's

---

elsewhere, is a distinctly dull read, his best memorial really being the portrait Bingley provides.
126   ibid. p. 253.

soundness of judgement as they sat once more, with clothes steaming, round Bron y Fedw's hospitable fire.

As his next objective, and in order to complete his plan of ascending Snowdon by all three main routes in use at the time, the indomitably energetic Bingley next repaired to Beddgelert. There he secured the services of a waiter, William Lloyd, at what is now the Royal Goat and was then the Beddgelert Hotel to guide him up Snowdon. Lloyd was also the village schoolmaster, though like a present-day Cuban doctor he found tourist tips in the brief season more lucrative than his pedagogic stipend. Bingley records how he found Lloyd through a poster displayed on the door of the hotel, the text of which he gives as:

> William Lloyd, conductor to Snowdon, Moel Hebog, Dinas Emrys, Llanberis pass, the lakes, &c &c. Collector of crystals and fossils, and all natural curiosities in these regions. Dealer in superfine woollen hose, socks, gloves &c.[127]

The route by which this one-man guiding service – and outdoor equipment retailer/manufacturer too, no doubt, in the long winter evenings – led Bingley to the summit starts from the prominent glacial erratic of Pitt's Head[128] near to Ffridd Uchaf farmhouse two miles north of Beddgelert village. It joins the modern and now-popular path from Rhyd Ddu at Pen-ar-lôn, where a quarry-path clattery with slates leads off east to Bwlch Cwm Llan, and climbs by way of Rhos Boeth on to the ridge above the cliffs of Llechog, before curving round east and north to reach the foot of Clawdd Coch, Snowdon's south-east ridge, at Bwlch Main. This was probably the most

---

127 ibid.
128 The likeness is amusingly close, and the name an index to this route's period of popularity – it is nowadays little used, parking being unavailable.

spectacular section on all the Snowdon paths in common use at the time, and Bingley describes it thus:

> This narrow pass, not more than ten or twelve feet across, and two or three hundred yards in length, was so steep, that the eye reached on each side, down the whole extent of the mountain ... in some parts of it, if a person held a large stone in each hand, and let them both fall at once, each might roll a quarter of a mile, and thus, when they stopped, they might be more than half a mile asunder.[129]

It might sound dramatic, but in fact this is a reasonably accurate appraisal, from a time when other writers delighted in fearful exaggerations, of the actual topography. The ridge above Bwlch Main *is* quite narrow and exposed in places, with considerable drops at either hand into Cwm Clogwyn and Cwm Tregalan, and only the petty-minded would quibble with Bingley's description. He himself was obviously not affrighted by it, and when, in order to spice up his narrative, he presents us with horrifying tales stemming no doubt from Lloyd of how people who had been guided across it in the hours of darkness, on returning in daylight would often baulk entirely or resort to crawling on hands and knees, there is the hint of a suspicion that the ascensionist of Clogwyn Du'r Arddu is mildly entertaining himself at the expense of other people's credulity.

This generation of poets, writers and painters, following hard on the heels of Pennant and his predecessors to Snowdon, initiated a half-century of extraordinary popularity and change for the mountain. In 1797 the only useful map of the region was that by John Evans, called by Bingley 'the

---

129   ibid. pp. 385–386.

correctest map I ever travelled by'. It sold at eighteen shillings – an extraordinary sum equal to three weeks' wages for an agricultural worker at the time. Telford's later A5 road from Betws-y-coed to Bangor was shown on it merely as a projected route, and the only extant road through the mountains went from Caernarfon by way of Betws Garmon, Beddgelert, Aberglaslyn and Tan-y-bwlch to Ffestiniog. The carriage route over the Llanberis Pass did not open until 1830, by which time the copper-mines in Cwm Dyli (of which more in the next chapter) had long been in production, the ore from them transported – this fact beggars belief! – on men's backs up to Bwlch Glas at the top of the zigzags on the Miners' Track, and thence on horse-drawn sleds down what is now the Snowdon Ranger Path to Cwellyn. The first one-inch Ordnance Survey maps to the mountain appeared between 1840 and 1841, and on them Snowdon was inconveniently divided between several quarter-sheets. Even on these the sole path to be prominently marked is the beautifully-engineered green track that leaves what is now the Watkin Path, crosses Afon Llem ('the leaping river', an apt, descriptive name, given as Afon Cwm Llan on the OS map) on a high single-span bridge formed from one slab of rock, winds through stands of Scots Pine which are one of the few and favoured haunts of crossbills in Snowdonia, and contours across the southern slopes of Y Lliwedd to reach the dramatic and dangerous rift-mines at the head of Cwm Merch.

Yet by the time the last of our trio of authors of great Welsh tours[130] arrived to make his ascent of Snowdon, Wales was an

---

130 I should confess here that I am skipping over libraries' worth of lesser productions, that appeared with unerring regularity over decades at the rate of several a year, specimens of all of them now languishing in the *Welsh Tours* collection of the National Library of Wales in Aberystwyth, where those

industrialized nation – more so perhaps than it is today, when post-industrial is the more fitting tag and the relics of former industries have become major attractions to the industrial archaeologist and the nostalgic or inquisitive tourist. And with its industrialization came the complex infrastructure that also facilitated tourism.

It was the summer of 1854. The militarism consequent on the Crimean venture was rampant. C. E. Mathews paid his first visit to the Pen-y-Gwryd Hotel, and we shall hear more of both in due course. In the Bernese Oberland, Alfred Wills made the ascent of the Wetterhorn to initiate a so-called 'Golden Age' of British activity in the Alps. And George Borrow, racing down Telford's new road alongside a teetotal market-gardener from Ogwen to Tyn-y-Maes, arrived in Bangor, having travelled on foot circuitously from Llangollen. He could conveniently meet his wife and step-daughter Henrietta, who had travelled by rail, at the Albion Hotel by the station (the name is still there emblazoned on the building's cracked stucco, no student-member of Cymdeithas yr Iaith yet having seen fit to deface it). Borrow, in his endearing way, spends most of a chapter discoursing on verses by two minor early-seventeenth-century Welsh poets that appear to him to predict both the coming of the railway and the two bridge-crossings of Afon Menai:

---

of tested stamina and truly eccentric interest may search them out if they consider what are in the main endless reiterations of and variations upon the language and inventions of Joseph Cradock worth the effort. There are exceptions to be made, of course, but they are few. My favourite from among them would be the charitable and good-humoured Richard Fenton's *Tours in Wales 1804–13* (but not published until 1917), which contains a good deal of interesting antiquarian material wittily expressed, and might best be viewed as a useful adjunct to the work of Thomas Pennant by an altogether-more-pleasant character.

... Lleiaf's couplet was verified. But since Telford's [bridge], another bridge has been built over the Menai which enables things to pass which the bard certainly never dreamt of ... a bridge over which thundering trains would dash, if required, at the rate of fifty miles an hour.[131]

And the second bard had predicted this too – proof, surely, of his being gifted with the second sight! *Wild Wales*, Borrow's enchanting, garrulous, quixotic account of his 1854 three-month visit to Wales, first published in 1862 to poor notices and worse sales, is crammed with odd little digressions like this. It is perhaps the greatest travel book ever written on any part of Britain. Immensely erudite and distinctly strange, it toys both with its reader and a presiding Victorian morality.[132]

Above all, *Wild Wales* is wholly enamoured of its subject, of which it presents a personal and original view with some notable contemporary distortion and omission (it also, incidentally, contains several remarkably good and well-concealed jokes, as well as certain fictive passages which might best be described as proto-Sebaldian). Borrow has often been criticized as having no interest in landscape and scenery, and a tendency to dismiss all mountains in generalized terms. And yet, in *Wild Wales*, he gives us a whole chapter on his ascent of Snowdon which is not only revealing of character and interesting as a historical record, but is surely also one of the most amusing and curious pieces ever written about the mountain.

---

131 George Borrow, *Wild Wales* (Collins, 1955) p. 155.
132 This Victorian morality would have been very well entrenched by 1862, when the kind of naked mixed sea-bathing by which Hucks and Coleridge had been mildly taken aback sixty years earlier at Abergele, would have been considered nationally scandalous. In Coleridge's case, it is more likely that he had been a little envious for, as a gentleman, he would have been unable to join in.

He and his wife and Henrietta arrive in Llanberis, where Borrow engages a young lad as their guide and deposits his wife at the hotel, she 'not deeming herself sufficiently strong to encounter the fatigue of the expedition'. George and Henrietta 'then commenced the ascent, arm in arm, followed by the lad', and with Borrow singing at the top of his voice a Welsh verse that he gives only in translation, where it sounds suspiciously like something sung by Autolycus in *The Winter's Tale*:

> We were far from being the only visitors to the hill this day; groups of people, or single individuals, might be seen going up or descending the path as far as the eye could reach. The path was remarkably good, and for some way the ascent was anything but steep. On our left was the vale of Llanberis, and on our other a broad hollow, or valley of Snowdon, beyond which were two huge hills forming part of the body of the grand mountain, the lowermost of which our guide told me was called Moel Elia, and the uppermost Moel y Cynghorion.[133]

All this is admirably exact ('Moel Elia' is, of course, Moel Eilio), and interesting too in the absolutely straightforward way it describes an established, easy and popular path which had not been an option for those earlier tourists, to whom Llanberis was an inconvenient and near-inaccessible hamlet reached only by crossing the mountain from Cwellyn or rowing up the lakes from Cwm-y-glo. He continues:

> On we went until we had passed both these hills, and come to the neighbourhood of a great wall of rocks constituting the upper region of Snowdon, and where the real difficulty of the

---

133   ibid. p. 163.

ascent commences. Feeling now rather out of breath we sat down on a little knoll with our faces to the south, having a small lake near us, on our left hand, which lay dark and deep, just under the great wall.[134]

They were sitting before the steep rise now known as Allt Moses, somewhere in the vicinity of where the old mine track branches off towards Clogwyn Coch and the mine barracks, looking down on Llyn Du'r Arddu and across to the great cliff that Williams and Bingley had climbed fifty-six years before. And there is not a glint of recognition accorded to this in Borrow's account. It's one of the book's inexplicable omissions (another is the total lack of mention of the contemporary 'Blue Books' educational controversy, which was then striking at the heart of Welsh-speaking Wales). One thing that is certain is that Borrow would never have made a rock-climber. With the most magnificent cliff in Britain right before him, what impresses him most are the crumbling bluffs of Clogwyn Llechwedd Llo.

Beneath these, incidentally, the remains of the unfortunate Reverend Starr whose grave at Nant Peris we visited in the introduction were found in mysterious circumstances at the beginning of June in 1847, only seven years before Borrow's ascent of Snowdon. It seems fitting at this point, Borrow himself being one of the consummate practitioners of lengthy digression, to give you the story, as being one of the most disturbing from the early Victorian period of our mountain's history, and reflecting on practices and concerns within the local community about the increasing visitor numbers.

Henry Willington Starr, the 32-year-old curate of All Saints Church in Northampton, had arrived in Caernarfon at

---

134   ibid.

the outset of a walking tour in Wales on the 14th September, 1846, taken lodgings in Pool Street, and on the following day (the one on which, according to his epitaph on the tombstone he perished), he travelled on to Llanberis and put up at the Dolbadarn Hotel. On the morning of Wednesday 16th September, which was misty, he set off to climb Snowdon. Thereafter, nothing was heard from him and his name did not appear in the summit visitors' book. He had left a carpet bag and great-coat at the Pool Street lodging, and these were not collected. Two reported sightings placed him by Cwellyn on Tuesday and descending from the Glyderau on the opposite side of the Llanberis Pass from Snowdon on Wednesday evening, but neither could be verified. Searches were mounted, rewards offered, and all were to no avail.

Nine months later, on 1st June 1847, a solitary huntsman was out with dogs and gun after foxes in the rough and bouldery ground under Clogwyn Llechwedd Llo when he came across what is described in contemporary accounts as 'a red shawl'. When he showed it later to the landlady at the Dolbadarn Hotel, she recognized it as having belonged to the Reverend Starr, and it soon came out that Starr's haversack had been found a month previously close to the same point. The next day the huntsman and the landlady's son-in-law returned to the boulders beneath Clogwyn Llechwedd Llo, and after a brief search they came across the fox-gnawed remains of the Reverend Starr. These were formally identified, an inquest was opened, and William Williams the botanical guide (also boots at the Victoria Hotel, hence his nickname of 'Wil Boots'), was called as a witness.

The latter surrendered to the authorities a watch, identified as the Reverend Starr's, which he claimed to have found on the morning of 2nd June, after having heard about the discovery of the red shawl. That the watch was rust-free and in perfect working order despite – if Williams' story were true – having lain on a hillside throughout a Snowdon winter – drew from the coroner a reprimand for conduct likely to cast doubt on his integrity, but in a community becoming increasingly reliant on tourism, the point was not pursued. Williams' account of how he came by the watch changed over the next fourteen years, until the June day of his own death in a fall from Clogwyn y Garnedd. That is the sum of this odd and disturbing story, and we can now return to Borrow and his stepdaughter as they look across unwittingly at the location where the Reverend Starr's bones had been found only a very few years before.

> Here we sat for some time resting and surveying the scene which presented itself to us, the principal object of which was the north-eastern side of the mighty Moel y Cynghorion, across the wide hollow or valley, which it overhangs in the shape of a sheer precipice some five hundred feet in depth.[135]

No match for Bingley in terms of exactitude, Borrow's real interest, as always philological, stands revealed:

> Struck by the name of Moel y Cynghorion, which in English signifies the hill of the counsellors, I inquired of our guide why the hill was so called, but as he could afford me no information on the point I presumed that it was either called the hill of the counsellors from the Druids having held high consultation on its top, in time of old, or from the unfortunate Llywelyn having consulted there with his chieftains, whilst his army lay encamped in the vale below.[136]

---

135   ibid.
136   ibid.

Borrovian conjecture is one of the recurrent pleasures of *Wild Wales*, and by no means always entirely unsound. However, it's not helping us to reach the summit of the mountain:

> Getting up we set about surmounting what remained of the ascent. The path was now winding and much more steep than it had hitherto been. I was at one time apprehensive that my gentle companion would be obliged to give over the attempt; the gallant girl, however, persevered, and in little more than twenty minutes from the time when we arose from our resting place under the crags, we stood, safe and sound, though panting, upon the very top of Snowdon, the far-famed Wyddfa.[137]

Small wonder they were panting – that's probably the earliest extant description of fell-running, Allt Moses up which they had raced being the steepest section of the ascent from Llanberis. What they found at the top he describes as follows, giving a very useful impression of the summit at the time:

> The Wyddfa is about thirty feet in diameter and it is surrounded on three sides by a low wall. In the middle of it is a rude cabin in which refreshments are sold, and in which a person resides throughout the year, though there are few or no visitors to the hill's top except during the months of summer.[138]

Having attained their objective, and before repairing to the rude cabin for excellent coffee (no longer thus, sadly) in Henrietta's case, and tolerable bottled ale (this, too, would

---

137   ibid.
138   ibid. p. 164.

be stretching a point) in that of himself and the guide – the summit refreshment hut having been licensed, except on Sundays, since 1845 – he proceeds to deliver himself of an extraordinary peroration:

> 'Here,' said I to Henrietta, 'you are on the top crag of Snowdon, which the Welsh consider, and perhaps with justice, to be the most remarkable crag in the world; which is mentioned in many of their old wild romantic tales, and some of the noblest of their poems, amongst others in the 'Day of Judgement' by the illustrious Goronwy Owen, where it is brought forward in the following manner:
>
> > Ail i'r ar ael Eryri,
> > Cyfartal hoewal a hi.
>
> The brow of Snowdon shall be levelled with the ground and the eddying waters shall murmur round it.
>
> You are now on the top crag of Snowdon, generally termed Y Wyddfa, which means a conspicuous place or tumulus, and which is generally in winter covered with snow; about which snow there are in the Welsh language two curious englynion or stanzas consisting entirely of vowels with the exception of one consonant, namely the letter R.[139]

Borrow then proceeds to recite the said verses in his habitually stentorian tones, observing as he does so the audience that had gathered round his small party:

> Such was the harangue which I uttered on the top of Snowdon; to which Henrietta listened with attention; three or four English, who stood nigh, with grinning scorn, and a Welsh gentleman with considerable interest.[140]

---

139 ibid.
140 ibid. 165.

Note that pointed national adjective standing as a noun! We will hear more of this. Meanwhile, back to the sharply-differentiated 'Welsh gentleman':

> The latter coming forward shook me by the hand exclaiming:
> 'Wyt ti Lydaueg?'[141]
> 'I am not a Llydauan,' said I; 'I wish I was, or anything but what I am, one of a nation amongst whom any knowledge save what relates to money-making and over-reaching is looked upon as a disgrace. I am ashamed to say that I am an Englishman.'[142]

Small wonder the book didn't sell well on its first London publication! A century and a half on, I still find myself both amused and astounded by this passage and the rhetoric in which it is couched (in the matter, for example, of the Welsh gentleman addressing him in the familiar and not formal way, implying as that does acceptance and friendship). It seems to me that what Borrow is doing here is providing a much harsher and more direct criticism of contemporary society than the implied one in its earlier counterpart, the famous conversation – one of those passages from literature that at one time almost every reader would have had by heart – on Mousehold Heath with Jasper Petulengro that concludes chapter 25 of his distinctly fictive, quasi-autobiographical masterpiece *Lavengro* of 1851. That great passage encapsulates the author's system of values, which was so much at odds with those of

---

141   That is, 'Are you Breton?' A recurrent joke in *Wild Wales* is against his own Welsh accent (at one point on Anglesey a man he addresses in Welsh – to Borrow's supposed amazement – responds in Spanish). Some have seen this as a lack of awareness of its oddity, but Borrow is a much trickier literary operator than many assume, and it is entirely of a piece with other of his stratagems in books like *Lavengro* and *The Romany Rye*.
142   *Wild Wales*, op. cit. p. 165.

his contemporary society. By the 1860s and the publication of *Wild Wales*, the Borrovian astringency had become all the more marked.[143]

Once again, Snowdon has exerted its phenomenal typological potential and been enlisted as stage for a blast against the materialism and philistinism of the English nation. No wonder the Welsh gentleman-bystander was pleased, the continuing cultural resistance of his country having been endorsed by one of the 'seed of the coiling serpent' – a representative of the nation that had conquered the kingdom of Gwynedd six centuries before. I love these incandescent little valuative sunspots (some might call them airings of prejudice) that flare out periodically from Borrow's prose. That Snowdon should have elicited one is entirely appropriate. And we had better now let George, his apparently rather taciturn stepdaughter, and their young guide, having partaken of their refreshment, go their way, along the course of which they offer an ironic glimpse into another, and soon to be extremely destructive, aspect of that acquisitive national character he so deplores:

---

143 'There's night and day, brother, both sweet things; sun, moon and stars, brother, all sweet things; there's likewise a wind on the heath. Life is very sweet, brother; who would wish to die?'

'I would wish to die – '

'You talk like a gorgio – which is the same as talking like a fool – were you a Rommany Chal you would talk wiser. Wish to die, indeed! A Rommany Chal would wish to live for ever!'

'In sickness, Jasper?'

'There's the sun and stars, brother.'

'In blindness, Jasper?'

'There's the wind on the heath, brother; if I could only feel that, I would gladly live for ever.'

George Borrow, *Lavengro: The Scholar – The Gypsy – The Priest*, (Thomas Nelson), p. 166.

...very much refreshed, we set out on our return. A little way from the top, on the right-hand side as you descend, there is a very steep path running down in a zig-zag manner to the pass which leads to Capel Curig. Up this path it is indeed a task of difficulty to ascend to the Wyddfa, the one by which we mounted being comparatively easy. On Henrietta's pointing out to me a plant, which grew on a crag by the side of this path some way down, I was about to descend in order to procure it for her, when our guide springing forward darted down the path with the agility of a young goat, and in less than a minute returned with it in his hand and presented it gracefully to the dear girl, who on examining it said it belonged to a species of which she had long been desirous of possessing a specimen. Nothing material occurred in our descent to Llanberis, where my wife was anxiously awaiting us. The ascent and descent occupied four hours. About ten o'clock at night we again found ourselves at Bangor.[144]

And we, in accompanying them, have glimpsed stately old George's own moment of prescience and second sight. We have come a long way from the herbalists and simples-collectors of earlier centuries now. That summit harangue of his will soon feel all too well justified.

---

144   *Wild Wales*, op. cit. p. 166.

6

The Human Imprint

Recently, sociologically inclined art historians have insistently argued that the omission of, say, rural poverty and the
signs of industrialization from much nineteenth-century
landscape painting, was somehow morally, or imaginatively,
reprehensible – 'escapist', rather than desirably 'realist'.

But I believe this argument needs to be stood on its
head: for the Higher Landscape was wrecked not so much
by a flight from reality, as through its progressive intrusion
and impingement in a way which threatened the 'potential
space'.[145] — PETER FULLER

In *Climbing Days* – her amiable and humorous memoir of
adventures on British and Alpine mountains,[146] often in the
company of her husband, the literary theorist I. A. Richards
– Dorothy Pilley gives an account of a Christmas spent on
Snowdon summit sometime in the early 1920s. She prepared
for it by making a trip to Selfridge's (a good index to the social
register of climbing at the time) and laying in a stock of all
the food that appealed, including pink jellies, heavy plum-cake
and a prize ham. Her party, which included Richards, Dorothy

---

145   Peter Fuller, 'The geography of Mother Nature', in Cosgrove & Daniels,
eds., *The Iconography of Landscape*, (Cambridge University Press, 1988), p. 26.
146   Dorothy Pilley, *Climbing Days* (G. Bell, 1935). All quotations are from
the 2nd, revised edition (Secker & Warburg, 1965).

Thompson and C. F. Holland, rented one of the summit huts. Their provisions were conveyed by means of a small donkey to Halfway House on the Llanberis path and relayed on their backs from there to the top:

> We were treated somewhat like fools or lunatics or cinema performers, since everybody knew 'that the place was uninhabitable'. Even the hotel at Llanberis, from whom we rented the shack for a modest ten shillings a week, paid in advance, did not conceal their belief that they were getting something for nothing and that we should be down again after one night at most.[147]

In the event they stayed up there for most of a week, but it was a dismal experiment. The floor of the shack was covered with a thick sheet of ice; there were no dry boards on which to unroll their sleeping bags; displaced sheets of tattered linoleum took to the air and flew around like magic carpets; the rusting stove that was fuelled by coal from the Summit Station filled the hut with dense and acrid smoke. When the flue did finally heat up and the stove began to draw, matters deteriorated still further, as the ice encasing the hut's walls melted and soaked everything. Rain fell and the mist swirled, a gale whistled round the chimney-stack and sang in the wire stays that anchored the hut to the rim of Clogwyn y Garnedd. The wooden lining to one wall suddenly bulged inwards and crashed down on the floor. Expecting the whole structure imminently to be whirled into the void, they fled to a smaller neighbouring shack for safety, and huddled there by candlelight for two further days in a 'little dark hole no larger than a bathroom'. The blocking of its chimney by snow all but suffocated them and put an

---

147   ibid. p. 48.

end to their marathon of endurance. Trailing plum-cake, ham and jelly, as well as sooty, sodden sleeping bags, they fled for the shelter of the Pen-y-Pass Hotel, warm baths, tables laid for dinner in front of roaring fires, and brass beds with clean sheets to follow.

As a glimpse into the squalor that had come to characterize the summit area of Snowdon in the early decades of the last century, this is peerless – Pilley's own complete lack of fastidiousness and perfect good humour only enhancing the effect. By the time of her brief summit sojourn, this 'little town of Snowdonia, as the guides called it'[148] had been growing (and then as rapidly decaying) for a century. A circular shelter was noted by Pennant and had probably been constructed from the stones of a putative Bronze Age summit cairn, the original Carnedd Rhita. (Carr and Lister's book, *The Mountains of Snowdonia*, suggests the building material came from the stone boundary wall near the summit, which for various reasons I think less likely.) Royal Engineers working with the Ordnance Survey erected the massive cairn alongside this shelter in 1827, and in 1841 the cairn was further augmented and furnished with a tall pole that appears in the very earliest photographs. For the history of the earliest refreshment huts on the summit, we need to turn again to the detailed local knowledge in D. E. Jenkins' book of 1899:

> The excellent idea of providing refreshments on the summit of Snowdon is now over sixty years old, and belongs to a miner, who was at the time working in Clogwyn Coch copper mine. His name was Morris Williams, and his native place Amlwch, in Anglesey. It was while busily engaged in the

---

148   H. Humphreys, *Guide to the Summit of Snowdon* (Caernarfon, 1850), p. 19.

mine that it occurred to him how large a number climbed Snowdon in the summer months, and that perhaps it would pay him to provide a small hut near the summit, where they might get something to refresh themselves. He tried the experiment once or twice without the hut, taking with him tea, coffee, butter, bread, and cheese, and was soon convinced that a living could be made there.[149]

This suggests that the Llanberis Path – which was visible for much of its length from Clogwyn Coch, unlike the other paths, and which is perhaps the most popular ascent-route of the present day, though not mentioned by the earlier writers on Snowdon – was already becoming busy by the 1830s. As we saw in the last chapter, it was the one used in 1854 by George Borrow. Jenkins relates the story of Morris Williams' business enterprise:

> The first hut was built about 1837 or 1838, and was situated below the summit cairn, on the property of Hafod y Llan. Its outer walls were of stone, and its inner lining of neatly planed boards. Morris Williams could neither speak nor understand English, and his business suffered in consequence. In order to get over this difficulty he took one of the guides, William Williams by name, into partnership; and he, thinking to add to the attraction of Snowdon, dressed himself in a suit of goat-skin, consisting of cap, coat and trousers, which made him appear like a savage from the land of perpetual snow. This strange dress did its part well, and the flocking visitors soon made the humble summit hut a paying concern.[150]

149   *Beddgelert: Its Facts, Fairies, & Folk-Lore*, loc. cit. pp. 182–3.
150   ibid. p. 183.

We learned something of the story of this quasi-Inuit, William Williams (known as 'Wil Boots' from his role at the Victoria Hotel in Llanberis), and of one of the enduring mysteries of Snowdon and his own untimely demise, in the introduction and previous chapter. Williams was primarily a botanical guide, and it is interesting to encounter him already ensconced on the summit at such an early date. Another guide now enters the narrative – John Roberts, also from Llanberis – and a bout of cut-throat competition ensues. The boundary between Hafod y Llan and Bulkeley Estate land crossed the summit, as the supposedly-robbed wall (it was actually quite recent, only dating from the era of the Enclosure Acts), slight remains of which are still to be seen, testifies. Roberts was distinctly entrepreneurial in a small way at the time – he had married into the Closs family of Llanberis, at whose Nant Peris inn Pennant had stayed, and with his wife he founded the Pen-y-Gwryd Hotel, of which more in the next chapter. Local tradition has it that Roberts discovered a hoard of Roman coins on the site of the Penygwryd marcher camp, and emigrated to California on the proceeds in about 1845. Before then, and before opening the Pen-y-Gwryd Hotel, he had canvassed Sir Richard Bulkeley for permission to build a hut on his land. It was given, and the new enterprise, according to Jenkins, 'soon took away the greater part of the business done'.[151]

Roberts compounded his success by securing a liquor licence to sell alcohol from his premises – a vexed point in the Calvinist Wales of the time – and a degree of feuding went on around all these issues until they were finally resolved at the end of the century, when the Snowdon Tramway Company

---

151   ibid. p. 184.

bought out all those interests that had survived various take-overs, termination of leases and orders to quit. Humphreys' 1850 *Guide to the Summit of Snowdon* gives a vivid picture of the little summit-settlement in its mid nineteenth-century heyday:

> This town consists of four huts made of wood. One of which is called Saxony, because the King of Saxony dined in it – or sat in it, or possibly dozed in it, – perhaps all three . . . Supper, a bed, and breakfast, are procurable there for five shillings; and during the summer seasons vast numbers of tourists avail themselves of the wretched accommodation afforded there, for the sake of seeing the sun set and rise – a truly glorious sight! Those huts are to be immediately papered, and to be provided with good fires, and they say, good beds too, and, strange enough, views – guidebooks – stationery, &c., are to be bought there.[152]

The distinctly sceptical tone here with regard to promised future comfort and convenience is compounded when Humphreys goes on to describe the 'hotel' as in reality it was:

> . . . a vulgar, and very dingy hut, about twelve feet long and nine feet wide, a rusty stove in one corner, and a black coffee-pot keeping itself warm upon it! The wooden floor damp and wet as that of a vault, the paper black and falling off, the windows about eighteen inches square, frames inclusive. My friend W. was seated on a three-legged stool, I was perched on one end of a bench, and the guide on the other, with a clunch[153] of bread in his hand of at least half-a-pound weight, indicating that the whiskey [drunk by him on the ascent] had

---

152   H. Humphreys, *Guide to the Summit of Snowdon*, op. cit. p. 20.
153   *Oxford English Dictionary*: 'A lump, now dialectal'.

not taken away his appetite. In the course of conversation with the guide (on W.'s recommending him to plant flowers about the huts) it was replied, that they would not grow there, and that potatoes, which he had planted about 100 yards below the peak, did not produce tubers.[154]

Not so far removed, then, from the conditions of Ms Pilley's day. In photographs of the summit from the nineteenth and early twentieth centuries you can see these extraordinary, lashed-down, tottering wooden structures still clustering close around the cairn, in the later pictures towering above the first summit station building of 1898. The sight of them gives a clear impression of what that gale-blasted 1920s Christmas sojourn on the peak must have been like. The railway station itself (we shall come to the Snowdon Mountain Railway below, having dispensed with the history of its terminus), was replaced in 1934/35 by one to a design commissioned from the local landowner and architect of the Italianate village of Portmeirion on the Dwyryd Estuary, Sir Clough Williams-Ellis. It was not one of his more notable achievements. The kindest thing to say about this building, which lasted for the next 72 years until work began on its replacement, built at a cost of more than £8 million and opened in 2009 as Hafod Eryri, is that it was functional – a metal-frame-windowed, reinforced-concrete rectangle let into the slope, where visitors arriving by train could step straight from carriage to café without ever having to brave the elements.

The point to be made, of course, is that any building on this site has to withstand a fearful battering from the elements. I have little doubt that Hafod Eryri itself will have become a crumbling slum not so very unlike its predecessor after three or four decades of rain-lash and winter freeze, as anything in this location must. I remember a dank winter's day in 1968 when I guided a director from the Bradite paint company of Bethesda up to the summit by way of the Pig Track (the Llydaw causeway being flooded), carrying large tins of a new and purportedly all-weather paint his chemists had developed, to daub test-strips across the station's concrete walls and roof, hoping to win the contract to paint for which the company was tendering. The weather was so dire at the top that we could only find one small area in the lee of the building sufficiently dry to take the test-strips.

On the way back, entirely soaked, to avoid that long return ascent on the Pig Track to Bwlch Moch we willingly if not entirely happily waded waist-deep in freezing water across the Llydaw causeway, a buffeting wind slapping the small waves against our chests and their spray in our faces, little waterspout squalls chasing each other down the length of the grey, foam-streaked lake towards us and every forward step an anxious one. I never heard what decision the railway company people made about the paint. They had long been battling with the elements in maintaining the place, and I doubt even that ambitious local manufacturer could have provided them with a satisfactory remedy to all their woes.

In terms of the human imprint on our mountain, the presence of the railway is probably the most contentious point of all, and has been so from the outset — one of the founders of the National Trust, Canon Rawnsley, being most vehement in his opposition. (Nowadays, of course, the National Trust owns many of Eryri's peaks, Snowdon among them.) It came about in the following manner. A branch line had been opened from Caernarfon to Llanberis in 1869 — it was one of Dr. Beeching's first casualties in 1961 — and the summer and holiday-time trains arriving in the town would be met by the selfsame hustling throng of guides, conveyances and ponies for hire that now greet the modern World Heritage Site traveller who steps out of the station at Agra, arrives in Buda or leaves the boat at Kilronan. The railway consolidated the status of Llanberis as a tourist town. There was, however, considerable competition at the time between Llanberis and Beddgelert to become the major centre for the ascent of Snowdon. This inter-valley rivalry was nothing new in the region. In 1854 George Borrow had been harangued in the following terms by one of the Snowdon guides – the venerable Snowdon Ranger himself, John Morton – on the respective merits of Cwellyn and Beddgelert:[155]

'Do many people ascend Snowdon from your house [asked Borrow]?'

'Not so many as I could wish,' said the ranger; 'people in general prefer ascending Snowdon from that trumpery place Beth Gelert; but those who do so are fools – begging your honour's pardon. The place to ascend Snowdon from is my house. The way up from my house is wonderful for the romantic scenery which it affords; that from Beth Gelert can't be named in the same day with it for scenery; moreover, from my house you may have the best guide in Wales; whereas the guides of Beth Gelert – but I say nothing. If your honour is bound for the Wyddfa, as I suppose you are, you had better start from my house tomorrow under my guidance.'[156]

---

155 W. P. Haskett Smith, in the earliest of British guidebooks to treat of rock-climbing, suggests that the house of the Snowdon Ranger (still extant and now a hostel belonging to the YHA) was one and the same with the 'Guides' House' of Bron y Fedw. He is, I think, in error here, Bron y Fedw Isaf and Bron y Fedw Uchaf both being the best part of a mile away towards Rhyd Ddu, above the road close to the eastern end of Cwellyn.
156 *Wild Wales*, loc. cit. p. 235.

The old tribal and martial spirit of the House of Aberffraw clearly still held sway in mid nineteenth-century Eryri (and still does every Friday and Saturday night on the streets of Caernarfon, as anyone who has witnessed the rampagings there of the young warriors down from their hill settlements will testify). Borrow in a remarkably tactful manner checked the lucubrations of this fount of modesty, and elicited from him a sense of the material with which he regaled his clientele:

'I suppose you are acquainted with all the secrets of the hills?'

'Trust the old ranger for that, your honour. I would show your honour the black lake in the frightful hollow in which the fishes have monstrous heads and little bodies, the lake on which neither swan, duck nor any kind of wildfowl was ever seen to light. Then I would show your honour the fountain of the hopping creatures where, where ---'[157]

We have met these stories before, and elsewhere, and Borrow seemed to think so too. Of the inter-valley rivalries, or even inter-settlement rivalries along the same valley, the gradual opening in the 1870s and 1880s of the Welsh Highland Railway to Snowdon Ranger, Rhyd Ddu, along the Nant Colwyn to Beddgelert and eventually by 1923 to Porthmadog (the line, in the face of some controversy, was recently restored and reopened), presented a clear threat to Llanberis' desired touristic hegemony. Most of the region around Llanberis had been 'grabbed' by the Assheton-Smith family of Vaynol through an Enclosure Act of 1806, and though a bill came before Parliament in 1871 for the formation of a company to build a Snowdon mountain railway, George Assheton-Smith,

---

157   ibid.

the family head of the time, had it thrown out on the grounds that it would spoil 'his' scenery, and his shooting as well.

Nonetheless, the new railway along the valley to the west of Snowdon, the renaming in 1894 of the station at Rhyd Ddu as the Snowdon Station, and the effect the popularity of this line was having on tourist revenues in his Llanberis domain concentrated Assheton-Smith's mind wonderfully. Having been against it, he was now persuaded to come out for it, whilst at the same time warning his Llanberis tenants not to give the place a bad name by overcharging the expected influx of visitors. In November 1894 the Snowdon Mountain Tramroad and Hotels Company Ltd. came into being, and acquired land from the Vaynol Estate, as it then was, and a lease on the Royal Victoria Hotel, as it now was (the Queen herself having arrived along the new turnpike road as early as the 1850s to confer the status).

In little more than a year an astonishing feat of engineering was accomplished, despite the bouts of severe weather. It was said to have been made possible in part through the employment of slate-quarrymen whose work had become jeopardized through the roles they had played in agitation preceding the First Penrhyn Lock-Out – one of the crucial events in the history of slate-quarrying in North Wales, when an heroic workforce for the first time took organized action against an oppressive management system. The dates, however, would seem to tell against this argument, and what Douglas-Pennant, who could be a notoriously vindictive employer, might have had to say to Assheton-Smith on this point and its bearing on the operation of their cartel is amusing to conjecture![158] Whatever the truth, a narrow-gauge track

---

158   For anyone wishing to read further on this crucial period in North

using the Swiss Abt rack-and-pinion system was laid to the summit of Snowdon alongside the path from Llanberis in an extraordinarily short space of time.

Locomotives were brought to Llanberis from Switzerland (one of them, *Enid*, is still in use today), and the first trains to carry fare-paying passengers left for the summit on Easter Monday, the 6th of April, 1896. It was a spring morning of blue-skied brilliance; all went well on the way up, and both trains reached the summit. The descent, unfortunately, did not go quite so smoothly. There is a very steep section of line just above where the Llanberis Path is crossed by a bridge near Clogwyn Station. On this severe incline the engine of the first train down became detached from the rack-and-pinion, accelerated down the line, and at some point before Clogwyn Station, above what was to become known as 'Cwm Hetiau' from the number of hats blown off the heads of passengers in the early open-topped carriages that ended up there, it shot over the rim of the ridge and bounded down by the side of Cyrn Las to its destruction in upper Cwm Glas Bach. This dramatic event gave rise to a score of apocryphal tales about terrified mountaineers looking up to see an airborne steam engine strewing fiery coals heading out of the mist towards them (Snowdon having performed its habitual conjuring trick and turned a clear morning to a cloudy day).

But what, you might ask, of the carriages and the passengers?

The engines on the line always pushed the carriages to the summit, and coming down in the same order, acted as brake

Walian industrial history, the indispensable work is R. Merfyn Jones' impassioned and scholarly *The North Wales Quarrymen 1874–1922* (University of Wales Press, 1982). An impressive and lucid piece of writing, it is also the best account of the social conditions that prevailed in the industry throughout this period.

for them on the descent. They were not coupled, and each train also had a carriage brake-man – on this Easter Monday it was the railway manager. He acted quickly and brought his carriage to a halt. However, when the engine of the first train had gone over the rim, it had taken out the communications cables with the summit, and these then short-circuited and rang the 'all clear to leave' bell at the top. So the second train began its descent, unable to see the situation that had developed further down the track. It descended, fortunately, at a crawling pace, and the only effect of the ensuing collision between the second engine and the first train's carriages was to shunt the latter into the passing loop at Clogwyn Station. Miraculously, there was only one casualty from the entire episode. A passenger – Ellis Roberts, proprietor of the Padarn Villa Hotel on Llanberis High Street – had seen driver and fireman jump from the engine of the first train before it went over the rim, and thought to follow the same course of action. A carriage wheel crushed one of his legs, which had to be amputated at the Dinorwig Quarry Hospital, and he died there in the early hours of the morning.

An inquest into his death established the cause of the accident – a combination of icing and settlement of new track – and to prevent its repetition, gripper-flanges were added to the central cog-rail, ensuring the locomotives could not disengage. The railway has run safely ever since, now carrying in the region of 150,000 passengers a year, its position secure as one of the region's major tourist attractions. The Snowdon guides, too, still continue to ply their trade, though nowadays they do so under a strict professional scheme of certification which even enables them to practice as alpine guides in Europe. And they no longer bound like young goats down the crags to secure specimens for their clients, or swoop upon walkers at the summit to offer Holly Fern roots at sixpence a time, as they did during the height of the Victorian mania for fern-collecting, when the mountain was stripped ruthlessly of many of its rarest plants. Consciousness of the harm caused by these activities came only just in time to save Snowdon's relict arctic-alpine flora from extinction, and we can attribute this growth of awareness to figures like the old quarryman Evan Roberts, who became himself a qualified mountain guide and also a world authority on this flora; and to the great twentieth-century field-naturalist Bill Condry, who wrote two volumes on Wales for Collins' magisterial publishing project, the *New Naturalist* series.

In the opinion of many the Snowdon Mountain Railway is to be counted as one of the ravages visited by industry on the mountain, since tourism (particularly under its subheading here of recreation) can reasonably be considered as Snowdon's longest-established industry, and in contemporary terms is certainly its most important. Nor is there much question about the ravage aspect. Hillgoers in their evangelical way would certainly argue that mountains are no place for railways, hotels, and other such facilities for a tourist-tribe from which they would wish to mark out a clear distance for their own interest. Leave out the small matter that the hillgoers' own paths for the last several decades have grown and spread as pale, continuous scars visible from many miles away – the hillwalkers would simply retaliate by pointing to the spaceship-reflection of the setting sun in Hafod Eryri's west-facing phalanx of glass and cry foul.

Perhaps all you can say in response to this squabbling is that Snowdon in large measure inevitably became a victim of its own popularity. It is so grand, so accessible, and by far the most desirable peak to ascend in many people's imaginations that it has inexorably been given over – call it sacrificed if you will – to the demands of the majority. Management plans have been put in place, revised, overseen; a warden service, both professional and voluntary, has been recruited and trained; National Park legislation and National Nature Reserve designation have been brought in, and all these ensure at least some degree of protection and supervision for the mountain and the crowds who flock to it.

Tourism, lengthy though its development has been, is by no means the only human agency and interest to have left its mark on the mountain, and nor is it the only one to have marked and marred the landscape. There is an argument that can perfectly reasonably be sustained about the effects of sheep-farming on the mountain over centuries – an industry still in operation, although it has been in decline for decades due to changes in dietary fashions. On the one hand, it created a traditional way of life in the Welsh uplands, and a hard one that has often been highly romanticized by those who would scarcely be able to endure its rigours through the yearly round; and on the other hand, through overgrazing, it produced a landscape radically different from the one that had existed before its arrival.[159]

Having worked in this industry in the last years of its traditional practice, I have a great deal of sympathy for it, and a liking for the men and women who sustained it; and a fascination too with the ways in which they kept alive folk memories and awareness of the land in all its aspects. But sheep changed the land even more comprehensively and ubiquitously than the influx of recreationalists and visitors that

---

159   . . . lambing, gathering, shearing, dipping, market day and its associated drinking, the annual visit to London's Smithfield Show (over the antics at which a veil is best drawn), dreaming up imaginative ways of exploiting subsidy systems. And so on and so on, rain, snow or shine.

has risen to a crescendo over the last two or three decades. They made replicant and uniform skinheads of the mountains, transformed the region's appearance from a place enlivened by the seasonally-varying textures of self-regenerating woodland and heather to one of smooth hillsides of short-cropped turf – a change the conservation agencies are now attempting, with some success in a few limited areas, to reverse. I don't know what the outcome of this will be in the future, and whilst I respect the arguments focused on that cant[160] word biodiversity, nor am I entirely sure of the project's validity. These issues are complex, and the application of rigid ideologies invariably results in misrepresentation, oversimplification, antagonized communities, the uninformed taking of sides and stances.

My sympathy on this last point is generally with the shepherds and small hillfarmers with whom I worked forty years ago in one of the most entirely satisfying and educative phases of my life. Moving on, I can say without ambivalence or ambiguity that abominations like the Cwm Dyli pipeline which plunges from by the outflow of Llyn Llydaw down to an architecturally pleasing old power station at the head of Nant Gwynen,[161] have no place in a wild and beautiful environment like that of Snowdon. It is the single most offensive blemish on the mountain, and questions were being raised in parliament

---

160 *Oxford English Dictionary*: 'a set form of words repeated mechanically; a stock phrase temporarily in fashion'. It is the mechanistic and unthinking employment of words like this – and I can think of several more to which current eco-religiosity bends the knee ('organic'? 'renewables'? 'green'?) – not bad in themselves, perhaps, but nowadays more in the nature of shibboleths than statements and definitions of individually reasoned and thought-through positions.

161 A 'renewable energy' scheme, this, that was replaced and renewed rather than the opportunity having been taken for its proper removal twenty years ago, and which originated in a power-generation project set up under statutory powers at the less environmentally-sensitive date of 1903.

about the associated disfigurations of the hill-environment as long ago as 1927. Yet even now in our 'eco' age, no steps have been taken to remove or conceal it. I've long meditated on the possibility of forming a Cambrian Chapter of the 'Monkey Wrench Gang'[162] dedicated to ridding Snowdon of its presence (and the Welsh hills of wind-factories whilst we're at it).

To return, with regret, to the reasoned world of realism and history: railway, sheep and pipeline are by no means the only evidences of harm done by industry to this mountain environment. In fact, there are two significant economic activities which formerly took place here that have left their very visible scars across several large areas of Snowdon. We tend to excuse these, or even look with sympathy and perhaps a degree of nostalgia upon them, because they now fall to the remit of that new, post-Thatcher interest group, the industrial archaeologists; and to social historians who present us with moving and graphic depictions of the hard conditions endured by the men who were engaged in them. The history of both on Snowdon deserves to be outlined in some detail, so let us examine the earlier of them first.

The first of these two industries to affect Snowdon was copper-mining. This had been pursued in north Wales as early

---

162   After the title of Edward Abbey's heartening and mischievous 1975 novel, which advocates direct action and sabotage against environmentally damaging projects. It has become an enormously influential text with such admirable and principled organizations as Earth First! and the Earth Liberation Front (ELF). My heart is with these people, and I've long thought the Cwm Dyli pipe-line (along with the proliferating groups of massive wind-turbines farther south in Wales, which do not need to be sited there, and have brought about the affective destruction in particular of the Elenydd as a wild landscape) would be prime and easy targets for their activity. It's just a question really of where to lay your hands on enough Semtex. One thing I particularly like about ELF is that the only permitted spokespersons for it are those who have been imprisoned for the cause. A good way to cut out the bullshit and the posturing . . .

as the Bronze Age (2000 BC to 600 BC approximately) on the Great Orme; and since Roman times on Anglesey's Parys Mountain and perhaps also at Drws-y-coed by the road down into Dyffryn Nantlle from Rhyd Ddu. (The scene towards Snowdon, looking back up this valley across Llyn Nantlle, was the one Richard Wilson painted so often, as mentioned in the previous chapter). Here a honeycomb of mines around Simdde'r Dylluan and Talymignedd farm, with its numerous adits and shafts over 500 feet deep in places, was creating a hollowed hillside like that of Cerro Rico above Potosi, from which the silver wealth of the Spanish Empire derived. Steeply increased demand for copper to line the hulls particularly of naval ships during the eighteenth-century expansions of trade and empire, and through the protracted times of war that lasted from the Boston Tea Party to the Battle of Waterloo, acted as catalyst to a surge of exploratory activity in a region where extensive copper deposits were known to exist. This led to the discoveries (or more properly rediscoveries) within sight of Yr Wyddfa at Drws y Coed in 1761, where the mine continued to operate until 1918, and of a huge high-grade lode in the workings on Parys Mountain in 1768, which remained productive for a century until its final abandonment in 1871.

Naturally enough, these finds acted as catalysts in the search for other deposits in the area, and Snowdon became an obvious hunting-ground. The workings on the Llanberis side of Nant Peris were already active by the 1760s. Ore from them was conveyed on boats down the lakes and eventually to Caernarfon for shipping, until a tramway was opened in 1824 to connect with the new quay at Port Dinorwic – now Y Felinheli. (As we saw in the last chapter with the first Ordnance Survey maps, the degree to which later tourist routes and paths came to use mine and quarry access-routes is noteworthy.) The historian A. H. Dodd records that 'Before the end of the eighteenth century from eighty to a hundred men and boys were employed there [i.e. at Llanberis], and the ore proved very productive through the first half of the nineteenth century.'[163] Productive did not necessarily mean profitable, and variables of quality at which the ore assayed, transport costs and current market prices negatively affected any putative profits. The Llanberis mine, until a late and blatant attempt at fraud[164] in 1870, never produced high-grade ore, and is today best remembered as location for one of the recurrent modern legends of the region.

This was the work of Mrs Williams, whose home-made lemonade – sold at Halfway House on the Llanberis Path up Snowdon – was among the regular and pleasant indulgences for young enthusiasts of my generation on their way to attempt some of the classic hard rock-climbs on Clogwyn Du'r Arddu. Mrs Williams and her daughter – notable flirts, both of them – used to tease all us climbers who were her regulars with tales of the two young boys from Llanberis who made their way into the mine-workings near Nant Peris one morning and wandered lost for several days through echoing, vast caverns with only candles to light their way, before eventually emerging out of one of the adits high on Clogwyn Coch. If she wasn't too busy, Mrs Williams would take you outside and for dramatic effect point out the very one by which they had made their escape. She would vary her story at times too. For a party

---

163   A. H. Dodd, *A History of Caernarvonshire 1284–1900* (Caernarvonshire Historical Society, 1968), p. 244.
164   These were a recurrent theme in the mining history of North Wales, their success deriving from memory of the astonishing 1768 discovery at Parys Mountain. The credulity on which they thrived is still around today, of course, as evidenced by the success of the National Lottery.

of walkers who had climbed Snowdon by way of the zigzags to Bwlch Glas and were descending by the Llanberis route, it was into the mines at Glaslyn that the boys had ventured. All of which demonstrates that the ancient traditions of the *cyfarwyddion*[165] lingered long on the slopes of our mountain, adapting themselves as the centuries passed to changing circumstances. The more literal-minded have been pondering the probability, or even possibility, of those connections for decades. David Bick, author of the standard work on copper-mines in Snowdonia, dryly observes that 'Rumour has it that Snowdon and Clogwyn Coch communicated underground, but this has not been confirmed.'[166]

Success or failure of the Llanberis mine (and its likely geographical extent) notwithstanding, in the course of the nineteenth century there were at least eight copper-mines working at various periods on the mountain. The open-cut workings of Ffridd Isaf mine, for example, close to the present-day Rhyd Ddu car park and path, date from the 1850s, and were on a small scale. A denser concentration of mining activity took place in Nant Gwynen, where there were mines at Hafod y Porth north of Dinas Emrys, Braich yr Oen in Cwm Bleiddiaid, and on land belonging to Hafod y Llan a short way east of the Gladstone Rock on the Watkin Path. Worked intermittently throughout the nineteenth century, none of these difficult mines in remote locations (they feel thus even today) was remotely lucrative, and by 1890 they had all ceased operation.

The most important mine in this immediate area we have already encountered. Known as the Lliwedd mine, its finely

---

165   The itinerant story-tellers of medieval Wales.
166   David Bick, *The Old Copper Mines of Snowdonia* (3rd edition, Landmark 2003), p. 111.

engineered access track that we descended in Chapter One leaves the Watkin Path above the waterfalls and leads at a gentle gradient with sumptuous southerly views over Nant Gwynen to the extensive abandoned workings at the head of Cwm Merch. This is one of my favourite approaches to Snowdon, the view into and across Cwm Dyli as you reach the ridge at Lliwedd Bach to which it gives access being one of the grandest and most surprising on the mountain. The Lliwedd mine's three lodes were being worked by open-cut from the first decade of the nineteenth century, and activity here faltered on into the early years of the twentieth century. Despite frequent reinvestment, its location weighed against its potential for profit. A dismantled waterwheel made at the Hawarden Iron Works still lies at the side of the old track, too remote to have been carried away for scrap. By the outbreak of the Great War all was finished here, and only the danger remains, for the unwary.

The same fate awaited the most conspicuous and important copper-workings on Snowdon, active from the end of the eighteenth century and noted by William Bingley on his explorations of the mountain in 1801 as having started up only a few years previously. These were the mines beyond Llyn Llydaw, around Glaslyn. Even in their present ruin, the scale of these workings is impressive. We have already seen in earlier chapters how they were responsible, in the interests of easing access, for the lowering of the level of Llyn Llydaw and the building of the causeway in 1853. Associated structures included the mine barracks, the ruins of which are to be seen below the Miners' Track by Llyn Teyrn (on the slope beyond the lake, there are dark scars where the miners billeted here cut peat for fuel). In the earliest days of the mine, the ore was conveyed, as mentioned before, on men's backs up from

Glaslyn to Bwlch Glas by the zigzags, and thence in six-hundredweight loads on horse-drawn sleds shaped rather like wheelless wagons, for the passage of which what is now the Snowdon Ranger Path was eased and improved. The crushing mills and smelting furnaces still to be seen at the head of Llydaw were built, as was the track itself, for the Glaslyn mines. The first of the cafes on Snowdon opened by the forge alongside Llydaw, serving cups of tea to early tourists who came this way and thus augmenting the miners' meagre wages.

Most of these industrial remains were the work of a Cornish mine captain, Thomas Colliver, previously encountered in the folklore chapter, who was employed here from 1852. He laboured under considerable difficulties of climate with a largely French workforce, no budget and little credit, and the scale of his achievements are truly monumental. And what we see is only what's left on the surface. Underground the extent of the workings at Glaslyn was considerable. Some of the adits here, interlinked by vertical shafts, penetrate the mountain for five or six hundred feet (not quite far enough to reach Clogwyn Coch, in case you were wondering, nor do the tunnels head in the right direction). They are exciting and atmospheric places to explore – dangerous, too, in places, with piles of rubble stacked on decaying wood above large drops – be warned! Consider the nature of the ground beneath your feet, lest at a moment's notice it pitches you into the void. But don't let this put you off the attempt either – the sense of the working lives spent here, the lovely mineral tints and hues picked out by your light along the walls in those workings that the spoilsport authorities haven't blocked off, the mining relics you still come across and the fascination of the mountain's inner geology are their own reward, and quite unlike any other experience Snowdon can offer. They have also, fortunately, not yet been turned into an official tourist attraction, with queues and turnstiles and guides and ice creams and bored, wailing children. But it may come, as it has in so many elsewheres.

The whole copper-mining enterprise at Glaslyn and Llydaw somehow continued working right through the time of the early rock-climbing explorations on Lliwedd to which we're coming in the next chapter, attracting capital expenditure for aerial ropeways and a manager's house on the shores of Llydaw, electricity generated from a waterwheel, and a motorable road right up to Glaslyn. This last phase in the mines' history took place against the steeply declining price of copper after 1901, and testifies to much money having been lost, for the returns in the years up to the Great War were pitifully low – only 124 tons of ore were mined in 1913. The outbreak of war and expectation of profit from increased armaments expenditure inevitably, sadly, desperately saw more money poured in, more plant built. In 1916 the bubble burst. The mine closed for the last time, the men marched away to the trenches and the grand edifices they had laboured to build were left to their long and certain destruction by the forces of entropy and mountain weather.

The final industry of any significance to have affected the physical fabric of Snowdon was the one that is automatically associated with the region, and of which Llanberis for a hundred and fifty years was one of the major centres. It was slate-quarrying, and if, on a clear day, you glance a degree or two west of north from the summit, on the slopes of Garnedd Elidir[167] opposite you gain an impression of the scale of it hereabouts. What you are looking at is the Dinorwig Quarry, worked from 1787 to 1969, in which latter year a huge landslide

---

167   For which, on the Ordnance Survey map, the invented nonsense-name of Elidir Fawr is given.

lasting for three days, the fall-line of which is still visible from Snowdon, took away all the electrics, hydraulics and roadways to the working levels at a time when large debentures had become payable, and the declining survivor of a monolithic industry was forced into closure and receivership.[168]

Nothing remotely on the scale of the major Welsh slate-quarrying enterprises – Dinorwig, Penrhyn, Dorothea, Oakeley, Llechwedd – took place on Snowdon itself, but there were significant workings, particularly around the Llanberis and Rhyd Ddu skirts of the mountain. The northernmost salient of the massif, the heathery whaleback of Cefn Du, was also extensively worked for slate right across the bwlch between it and Moel Eilio from the early days of the industry around the turn of the eighteenth century, with further quarries following the slate seams down from here all the way to the shores of Llyn Padarn.

They are redolent, bleak places these days, colonized by parsley fern, stonecrop and stunted birch trees, with the woodpeckers calling in spring from the oak copses below. Most of them – Caermeinciau, Cefn Du, Upper and Lower Glynrhonwy (the latter now the location of a small light-industrial estate, making pregnancy-testing kits and the like – all very useful in an area where the local population is neither wealthy nor blessed with full employment, and the diversions

---

168   It was bought at auction for a trifle by Sir Alfred McAlpine and Sons, and for an exponentially larger amount was then leased to the Central Electricity Generating Board, which had been looking for a site suitable for the pumped storage scheme which has subsequently desolated the shoreline of Llyn Peris and the once fine and wild upper cwm of Marchlyn. The membership of the board at the time makes for interesting reading. But hush! Insider trading was not a term that had any currency in those days – this was just good business practice at the expense of the public purse, and with the connivance of the usual suspects from among the political parties.

on offer are few), Cambrian, Goodman – were worked out and closed by 1930. The last of them, Cook and Ddôl,[169] had finished quarrying by 1937.

On the auction list for Cefn Du in 1930 appeared storehouses, a powder magazine, a sheltering shed, a miners' hut and a dinner shed. Roofless and decrepit, the ruins of these still stand up there on the windy and wide-horizoned moor. Here too is the gaunt brick shell of Marconi's wireless transmitting station of 1914, from the ten four-hundred-foot-high masts of which in 1918 was sent the first wireless telegraph message to Australia. What is perhaps the best of all approaches to Snowdon starts along this airy and spacious heather crest and follows the long ridge over Moel Eilio and Moel Cynghorion to join the Snowdon Ranger Path at Bwlch Cwm Brwynog. The Watkin and Rhyd Ddu Paths too on the southern and western approaches to the mountain lead you past old slate-workings and inclines at Bwlch Cwm Llan and Clogwyn Brith.

All these were abandoned by 1880, and since then they too have been going back into the silence of the hills – *y llonydd gorffenedig* – the accomplished, the finished silence.[170] Their memories find brief expression now in a slither of spoil or a flurry of wind through the glassless window of a *caban* long

---

169 Cook and Ddôl Quarry briefly found fame at a later date as the set for Michael Mann's 1983 horror film, *The Keep*, starring Ian McKellen and Gabriel Byrne – hence the new local name of 'Film-set Quarry'. Before that it had been a munitions dump. Bomb-disposal teams billeted in Llanberis' Castle Hotel – now flats and the village Spar – between bouts of hostility with the young braves from tribes indigenous to Llanberis and the surrounding villages cleaned it up as training exercises in the 1970s.

170 R. Williams Parry, *Cerddi'r Gaeaf* (Gee, 1952), 'Eifionydd'. You may be interested to note that R. Williams Parry was a first cousin to Rhyd-ddu's T. H. Parry-Williams (and to Thomas Parry, one of Wales' most eminent twentieth century academics – and another excellent poet to boot).

since stripped of its rafters and slates. There are other voices here now, and in a different language for the most part, speaking not of toil and privation and industry but of the freedom from those things which is now the mountain's gift. They tell of how the human imprint still stamped here no longer seeks to exploit these high places for the monetary wealth that might be won from them. That imprint no longer designs to extract and blast and drill; but instead it comes in quest of the riches of experience, that being here more intangibly, and more surely, brings.

7

Colonizing the Vertical

... climbing rocks must not be thought to have had then the connotations we now attach to the term rock climbing. To understand past history we have always, with difficulty, to put our minds back into a point of view no longer our own or that of our generation. Mountaineering had not then long been recognized as a sport or even given a name. The word climbing had not yet its specific meaning of a technique or skill. It is always hard to imagine that any popular activity ever could have had a beginning, especially so recent a beginning.[171] —
GEOFFREY WINTHROP YOUNG

There is a cloudiness worthy of Snowdon itself in Winthrop Young's comments here. Perhaps this is inevitable, given the nature of the subject. For most people, their understanding of the notion of climbing Snowdon comprises an ascent by one or other of the six best-known paths to the summit – several of them, as we've seen, adapted from their former roles as mine or quarry access routes – that had come into regular use for this purpose by the mid nineteenth century or earlier. The last of them to be established – significantly, I think, for of all the

---

171 Geoffrey Winthrop Young, 'From Genesis to Numbers', in *Snowdon Biography*, ed. Wilfrid Noyce (Dent, 1957), p. 31. Winthrop Young (1876–1958) was the major British mountain writer of the early twentieth century. More of him below.

ways to the top this is the one you are best advised to avoid[172]– was the Watkin Path,[173] a lengthy and interesting, albeit rather enclosed, route with a perfectly horrid final section. If you need to know why the Snowdon Horseshoe is invariably done anticlockwise, look no further than the Watkin Path's final diagonal rise across steep, loose scree from Bwlch y Saethau to join the north-eastern end of Clawdd Coch. Its start being a mere 57 metres above sea-level, it also has the most climbing of any of the paths, and was officially opened by Gladstone in 1892. (A plaque affixed to the glaciated bluff that now bears his name commemorates the occasion.)

Arriving at the summit by any of these routes, or even by the train if it comes to that, will certainly qualify you to buy an 'I climbed Snowdon!' tee shirt in the Hafod Eryri shop (if time and season are right and it's open). Dear old Geoffrey Winthrop Young, however, would still seek to exclude you from his definition of a climber. He was thinking only in terms of his own clan – for the early history of which he provided over many years an exclusive and distorting account – which became, after many metamorphoses, that of the modern rock-climber.

It is interesting to consider the versions of history provided by the chroniclers of this sport – for which Snowdon has some

172   Not only in ascent either – the top part of the Watkin Path, along with the descent along the railway track, in winter under snow and ice conditions is one of the mountain's major accident black spots.
173   The concept and finance for construction of the path – and hence its name – came from Sir Edward Watkin (1819–1901), the Salford-born anti-Corn Law campaigner, Liberal M.P., railway magnate and progenitor of the first attempt to construct a Channel Tunnel. The ruins of his house, 'The Chalet', can be seen alongside the National Trust's permissive access from Bethania to the track above Hafod y Llan. For all that it ends so brutishly, the Watkin Path was a philanthropic gesture by a great Victorian benefactor, and I would by no means wish to be thought dismissive of it.

of the notably fine and significant venues. The event with which most authorities agree that it began was the ascent, alone and unroped, by Walter Parry Haskett Smith – a young barrister, Eton-and-Oxford educated, of independent means – of the striking seventy-foot-high pinnacle known as the Napes Needle on Great Gable in the English Lake District, which took place in June 1886. There is a broad consensus among the commentators that this was the first 'real' British rock-climb (in the sense of its having been undertaken purely for recreational purposes), and many specious definitions of the latter have been adduced by them in support of their case.

In fact, this is nothing more than a convenient misrepresentation. Haskett Smith himself, before his ascent of the Napes Needle, had made several undoubtedly 'real' rock-climbs – albeit fairly easy ones which were accomplished unroped[174] – in the course of university reading parties in the Oxford vacations at Wasdale Head in Cumbria as early as 1881 and 1882. In the latter year, too, an ascent took place on Snowdon which was beyond doubt a 'real' rock-climb, with as good a claim as any of its rivals to being the first recorded in Britain[175] – though the two climbers involved did use a rope, which may (see note 174) have rendered their ascent invalid in the eyes of some of their contemporaries.

---

174   Haskett, in his own words, 'classed ropes with spikes and ladders, as a means by which bad climbers were enabled to go where none but the best climbers had any business to be'. This puritanical attitude held sway for some time during the early years of the sport in Britain. In alpine climbing, however, the use of a rope had been standard practice for several decades, The Alpine Club even endorsing one particular manufacturer of 'Alpine line'.

175   This does beg the question of whether or not Williams' and Bingley's 1798 ascent of the Eastern Terrace on Clogwyn Du'r Arddu can be considered a rock-climb. It is really a scramble with a couple of short rock-steps, and might possibly be classified as 'Easy' or 'Moderate' on the rock-climbing scale. See note 194 below.

The two men involved were A. H. Stocker and T. W. Wall – the latter a member of The Alpine Club. Their climb took place on the great, shadowy face of Y Lliwedd, the complex thousand-foot-high wall of rock towering above Llyn Llydaw which held the imagination of cliff-explorers in Wales for half-a-century, and has subsequently – particularly in modern times – been almost completely ignored by them. The pioneering pair looked across Cwm Dyli from the summit of Crib Goch during a New Year traverse of the Snowdon Horseshoe in 1882 and were, as Wall wrote, 'struck by the grand appearance of the Lliwedd cliffs, and hearing from Owen, the landlord of the Pen-y-Gwryd Hotel, that the northern face had never been climbed, the desire to make the first ascent naturally came upon us.'[176] So the next day they acted upon the impulse and attempted their precipice, choosing as line of attack that of the crag's Central Gully, which was not climbed direct until Menlove Edwards' ascent in 1938, and even then at a grade almost unprecedented for the day.

It was far beyond the capacity of Stocker and Wall, and had anyway become a watercourse in the rain that was falling (the modern guidebook warns that 'a party caught by heavy rain must get off immediately since the whole upper amphitheatre empties down this crack'). So they retreated back to the Penygwryd – leaving at the end of their stay a self-addressed postcard so that the landlord, Harry Owen, might advise them if any rivals showed up with like designs.

No-one did, and a year later, on 4th January, 1883, they were back at the foot of Central Gully. Instead of attempting to climb this direct, as they had the previous year, they now traversed out on the right towards the centre of the West

---

176   *The Alpine Journal* (1883), p. 239.

Buttress, and found a way up this by a line which has never been identified, though one of the Bilberry Terrace routes that were recorded later, by some difficult and unknown lower variations, is by far the likeliest candidate. I must confess to being a little bewildered as to why this ascent has not received more serious attention from the chroniclers of early climbing. It was undoubtedly a major rock-climb of some difficulty, as parts of Wall's account from *The Alpine Journal* make clear:

> ... the ledge was broken by a bold face of rock. One of us was pushed to the top of the smooth part, and finding he could not descend to the ledge on the other side, he ascended a little higher, anchored himself firmly to the rocks, assisted his companion up, and let himself down to the required ledge; then, throwing the rope over a pinnacle, he gave both ends to his companion to hold tight, and slid down the 40 feet of rope to join him.[177]

One thing apparent here, and confirmed by events in April of the following year, is that Stocker was the leader and driving force – but unlike Wall, he was not one of those gentlemanly members of The Alpine Club of London. The latter continues the account:

> After a few yards of easier work, we came to a ledge about six inches wide and four yards long; the rock above was nearly perpendicular, with no handhold and there was nothing below. It was the only way; we could not turn it, and somehow we got over, but neither of us wishes to be there again.[178]

What is being described here is beyond doubt rock-climbing.

177 ibid.
178 ibid.

Some commentators, betraying ignorance of Snowdon winters, when the mountain is as often free of snow as not, and making assumptions around the fact that the pair carried alpenstocks – normal practice at the time whether or not snow was lying, and along with a pipe particularly crucial when posing for group photographs in front of the Pen-y-Gwryd Hotel – have suggested that the climb was made under snowy conditions.[179] The text carries no mention of anything but rock, which is conclusive against their argument. Finally, Wall seems to have spoken only for himself when he claims that 'neither of us wishes to be there again'.

In April 1884 Stocker, this time with a different companion, A. G. Parker (Wall being conspicuous by his absence), was back at the foot of Central Gully and climbed the West Buttress by a different route to its summit – one to which he provided a precise and recognizable description.[180] He considered it to be markedly less difficult than the climb of the previous year – the latter a feat which the only reasonably authoritative (albeit now rather dated) general history of British rock-climbing described as 'the first major rock climb in Wales and one which was at least a decade in advance of its time.'[181]

These two ascents, then, have a surer claim than that of Napes Needle to the accolade of 'first British rock-climb'. For the purposes of this book, that they are both on a cliff

179   R. W. Clark & E. C. Pyatt, *Mountaineering in Britain* (Phoenix House, 1957), state that 'snow was almost certainly lying at the time', which is entirely conjectural. My experience of Welsh winters over fifty and more years suggests that it is quite *unlikely* for snow to have been lying particularly on the lower parts of Y Lliwedd (even the summit of which is over 600 feet lower than Yr Wyddfa) at this time of year.
180   Stocker later provided elucidating comments on the lines of both climbs in the Penygwryd 'Locked Book' (see below), which make their general lines identifiable if used in conjunction with the original descriptions.
181   R. W. Clark & E. C. Pyatt, *Mountaineering in Britain*. p. 49.

of the Snowdon massif is all to the good. Nonetheless, I think even their claim is debatable. Are we to discount the St. Kildans' annual egg-and-sea-bird-harvesting ascents of sea-stacks in their archipelago because the purpose of those was not simply recreational?[182] The well-authenticated 1876 ascent of the Great Stack of Handa in Sutherland – a far more difficult rock-climb than Napes Needle – by three men from the guga-harvesting community of Ness on Lewis seems to have been undertaken for recreation, though it may have been a reconnaissance for food sources or even a rite of passage. To go back to harvesting, the exploits of the men of Arainn, egg-collecting along the lateral breaks of the awe-inspiring precipice on the ocean side of Inishmore, and their occasional mishaps and fatalities, were well documented in the island's oral tradition, which in its turn has been recorded in the series of books and maps by Tim Robinson. And are we to disregard the hints given by Bingley as to the competence of the indigenous Welsh among their native hills – the ability and local knowledge of his companion Peter Bailey Williams for example, or the 'female of an adjoining parish' he mentions, who was famed as having often made the leap between Adam and Eve on top of Tryfan? Then there were the botanical guides, combing the cliffs for choice specimens which often grew in steep gullies or on ledges perilous of access. There was the unerring way in which Thomas Johnson, guided by a local lad, homed in on the mountain's prize specimens. And here's

---

182 It was far more serious than that, being closely monitored by the unmarried island-women, who were intent on selecting a biologically-suitable mate through his climbing prowess. Whether this motivation has ever been current elsewhere is open to question, though antics at some of the more prominent mountain-training centres in Britain suggest that it may have been. And there was also a tradition associated with the Eagle Stone on top of Baslow Edge in Derbyshire, but in all respects this is outside our area of interest.

John Henry Cliffe in conversation with 'Wil Boots' – last met strangely attired at Snowdon summit, in partnership with the Clogwyn Coch miner Morris Williams:

> He told us that some of the rarer species of plants, were, in consequence of the incessant researches of botanists, yearly becoming more scarce, and that in winter, when the snow was on the ground, and deep in some parts of the mountains, he had several times risked his life amongst the precipices and hollows of Snowdon, in pursuit of some rare plant which he had been commissioned to procure for some botanical enthusiast.[183]

The book (despite its slightly misleading title it is the best Victorian account of the Welsh mountains, incidentally) in which Cliffe gives these details was published in 1860. The following year, as his tombstone in Nant Peris churchyard records, the botanical guide William Williams 'was killed by a fall from Clogwyn y Garnedd June 13 1861 whilst pursuing his favourite vocation'. The fatal accident appears to have happened not from a failure of skill or nerve but by the snapping of a rope on which he was descending to one of his collecting sites. The difficulty of access to these was rivalled by that to the copper-mine adits worked from the end of the eighteenth century on Clogwyn Coch, below the Snowdon Mountain Railway track and left of the great buttresses of Clogwyn Du'r Arddu. Having climbed up to some of these, I can vouch that to do so involves the making of unprotected moves in exposed positions which, if encountered on a 'proper' rock-climb, might well be graded 'Severe'.

---

183   J. H. Cliffe, *Notes and Recollections of an Angler* (Hamilton Adams & Cº, 1860), p. 166.

The men who laboured here were palpably competent on and habituated to their native element of rock – more so, I have no doubt, than the English visitors who came to indulge in the occasional and irregular practice of their newly-invented 'sport'. I often wonder to what places the working people of the area might have ventured in their native hills before the English sportsmen arrived?[184] Certainly the instances cited above argue a fund of climbing expertise among communities where it was by necessity required which, if we are to judge by some of their achievements as revealed through the work of folk historians in places like Ness and St. Kilda, far outstripped the skill of the earliest recreational climbers.

What is very apparent, though, from reading the commentaries on the early recorded activities of this latter faction is that its nature was both exclusive and mythopoeic. The concern throughout is with the activity of small social groups convinced of their own elite qualities making holiday-visits to the two mountain hotels of Penygwryd initially (where the deeds of mountain-going guests, significantly, were recorded in 'The Locked Book') and later to Pen-y-Pass – a theme to which even the more modern chroniclers of rock-climbing return obsessively. I am less than convinced that this is all there was to the early climbing history of Snowdon. Picking at random from Geoffrey Winthrop Young's recollections of the early days of a sport that he lays implicit claim to his tribe's having invented (in the epigraph to this chapter – 'always hard to imagine that any popular activity ever could have had a

---

184   The early botanists and simples-collectors mentioned in a previous chapter are a special case here. An interesting local perspective on the long survival of that tradition is given in the portrait of Evan Roberts of Capel Curig by Llŷr D. Gruffydd and Robin Gwyndaf, *Llyfr Rhedyn Ei Daid* (Gwasg Dwyfor, 1987).

beginning, especially so recent a beginning'), I came across the following, which would, I think, be comical if it were not so utterly serious and self-confident about the pictures it draws:

It is unlikely that any mountain generation will see again the association of three more outstanding personalities. Pope, prodigious in his height, reach, splendid physique and controlled method, the product of cultivated atmospheres, with a typically Etonian and leisurely manner, a large, dark, humorous eye for all human ways, and, underneath, the soul of romance and poetic adventure. Herford, shapely, powerful, with a wind-blown fair mane and blue thoughtful eyes ... a poet at heart, coming and going at our meetings with the spontaneousness of the wind, so near to the light and wonder of the hills in spirit that his feats upon their cliffs seemed only natural. Mallory, the last to survive, was the greatest in his fulfilled achievement, and possibly the first man to reach the summit of the world's surface; so original in his climbing that it never occurred to us to compare him with others or to judge of his performance by ordinary mountaineering standards. A Galahad ... chivalrous, indomitable, the splendid personification of youthful adventure; deer-like in grace and power of movement, self-reliant and yet self-effacing, and radiantly independent.[185]

This effusion was written towards the end of 1924. Over thirty years on, re-remembering the same golden age and generation, he thinks to add that 'it says something for the calibre of the men first attracted by the romance of the hills, and of pioneer climbing, that of those who came on Pen-y-

185   Geoffrey Winthrop Young, 'An Impression of Pen-y-Pass, 1900–1920' in Carr & Lister, eds., *The Mountains of Snowdonia* (2nd edition, Crosby Lockwood, 1948) pp. 79–80.

Pass parties, as I look through the list of names, three earned the Order of Merit, four had the Nobel Prize, five became Cabinet ministers, seven were made peers and one a life peer, fifteen were knighted, and of course an indefinite number became honorary doctors.'[186]

Of course they did! And his statistics are no doubt accurate, and give the clearest possible sense of the social register from which these early participants were drawn. And of copper-miners and botanical guides and their ability in the hills and the possible extent of their explorations?

Well, how very interesting, old chap ...

The attitude towards such as these is most tellingly revealed in the inaugural presidential address of C. E. Mathews, a Penygwryd regular, to the Climbers' Club, the self-styled representative body of Welsh climbing, given at the Café Monico in – where else? – London in April 1898:

> It is a sport that from some mysterious cause appeals mainly to the cultivated intellect. 'Arry or 'Arriet would never climb a hill ... Above all, it is a sport that makes a man.

Imagine the stately, self-satisfied tone and accent in which these maxims and sentiments were delivered. Imagine the port-raddled audience's smug assent and booming applause, they being of the elect. Poor 'Arriet, her physical competence so impaired by all those dropped aitches, losing thus her chance to become that wisest and best of God's creatures, a *man*, obviously stood no chance among these demigods, and knowing her place should have felt honoured to be allowed to serve them their *Consommé Marie Louise avec Crème Chantilly*.

Some time before his death at the age of 70 in 1999, I

---

186   *Snowdon Biography*, ed. Wilfrid Noyce, loc. cit. p. 41.

was talking to Ioan Bowen Rees[187] about the lingering mis-
conception of the Welsh as a people ignorant of their native
hills. Ioan's reply was habitually crisp, and is one with which I
am entirely in agreement:

> Oh, I think that's quite simple. It's a matter of class, surely?
> The early mountaineers who stayed at the Penygwryd and
> such places didn't concern themselves with the activities of
> a lower class and the language in which they were expressed.
> They assumed pre-eminence for their own achievements.

In the words of Geoffrey Winthrop Young that I quoted
above, you have the naked assertion of that assumed pre-
eminence. 'Was there ever such a company of men as ours?' For
Winthrop Young, the existence of the denizens of the Welsh
hills is even less substantial than that of those paid employees
the professional guides – Josef Knubel in particular – who led
him up the pre-Great War alpine climbs on which Young's
reputation was built. The professionals, it should be noted,
were yet another category of the invisibles, only the deeds
of the 'amateurs' being worthy of record. The same vicious
social distinction held true in the game of cricket until the
1960s or beyond. The Welsh are certainly there for Young – as
hosts or servants of the hotels he patronizes, or to drive the
carriage up from the railway terminus. Beyond that, the roll of

---

187 Ioan Bowen Rees (1929–1999), former head of Gwynedd County
Council, was a poet, White Robe Druid of the Gorsedd of Bards, a mountain
writer and essayist of real distinction, and father to Gruff Rhys of Welsh
rock band Super Furry Animals. In collections such as *Bylchau* (Gwasg
Prifysgol Cymru, 1995) Ioan reveals himself as the finest of all writers from
his native Wales on mountain themes. His anthology, *The Mountains of Wales*
(University of Wales Press, 1992) is far and away the best introduction to its
subject, and indispensable. I miss Ioan's combative friendship enormously. He
was a significant influence in my life.

honour belongs to his own caste. And his reciting of it in those resonant, proud terms takes us back a very long way indeed.

For all its surface polish, his sentiment is primitive in style and intent. It hints at the mythologizing in those stories we heard in the second chapter. It resonates with Homer, who celebrated warriors thus in *The Iliad*. Its phrases – that one about Mallory being 'deer-like in grace and power of movement' in particular – have their exact counterparts in epithets bestowed upon warriors in *Y Gododdin*, the earliest extant Welsh poem, ascribed to Aneirin and relating the story of a battle that took place at Catraeth (Catterick) in about AD 600. Winthrop Young's implicit values, in their arrogance and lack of interest in or awareness of any caste but his own, are those of an imperial and dominant warrior class, as surely as were the values of the three-hundred-strong aristocratic warband that rode to its destruction at Catraeth.

The irony here is that Winthrop Young himself was a more rounded and complex character than this would allow. I had better give some sense of the man here, since he is an undeniably important, albeit significantly biased, source of information about early twentieth century climbing on Snowdon in particular. He is also someone for whom the climbing world, rightly but I would hope not blindly, retains a long fund of affection. Though his Establishment credentials were impeccable – father a baronet and charity commissioner, Winthrop Young himself educated at Marlborough and Trinity College, Cambridge, where his pleasant if facile poetry twice won the Chancellor's verse-medal – there were more difficult passages to be negotiated in his life than this easy progress might suggest.

He was quietly removed from his five year spell of employment as assistant master at Eton, which he took up after Cambridge, for behaviour that in his day was certainly illegal though widespread within a particular social stratum, and in our time, when a gentleman's peculiar and predatory appetencies are less easily tolerated, would have earned him tabloid vilification, a substantial prison term and a place on the sexual offenders' register. Instead, the discretion of polite society ruled and influence rescued him. At the remarkably young age of 28 he became an inspector of secondary schools. At the outset of the Great War, a peace protester, he went to command a Friends' Ambulance Unit set up by Cambridge Quakers in Belgium, his conduct there earning him mentions in dispatches and decorations including the *Légion d'honneur* for his courageous and humane actions at Ypres. After Belgium he joined his good friend the historian George Trevelyan as the unit was transferred to northern Italy. Here, at the battle of Monte San Gabriele, he received wounds that led to the amputation of his left leg.

His refusal to accept this as an end to his stellar pre-war alpine career is rightly admired, his adaptation as rock-climber and alpinist to the artificial limb an example to many, and the book, *Mountains with a Difference*, in which he records these climbs has a flickering wry humour and not a trace of self-pity about it. He married Eleanor ('Len') Slingsby at the end of the war, and the tradition of the Pen-y-Pass Easter parties, which had faltered during the time of carnage, was resurrected – and I think grew a little more inclusive over time. Certainly the slightly louche and bohemian figure of Young had by this time become a revered institution. As the 1920s progressed, and Geoffrey and 'Len' Young were established in Cambridge at 5 Bene't Place, where the two held Sunday evening mountaineering and intellectual *salons*, a new generation of university climbers was invited along to Pen-y-Pass.

Jack Longland was one of them. He described the tenor of Pen-y-Pass Easter parties as 'a social and intellectual background which is quite foreign to what I know of climbing today'.[188] But the saga of Penygwryd and Pen-y-Pass, as related by Winthrop Young and those later commentators who borrow heavily from him, conceals as much as it reveals. It presents a received version of our mountain's climbing history which is little different in essentials to the lists of dates and victories, commanders and monarchs propagated by any victorious faction, and behind which there are many differently interesting and suppressed demotic stories that we can now only piece together from chance and gratuitous fragments, or clues that the 'conquerors' themselves unwittingly supply.[189] This brings us round again to the early history of Lliwedd and a possibility – a distinct possibility – which, if it were the case, effectively trumps Winthrop Young's whole mythologizing and colonialist project.

---

188   As an eighteen-year-old freshman at Cambridge in the mid 1920s, as though to prove that old habits died hard, Jack was sexually involved with both G.W.Y. and 'Len' Young, a fact on which he swore me to secrecy as long as he lived, and – typical, this, of the mischievous aspect to his character – commanded me to divulge as widely as possible after his death (which was in November 1993). Jack's wife Peggy had her own contribution to make about Geoffrey's eccentricities, asking if I remembered the cloak he wore in several well-known photographs, and going on to tell of how he would come into the women's bath-house at Pen-y-Pass and with a flourish swing it aside to reveal himself naked underneath: 'We would merely giggle at this – there was nothing there to make a girl feel afraid on her wedding night.'
     Arnold Lunn's summary and elliptical comment in his D.N.B. notice for Geoffrey tells of how 'Len' had 'an affectionate understanding of his endearing weaknesses'. Which neatly defines the Establishment's contemporary view of these issues.

189   Mountaineering historian Alan Hankinson tersely sums up the problem thus: 'Unfortunately, Young's writings form not only the chief, but almost the only source of information. He cannot be claimed as an impartial witness.' Alan Hankinson, *The Mountain Men* (Heinemann Educational, 1977), p. 120.

I first became aware of the material that follows over forty years ago, when I was shown by a very excited Peter Crew[190] in a copy of the Abraham Brothers' *British Mountain Climbs* that he'd just bought a marginal note written in pencil by the description to Slanting Gully on Y Lliwedd, a thousand-foot Severe the first ascent of which was claimed by the Abraham Brothers at Easter 1897. The note indicated that this feature had in fact first been climbed by copper-miners from Nant Gwynen – relatives of the note-writer – in the *early 1860s* – a quarter of a century before Haskett ventured up Napes Needle.

We know from the preceding chapter that the Snowdon copper-mines were active at the time. The miners at Llydaw looked across at Y Lliwedd every working day. They knew the legends about Arthur's gold being hidden in Ogof Llanciau Eryri – the prominent cave near the top of Slanting Gully, to which the shepherd boy had supposedly found his way.[191] Also, if Arthur's riches were not still there, guarded by his sleeping knights, who knows what rich lodes of copper might be in their stead? For anyone who thinks that these men could not possibly have been capable of reaching the Slanting Gully cave and carrying on beyond it, I would again recommend that they try wandering around the adits on Clogwyn Coch. All this merely establishes possibility; but there is more, and it shades the matter into what I would take to be probability.

When the Abraham brothers of Keswick made their ascent in 1897 they came across what they described as a 'piton' that – according to which of their two accounts you read, and it does change – either crumbled to rust at their touch or was so loosely attached that it simply fell out. How had this 'piton' – a

190   See Chapter Two, note 25.
191   And would have known too of John Roberts' recent discovery of the Roman silver coin hoard at Penygwryd.

device the use of which was more or less unknown to British climbers at the time – come to be there? The supposition of the Abrahams and others was that it had been placed by an Oxford dictionary editor, Mr Mitchell, who had attempted the climb solo in August 1894. An ascent of this magnitude for its time, then as now, came under the closest scrutiny. Mitchell was watched as he moved out on to the crucial slab pitch by the cave, faltered, ground to a halt unable to return to his previous position, and eventually fell to his death. Had he made any attempt to place a piton, it would have been observed and commented on. He can have made no such attempt.

For a miner, though, the placing of metal spikes to safeguard and assist on dangerous ground was an everyday procedure. The Abraham brothers' claimed first ascent of Slanting Gully took place at Easter 1897, over thirty years after the period given in the marginal note for the miners' ascent. That is more than enough time on a wet Welsh crag for an iron spike to rust into flaking ruin. Two and a half years is not. I see no reason to doubt the chance surviving testimony of the marginal note. To my mind, the ascent by the Nant Gwynen miners, pre-dating Haskett on the Napes Needle by twenty-odd years and the Abraham brothers on Slanting Gully by over thirty, ought to be recognized as in all probability the earliest recorded ascent of a 'proper' rock-climb – at least on Snowdon (my *caveat* regarding the St. Kildans and others I would wish to retain).

What would Winthrop Young, or that humorous old barrister Haskett Smith, have made of the case? It would have been fascinating to have argued it out with them. Though there is another ironic element here, which is that support for the Abraham brothers' first-ascent claim could well have been less enthusiastic than we might assume. George Abraham, a shop-keeper and professional photographer – a mere tradesman, therefore, in the eyes of the Winthrop Young elite – in one of his later books commented on 'the dog-in-the-manger idea which then prevailed, that the joys of the mountains were only for men of liberal education and of the higher walks of life'. As expressed in the orotundity of president Mathews, perhaps? Elsewhere he noted that he and his brother 'had always found it most difficult to obtain accurate information regarding the newer climbs. The authorities, with a few notable exceptions, were very reticent and gave us but little practical encouragement'. He moves on from these general charges to plunge his knife into the heart of the Penygwryd clique's integrity:

> Often we have started out for a gully on the strength of an assurance that it was a well-known climb, and almost as frequently have we encountered difficulties far beyond what were anticipated. In many cases these gullies had not even been visited.

This is a sharp perspective indeed on the early records of climbing in Wales, but it is one the import of which we need to hear. A self-professed elite will always acclaim and inflate its own deeds, and rest satisfied with its own supposed excellence. It will, as we have seen with Winthrop Young, find its own myth-maker and celebrant and applaud his tales.[192] The result

---

192   The most notable example of this in British climbing history is the obsession with George Mallory's doomed 1924 attempt on Chomolungma, 'Mount Everest'. Even as I write, yet another expedition is on the mountain searching for the camera carried by Mallory's companion 'Sandy' Irvine, which it is hoped will provide final proof that the pair 'conquered Everest' as the odious media phrase has it. The supposed likely indices of this relate to the absence from his personal possessions, when Mallory's corpse was discovered in the place to which it had fallen below the crucial 'Second Step' in 1999, of a photograph of his wife Ruth which he had apparently vowed to place on the summit; and also to the fact of his snow-goggles being in his pocket, which has suggested to some that he had reached the summit and was descending in the dark.

of this complacency in Welsh climbing was that it lagged far behind the Cumbrian version – which was not so hide-bound by class issues and the assumption of superiority – for decades. There is nothing in our gentlemen's Welsh preserve that for contemporary achieved difficulty can remotely compare with Godfrey Solly's Eagle's Nest Ridge Direct on the Napes from 1892; Collier's Climb on Scafell from 1893; Fred Botterill's eponymous slab on Scafell from Whitsun 1903; Herford's and Sansom's epochal ascent of Scafell Central Buttress in April 1914; J. I. Roper's two futuristic climbs on Dow Crag in 1919 and 1920.[193]

Other modern commentators have stated that, 'As for climbing difficulties, Mallory is known to have climbed comfortably at Hard Very Severe in Wales'. This is simply not true. The hardest climb by a verified route that Mallory is known to have accomplished in Wales was his eponymous rib on the Nantlle Y Garn, which is graded Mild Very Severe and the difficulties on which were led in fact by H. E. L. Porter, and not by Mallory himself. We are back here with Winthrop Young-esque mythopoeia. There is nothing whatsoever in Mallory's climbing record to suggest that he was remotely capable of climbing at extreme altitude a cliff of the difficulty of the Second Step – and especially not when carrying heavy oxygen cylinders, and exhausted at the end of a long and gruelling expedition.

That the British mountaineering establishment still ardently wishes that it had been Mallory who had 'conquered' the mountain, instead of an Antipodean bee-keeper and his Nepalese climbing partner, scarcely needs further comment – the Winthrop Young passages are the best gloss here. As to the Anglo-American industry that has built up around the myth, it has proved a nice little earner for *National Geographic* and sundry mountaineers and camp-followers funded by that organization, and will no doubt continue to grow for as long as the dollars are forthcoming for its maintenance.

The hills of Snowdonia, meanwhile, can provide their own testimony as to Mallory's competence on rock, and it is not a substantial one – a pleasant little V. Diff. soloed to collect a forgotten pipe; a one-move Hard Severe where the use of an ice-axe – as was the case on Mallory's ascent – reduces the grade to about Difficult; a debatable climb on Llechog and an easy Very Severe on the safe end of a rope – harsh summary perhaps, but inflated and dishonest claims need to be tempered thus.

193 'Joe' Roper was one of British rock-climbing's exceptional shooting-star talents – an I.L.P. member from Barrow who studied Economics at Ruskin

I would happily argue that this situation of Cumbrian pre-eminence over Wales – on balance, and disregarding for once Chris Preston's remarkable Suicide Wall in Cwm Idwal (though in essence this was a top-rope-rehearsed outcrop climb) lasted right through to the early 1950s, when Joe Brown of Manchester and Don Whillans from Salford finally achieved parity with the climbs of Dolphin and Greenwood, who were the leading post-war Cumbrian pioneers. But this is both a broader perspective and to move too far ahead. We need to consider what – unreliable and self-serving accounts of the gentry aside – was happening on Snowdon once the sport of rock-climbing had achieved a certain impetus in the decade or so before the Great War.

Behind all the colonialist and elitist obfuscation and self-celebration, discernible trends and truly significant figures were emerging in the story of climbing on Snowdon in these years leading up to the outbreak of war. There were technical developments in safety and equipment: a better understanding of the use of the rope and of belaying techniques; the introduction of specialist nails (tricounis, clinkers, star-muggers) for climbing boots, and of rubber shoes for use in dry weather; even the occasional use of the rope sling or rock-piton to safeguard or facilitate progress. There was both a promiscuous search for new cliffs to be climbed – the first climbs on Dinas Mot, Llechog, Cyrn Las and the Teyrn Bluffs belong to this period – and there was intense exploratory

---

College and dedicated his life to work with the W.E.A., his two Dow Crag routes, Great Central Route and Black Wall, were exceeded in difficulty by very few British rock-climbs before the 1950s revolution in the sport. Colin Kirkus fell off the easier pitch of the former, and Menlove Edwards had to be rescued from the latter. And these were the two leading Welsh climbers of the 1930s! I wonder what G.W.Y. would have made of Roper, and vice versa?

activity concentrated on Y Lliwedd. Like Clogwyn Du'r Arddu from the 1920s through to the 1980s, here was a cliff where potential for pioneering and the achieved standards of contemporary climbing ability were remarkably consonant. The rock-structure lent itself to a range of grades from the easier Difficults to the harder Severes.[194] The pioneer who emerged to avail himself most prolifically of this natural gift was a clergyman's son and Cambridge Classicist who from 1884 onwards was a master at the Friar's School in Bangor. He was taciturn, depressive and essentially solitary. His name was James Merriman Archer Thomson.

Along with local companions, Archer Thomson more or less instigated the habit of regular weekend climbing, and seems to have been interested exclusively in Welsh rock without any need for an alpine frame of reference – his home crags became not a training ground for greater things, but an end in themselves, which was an enormously significant paradigm shift that has gained in force and popularity down the decades. There is a sense in which his relationship with this single cliff

194   For those unacquainted with the British systems of grading climbs, briefly in its traditional form this was given as an adjectival progression from Easy through Moderate, Difficult, Very Difficult, Severe, Very Severe and after the Second World War on through to Extremely Severe (Exceptionally Severe held sway for a short time in the 1950s and early 1960s, but resulted in some manifest absurdities and was quickly dropped). All these grades could be qualified by the addition of Mild or Hard, and some constructions, striving for exactitude, could become remarkably clumsy at times ('Perhaps just Mild Very Severe, by a tradition' went one example from an interwar Tryfan guide.) A numerical grade for each pitch (passage of climbing between stances and belays) was introduced in the mid 1960s and had become prevalent within a decade. The grade of Extremely Severe by the mid 1970s, with the stratospheric rise in standards at that time, had become very crowded and was replaced by an open-ended system of E-grades allied to individual pitch-grades, so that, for example, a modern classic like Great Wall on Clogwyn Du'r Arddu would be given E4, 6a, 5c. At this point it is probably appropriate to take back those comments about the Pen-y-Pass coterie's capacity for elitist obfuscation . . .

of Y Lliwedd foreshadowed the whole future development of climbing – the searching out of boundless variation, the quest for difficulty, the probing into unexplored gaps, the logical sequencing of climbing pitches to construct a good climb. All this was typical of Archer Thomson's approach. His association with Y Lliwedd lasted from 1894 until his death, from drinking potassium cyanide, in 1912 – his last new climb on the cliff having been made only weeks before. With the Cornishman A. W. Andrews – another figure peripheral to the Pen-y-Pass group centred around Winthrop Young – he wrote the first British guidebook to a single cliff. And of course the cliff was Y Lliwedd, upon which he pioneered over twenty new climbs through the years of his association.

These included the Avalanche-Red Wall combination – a route of Very Difficult standard (see note 194) which was held up to my generation of tiroes as the very type of the Welsh mountain rock-climb. It was only to be undertaken wearing thick tweed or moleskin knee-breeches which would chafe your inside thighs red-raw, worsted-wool stockings and stiff boots, with laden rucksacks on our backs, and to be followed by completing the circuit of the Snowdon Horseshoe (in the wrong and clockwise direction). Finally we descended to the shabby old institution that the Pen-y-Pass Hotel had become by the early 1960s, with its old ladies there bringing the beer up from the cellar in great chipped white enamel jugs, and the stuffing from armchairs that had received the forms of Young and his contemporaries spilling out on to the slate-slabbed floor. Avalanche/Red Wall no longer seems to be a popular excursion, and for all the rest, progress, mortality and the Health & Safety Authority have long since swept them away.

Real history, as opposed to its climbing versions, intervened two years after Archer Thomson's death in the shape of the

Great War, and inevitably it decimated mountaineering's ranks. A hiatus in climbing on Snowdon lasted with very little interruption – a late climb on Y Lliwedd by George Mallory in 1919, a couple of pioneering efforts from I. A. Richards and Dorothy Pilley in the early 1920s, a climbers' guidebook to Snowdon and the Beddgelert district from Herbert Carr[195] in 1926 – until in the second half of that decade a new crag began to emerge into climbing consciousness and assume a pre-eminence it holds to the present day.

It would be wrong to assume that Clogwyn Du'r Arddu – the peerless and architectonic masterpiece of geology on Snowdon's northern flank below the ridge taken by the Snowdon Ranger Path – had not registered in climbers' imaginations before the series of ascents between 1927 and 1986 that established it as the most significant of all British cliffs. The Abraham Brothers had ascended a pleasant, if slight, couple of pitches here in 1905 that started from a point close to that on the Eastern Terrace where in 1798 Peter Bayley Williams had assisted Bingley with his belt. Mallory and Todhunter had laboured up the loose, dark and hideous cleft of the East Gully (a climb of no technical difficulty now only ever used in full winter conditions – when it is quite sporting

195 For all his sterling service, particularly to the Climbers' Club, both through the writing of his Snowdon guidebook and his role in the acquisition of the club cottage at Helyg in the Nant y Benglog, there were elements within the climbing world who blamed and never really forgave Carr for his part in the accident in Cwm Glas which killed the very promising Cambridge climber Van Noorden. Carr himself had lain beneath the crag with severe injuries for two days after their fall, his dead companion beside him, before being found. In later life Carr was an antiques dealer in the Cotswolds, and in his old age was rather lionized by celebrity-collectors among a younger generation of social climbers – attention which the by then very aged Carr seemed to enjoy.

and tends to hold what snow there is – or as access to the magnificent later climbs on its right-hand walls) in 1912, 'after an hour or two spent on more or less unprofitable inspection on the face'. Carr himself had made a series of vaguely worthy if vegetatious and rambling routes on the characterless expanses of the slabby Far West Buttress in 1919, and in the early 1920s the man who was later to become mountaineering's prolific and pre-eminent author, Frank Smythe, completed a couple of curious climbs at either end of the crag, one of them on the Far Eastern Buttress up 'rocks … indeterminate, evil, and untrustworthy' and the other taking the deliciously exposed slabby terrace above the Steep Band. None of these were anything more than prolegomena to the crag's real challenges.

In his Snowdon guidebook, Carr had written of The Pinnacle (the sharp crest of the East Buttress, bounding the upper basin of the Eastern Terrace on the left and overlooking the East Gully) that 'the scenery here is not surpassed on any crag in Wales' – still a reasonable and accurate statement. And of the East Buttress he recorded that it 'has never been climbed. The final wall is quite impossible, but the lower 200 feet below a broad green gallery, may yet be conquered by a bold and expert party. The sheer walls of this crag offer one of the most impressive mountain spectacles in Britain.'

Having delivered himself of these enticements with regard to the East Buttress, Carr then raised the tempo even further by his description of the West: 'No breach seems either possible or desirable along the whole extent of the West Buttress, though there is the faintest of faint hopes for a human fly rather towards its left side.' If ever words were guaranteed to set the human flies buzzing, it was these. In 1926 the Rucksack Club of Manchester dispatched a contingent including the gritstone

COLONIZING THE VERTICAL

experts[196] Fred Pigott and Morley Wood. These two climbers, 'as unscrupulous as they are invincible' in the words of a third member of the party, by various chicaneries involving inserted chockstones and rope-loops (the informality of climbing as a sport then as now means that the opportunities for what is basically cheating are legion) made progress on what appears to be the easiest line[197] on the front face of the East Buttress, up a line of corner-cracks in a blocky recess to the left of its smooth and sheer central wall. Their ruses failed to bring them success on either their first or second attempts.

Manchester terriers that they were, the following May they returned, and exercised even more guile even more inadmissibly; but it brought them successfully if by dubious means to that 'broad green gallery'. A psychological barrier, which in climbing is often the most significant of problems, had been broken. The East Buttress had been climbed, and not a Cambridge climber, G.W.Y. disciple or Pen-y-Pass-ite was in sight. The wheels of precedence had turned, and the Cambridge contingent had no wish to be left behind. An unclimbed buttress yet remained. Frank Smythe was reconnoitring it before the month was out, and was impressed by what he saw:

> I found myself gazing up the most impressive slab that I have seen in Britain. Two hundred and fifty feet high, it slants up to the left in one great sweep, sloping slightly outwards in the

---

196 'Gritstone' – properly millstone grit – is a coarse-grained and compacted sedimentary rock that outcrops extensively in the southern Pennines, particularly around Manchester, Sheffield and Leeds. Climbers love or loathe the steep, bold, frictional style of climbing it demands, and most advances in the British sport gained their initial momentum from those who had served their apprenticeships and become expert here.
197 Far from it, in fact – in the damp conditions that frequently affect the crag, the upper cracks of Pigott's still present one of the stiffest problems at their grade.

same direction. On the right it is bounded by an overhanging wall; and in the angle this formed is a narrow cleft of terrific aspect. The left-hand and outer edge of the slab is about twenty feet, and the inclination between seventy and eighty degrees. Up it the eye wandered fascinatedly while the mind speculated half-dreamily, awed to passivity.

That last sentence is one of the best short evocations I know of the appeal of unclimbed rock. And the passivity does not last, the speculation drawing you into action. By the end of the summer both Smythe (in company with Jack Longland) and Fred Pigott had separately reconnoitred the hinted line. Both failed. At Whitsun in 1928 both parties that had previously attempted the climb arrived on the same day at its foot, the Manchester group speculating in surprise at the discovery of a rope sling left by Smythe and Longland at Easter. 'Could it have been the early pioneers?' they wondered.

They themselves were the early pioneers as far as this cliff was concerned. After discussion, they joined forces. Longland was appointed leader, and the ascent was accomplished with Winthrop Young watching his own and his wife's young lover from the safe vantage point of bathing in the lake. Here's Smythe again:

Longland meanwhile with great difficulty changed into rubber shoes; but even with their aid his lead was a brilliant piece of climbing . . . Only a man at the top of his form, with nerve and skill working in perfect unison, could safely make it . . . those fifteen feet were overhanging; but more than fifteen feet of overhang were required to stop Longland at this stage . . . [he] settled the question in arbitrary fashion by clinging up the overhang – the solitary piece of pure gymnastics on the climb – and gaining the platform above.

In the space of a year, both of the formidable central buttresses of Clogwyn Du'r Arddu had been climbed. Welsh climbing in two bold strokes had been freed from the influence of those termed by E. A. Baker 'the torpids of Snowdonia [who] took life much too easily'. Its future now lay wide open, and was held in other hands than these.

Those new hands, even at the time of Longland's great climb, were already shaping themselves to the intricacies of rock. Anyone proud of their Welshness will delight to hear that their possessors both came from *Lerpwl* (Liverpool), the city that from the time of the industrial revolution had been the effective capital of north Wales. They were two men of near-identical age. One of them was the son of a car mechanic and was employed as a clerk in an insurance company office; the other was a medical student whose father, an impoverished and crippled parson, had lived and worked with and written upon the homeless and the unemployed – with tramps, in the terminology of the day. C. E. Mathews must have been squirming in his grave with appalled disbelief, though there's no evidence of dropped aitches with either of our new men. Between them Colin Kirkus and John Menlove Edwards – friends and contrasting characters differently honoured in the climbing community's collective memory, with Kirkus slightly the senior in his climbing experience – were to dominate the climbing history of Snowdon for more than a decade.

Kirkus was the first to make his mark on the mountain's history. He did so in momentous style three days before his twentieth birthday in June 1930 by pioneering a climb right up the centre of the buttress that had been hailed only four years before as unassailable, with no breach possible or desirable along its whole extent. In the event, although climbing the Great Slab was distinctly adventurous or even hazardous because of the tendency of grass which had spread over much of it to part company with the underlying steep, smooth rock, the technical difficulties of this seven-hundred-feet-long route proved not to be too demanding, and they eased as it gained height. By the line Kirkus took, the Great Slab is now firmly established as one of the classic expeditions in Snowdonia. A week later, on the Nose of Dinas Mot – a downhill walk from Pen-y-Pass – Kirkus climbed another of the finest Very Severe rock routes on Snowdon, the Nose Direct.

Floodgates were opening. Back on Clogwyn Du'r Arddu Kirkus went on to produce a series of ascents along the East Buttress and Middle Rock: Chimney Route, Curving Crack, Pedestal Crack and its Direct Start, Terrace Crack, Birthday Crack and the Bridge Groove (the latter in retrospect, along with the Javelin Blade climb in Cwm Idwal led by Jack Longland three months earlier, was the hardest technical climbing yet achieved in Wales, almost reaching the standards of the hardest Cumbrian climbs from a decade before). Together these constitute one of the most extraordinary series of exploratory ascents at or near the highest contemporary standards in mountaineering history.

The final new route Kirkus added here, in June 1932 and accompanied by those unscrupulous and cunning Mancunians Fred Pigott and Morley Wood, lay up the right-hand bounding groove of the Pinnacle Face above the Green Gallery. These climbs now constitute the cliff's middle-grade classic repertoire, and an addition to them was made by another Manchester climber, Maurice Linnell, the following summer, with Pigott once more holding the rope. This was the Narrow Slab, the hardest climb so far on the West Buttress (though by no means one of the best). Kirkus and Linnell were increasingly keeping company, and using the new Idwal

Cottage Youth Hostel at Ogwen, which had the inestimable advantage over the new club cottages of the Rucksack and of the Climbers' Clubs of being open to both sexes,[198] and was therefore lower on squalor and higher on entertainment. The future on all fronts was looking very bright.

In 1933 the old metropolitan/Oxbridge mountain establishment had excluded Kirkus from consideration for a place on Hugh Ruttledge's 'Everest' expedition on the grounds of his inexperience. They had had no such qualms about Sandy Irvine in 1924, though his mountain experience was limited to a few easy peaks in the Bernese Oberland – but then, he was an Oxford rowing 'blue' and Kirkus was the office clerk who was a car mechanic's son. As to Kirkus' mountaineering ability, he had climbed guideless on difficult routes in the Alps by this time, and in 1933 had been on an expedition to the Gangotri glacier in the Garhwal Himalaya where he and Charles Warren had ascended Bhagirathi III, which was the most difficult climbing at altitude achieved at that date.[199] This expedition was the reason for the 1933 hiatus in his explorations on Clogwyn Du'r Arddu. With the evidence of rock-climbs like West Rib, his 1931 climb on Dinas Mot which is still regarded as a serious lead at a grade of Hard Very Severe, and two other climbs from this period – Bridge Groove on the Middle Rock and Kirkus Corner on the gritstone edge of Stanage in Derbyshire, both of which now receive E-grades – it is apparent that Kirkus was on the verge of an advance

---

198 The group photographs taken at Idwal Cottage from this time show Kirkus, Linnell & co. looking very relaxed and happy in the company of some remarkably pretty young women.

199 How stupid of me to have forgotten here about Mallory and his conquest of the Second Step! It will put the Establishment and *National Geographic* Inc. in quite a sulk!

into new levels of climbing achievement. He also had climbers around him like Linnell and Menlove to support, compete with, raise each other's games . . .

At Easter 1934, with the snow on Snowdon, then as now, unreliable, Kirkus set off in Linnell's sidecar for some winter climbing on Ben Nevis. On a difficult buttress-climb called The Castle, Kirkus was leading through the cornice at the top of the route when a small slab-avalanche took his footholds away. He and Linnell, who had been pulled off his belay attempting to stop the fall, slid and bounced 250 feet down the rocks and snow, finally stopped by the rope between them catching across a snow-ridge. Kirkus was knocked out in the fall, but once he regained consciousness he climbed up to Linnell, who was unconscious and probably dead of head injuries. Kirkus secured him to the slope, completed the climb having found his own broken ice-axe, had the presence of mind to build a cairn to lead rescuers to Linnell, and with the serious head injuries he too had sustained causing him to lapse in and out of consciousness, he began to descend to seek help. He was found wandering by Alastair Borthwick[200] and taken to hospital in Fort William. His jaw was broken, and he had serious fractures to his skull, leg injuries, severe shock and concussion. Rescuers, guided by the signs he'd left, because of the dangerous conditions did not manage to reach Linnell's body until the following day. Kirkus himself was kept in hospital for three weeks. His sight was permanently damaged in the accident, but the psychological damage was even greater. His pioneering days on Snowdon were at an end.

---

200 Author of an evocative prelapsarian account of interwar Scottish climbing, *Always a Little Further* (Faber and Faber, 1939), to match Kirkus' own delightful reminiscent manual for young people, *Let's Go Climbing* (T. Nelson, 1941).

Climbers, through the nature and sometime consequences of their activity, are inured to tragedy, and climbing itself goes on. A curious little reversion to older norms was the next significant event in the history of Clogwyn Du'r Arddu – not of any great intrinsic significance, but a reminder of just how much the social structures of the sport had changed in the space of a decade or so. It was a little spurt of exploratory activity by a party comprising two Oxford students, Robin Hodgkin[201] and David Cox, and two from Cambridge, George and Ruth Mallory's daughters Clare and Beridge. They camped together for the month of June in 1937 beneath the cliff. 'The Mallory girls in one tent, David and I in the other', Robin vouchsafed, in response to my quizzical look. 'And as to our bathing together naked, of course we did but the tradition was that you didn't look. Though no doubt there was the occasional accidental glimpse . . .' They made the first ascent of Sunset Crack on the East Buttress – a climb with a distinctly effortful top pitch, and Robin, who was perhaps the most naturally gifted climber of his generation, also added significantly difficult variations to Pigott's Climb and to Great Slab.

The quiet and forceful Rucksack Club climber Arthur Birtwhistle visited briefly that summer too and climbed the last and probably the best of the straightforward entry pitches on the East, the Drainpipe Crack, but it led nowhere at any

---

201   Robin Hodgkin (1916–2003), a fine old Quaker educationalist and Headmaster of Abbotsholme, would surely have been one of the great names in British rock-climbing had he not lost his fingers and toes from frostbite on the 8,000-metre peak of Masherbrum in 1938. His great friend David Cox, a history don at University College, Oxford, was also a fine climber in his day. He caught polio from Wilfrid Noyce on their expedition to Machapuchare in the Annapurna Himalaya in 1957, which effectively ended his climbing career. In my time David was the most benign and approachable of mountaineering's elder statesmen.

grade possible for the time, so he retreated and left the cliff
to the ravens and the choughs and its profound and gathered
silences once more. Elsewhere on the mountain, climbers'
curiosity probed at different rocks. An intricate line of least
resistance was worked out in 1935 by two Rucksack Club
members up the statuesque main buttress of Cyrn Las,
towering over lower Cwm Glas, to provide the enjoyable and
atmospheric Main Wall climb, which is surely the best climb
at its grade of Severe in Wales; the ice-polished slabs of the
Nose of Dinas Mot were criss-crossed with climbs by Kirkus
and Menlove. Winthrop Young's Easter parties at Pen-y-Pass
continued in their long tradition, which meant that there was
always Y Lliwedd, overshadowed and old-fashioned though it
might now be.

Menlove Edwards was invited to Pen-y-Pass at Easter
1934 – the time of Kirkus' accident. A mutual fascination
grew up between himself and Winthrop Young, and Menlove
left a teasingly fond parody of his mentor's heroic style, which
implicitly conveys a good deal of how times, equipment and
techniques had changed:

> In the good old days climbing was a sport for men of iron
> and they wore deerstalker caps, were 6'3" in height and broad
> by comparison. When they climbed a climb they were brave
> and fine about it and they showed grit and determination of
> a high order. They took life seriously, these grand old men,
> and they called a spade a spade even if it was a trowel . . . But
> now the boot-nail of the ancients has lost its glory while the
> rubber shoe stalks abroad through the hills. Now our heroes
> are no longer men of iron but are made only of sorbo rubber
> guaranteed to bounce without bursting and there remains
> only an occasional outsider of stainless steel.

To Menlove, then, fell the task of making sense, of elucidating, all that had taken place since recorded climbing in Wales began on Y Lliwedd. He was to write a new guidebook to the cliff. A practising psychiatrist by now, he spent the month of August 1938 threading and re-threading Y Lliwedd's endless and often indistinguishable connections between one obscure terrace or ledge and another into coherent descriptive narratives. (A hallmark of climbing on the cliff is the route that starts a quarter the way up a buttress and finishes at two-thirds height on another face entirely, or some such, which makes life difficult for the guidebook-writer.) The subsequent volume was a perfect expression of the meeting between an idiosyncratic mind and an impenetrably undifferentiable precipice. It acquired a kind of legendary status as a text where charm of expression existed in perfect balance with total and incomprehensible indecipherability. But this was the effect of Y Lliwedd, and not the fault of Menlove. The cliff is essentially undescribable, though Menlove undoubtedly compounded this quality through several quirks of his own.

Most climbers will talk up their own discoveries and even annex the better part of those by others on the slightest pretext. Menlove, who would always talk down his own achievements, took the opposite tack and managed to distribute and ascribe a large proportion of his own considerable stock of new climbs without the least historical proof or justification among the legions who had gone on the cliff before him. Many reputations were substantially enhanced by Menlove's guidebook. His own tally at every possible juncture was minimized. Yet what he could not conceal, here and elsewhere through his climbing years, was the huge ability he possessed for climbing rock and the radical eye that he brought to its possibilities, searching out the places that few would have considered before him.

On Snowdon's great cliff of Du'r Arddu, on his own initiative[202] he made only one new climb, the Bow-shaped Slab of 1941, but it is the best of the older slab routes on the cliff, and distinctly the hardest and most serious of them. He produced a slim interim guidebook to this cliff too the following year – his own work, but characteristically the authorial credits for the guidebooks Menlove wrote were shared with others who generally contributed little to their production. In all his writings there is a remarkable flair and intelligence at play, an oddness and freshness of perspective and a dancing, quirky humour. He is by far the finest of all essayists about his chosen sport, and his work resonates far beyond its constricting boundaries.

In 1942 Colin Kirkus, who had managed to conceal the faulty vision resulting from the accident on Ben Nevis in enlisting for the RAF, was shot down in the Wellington bomber from a Pathfinder squadron of which he was navigator in a night raid over Bremen. And Menlove's story from this year onwards is almost unbearably sad, one of mental disintegration ending with his death in 1958 by taking potassium cyanide – the second of Snowdon's major climbing pioneers to die through this means. Yet of all the people who have climbed on Snowdon's cliffs, somehow it is the personalities of these two that attach most insistently to the great rocks on which they pioneered their routes, and whose writings convey with insight and enthusiasm the nature of the activity at which they excelled in the years between the wars. When the Second World War was over, a change as significant as that which had swept through the mountain society after the Great War came over climbing. Its results on Snowdon were to be phenomenal.

---

202   He had been second man to Kirkus on the ascent of Chimney Route in 1931.

We need to return to the interwar years to understand the genesis of what comes next in this chapter of climbing history on Snowdon. We've seen the shift away from the self-affirmed hegemony of a much-mythologized Oxbridge-and-alpinist social elite – an upper-class monopoly, more or less, which controlled the historical record and propagated versions of its own mastery and excellence. Menlove through his writings and Kirkus through his example had thoroughly subverted this fallacious construct in the 1930s, though it lingered on in pockets (particularly in the so-called 'senior clubs', with their exclusion of women, control of guidebook production, proprietorial attitude towards the historical record, assumption of regional representative status and Paleolithic social attitudes) until quite recent times.

However, a wider social movement was growing between the wars, particularly in the great urban centres of the North of England and Scotland, deriving its philosophy from Robert Blatchford's *Clarion* movement[203] (which in turn adhered to that of the great American transcendentalist writer Henry David Thoreau). It was particularly strong in the industrial cities of the north. *The Clarion* weekly newspaper, circulating

---

203 Robert Blatchford (1851–1943), writer and journalist, was the great populist among early British socialists. His *Merrie England* of 1893, copies of which sold worldwide by the million, was one of the founding texts of socialism in this country. His newspaper *The Clarion*, with its emphasis on intellectual advancement and healthy outdoor activity, gave rise to a countrywide outdoor recreation movement, expressed through Clarion cycling clubs, Clarion ramblers and so on – to all of which the landowning gentry, who had held their estates undisturbed for a century since the land-grabs of the enclosure acts, were significantly opposed. It was from within this movement that the agitation for open country access came that finally found expression in countryside and national park legislation from the post-Second World War Attlee government onwards. William Condry (1918–1998), the major writer on nature in Wales of the twentieth century, had a Clarionite background, as did the great South Walian Labour politician Aneurin Bevan.

in these deracinated settlements resulting from the starved-out rural diaspora, promoted an aspect of life there which had never quite gone away – the necessity for experience of natural surroundings in the limited free time[204] at the workers' disposal.

During the depression of the 1930s, this activity was very marked. Byne and Sutton, in their fascinating history of walking and climbing in the Peak District[205] – the expanse of wild, open country between Manchester and Sheffield – record how large numbers 'began to wander out into the Peak District each weekend, and eventually many became bogtrotters, rock-climbers and mountaineers'. After the Second World War this outdoor procession became even more marked, assisted by the widespread cheap availability of War Department outdoor clothing and equipment, including nylon ropes, pitons, karabiners. Public transport too, before the wholesale and short-sighted cuts, depredations and lack of investment by the Conservative government of the early 1960s, was extensive, frequent, cheap and reliable. From these same northern cities you could get into the Welsh mountains with relative ease for weekends. So the climbers came, and the next phase of Snowdon's story belongs to them.

---

204   The definitive description from Mrs Gaskell's 1848 novel *Mary Barton* is worth quoting here for background: 'There is a class of men in Manchester... who yet may claim kindred with all the noble names that science recognizes ... the more popularly interesting branches of natural history have their warm and devoted followers among this class. There are botanists among them, equally familiar with either the Linnaean or the Natural system, who know the name and habitat of every plant within a day's walk from their dwellings; who steal the holiday of a day or two when any particular plant should be in flower, and tying up their simple food in their pocket handkerchiefs, set off with single purpose . . . There are entomologists . . . the two great and beautiful families of Ephemeridae and Phryganidae have been so much and so closely studied by Manchester workmen . . . Such are the tastes and pursuits of some of the thoughtful, little understood, working men of Manchester.'
205   Eric Byne and Geoff Sutton, *High Peak* (Secker & Warburg, 1966).

It belonged particularly in the 1950s to three young men from Manchester who were to transform not just Welsh climbing but its practice worldwide. They were Joe Brown, Don Whillans and Ron Moseley, and I doubt if in their early days they could have mustered an aspirated aitch between them. 'Arriet would have loved them, and they her no doubt. Joe Brown, the eldest of the three and the man who went on to become without question the greatest all-round mountaineer Britain has ever produced, paid his first visit to Clogwyn Du'r Arddu in 1949. It was nearly his last. In poor conditions he fell from a continuation pitch above that Drainpipe Crack which had been climbed by Birtwhistle in 1937. Two strands of his hemp rope parted and he almost plunged over the edge of the ramp on which his second was belayed.

His luck and the last strand of the rope held. Two years later, after completing his National Service out in the Far East, he was back to begin the series of climbs on the cliff that was to equal and then surpass that of Kirkus twenty years before: Diglyph, Vember, The Boulder, The Black Cleft, The Pinnacle Flake, Spillikin, Llithrig, Octo, The Corner, Gargoyle, The East Buttress Girdle, East Gully Wall, Carpet Slab, Woubits, The Sceptre, The Mostest, November, Shrike, Boomerang, Woubits Left-hand, The Key, Sinistra, The Far East Girdle. Some of the finest rock-climbs in Britain are in this collection, the first of them climbed in 1951, the last in 1965. Nor was his climbing limited only to Clogwyn Du'r Arddu. He produced classic routes on Cyrn Las, Craig y Rhaeadr, Clogwyn y Ddysgl, Dinas Mot; made the first ascent under winter conditions of Slanting Gully on Y Lliwedd; in Nant Gwynen he monkeyed his way up excellent technical problems on the steep buttress of Clogwyn y Wenallt. As an exploratory campaign, this is peerless in the history of the mountain, and the nature of climbing here was changed by it irrevocably.

Not that Brown had it all his own way. On some of the climbs – Vember, Black Cleft, Spillikin, Pinnacle Flake, Woubits and so on – he shared the lead with his younger and more thrustingly aggressive companion Don Whillans. And on another notable occasion, in 1955, when Brown was back from his gruelling first ascent of Kanchenjunga – the world's third-highest peak – and was far from rock-fit, Whillans led him up the insecure, loose groove of Taurus on the front face of The Pinnacle after Brown had retreated from it, and gave the senior member of the party a tight rope when he came to follow (wearing, as was often the case with this wonderfully gifted and eccentric character, a pair of wholly inappropriate and unfamiliar mountain boots).

In that same year of 1955, taking advantage of Brown's absence and a week before the latter returned from the Himalayas, Whillans snatched the first ascent of Slanting Slab, a long and compellingly unpleasant climb on the West Buttress. And the third and perhaps least consistent of the triumvirate, Ronnie Moseley, in an intensely competitive manner, took in April 1956 what was perhaps the greatest prize of them all – the White Slab on the West Buttress, a route of over five hundred feet in length, sustained at a grade of mild Extremely Severe, which had been coveted for years and is considered by many to be the most enjoyable and elegant of all British rock-climbs.

There had been another intruder on this Manchester fiefdom four years earlier when another of the shooting stars of climbing history – a diminutive Trinidadian called John Streetly – had climbed the Bloody Slab[206] on the West. His

---

206 At one time a wonderful climb, though sadly rather less attractive and

ascent, without prior inspection or knowledge and in poor conditions with minimal protection, running out 300 feet of rope and making irreversible moves on loose, vegetated and unknown rock at a high sustained standard, has gone down as one of the finest leads in climbing history (and was again a reversion to social type, Streetly having been a Cambridge student – though this time G.W.Y. was rather too elderly, frail and ill for struggling up and bathing in the lake as he watched).

If the Rock & Ice Club of Manchester, to which Brown, Whillans and Moseley all belonged, had it mostly their own way on Snowdon in the 1950s, inevitably they too gave way to a new generation. They had given much to the development of the sport in their time – a different and bolder attitude towards apparent difficulty; greater gymnastic ability stemming in part from the toned muscle built up in their manual work and also from time spent training in the gym; a better grasp of the use of equipment and the techniques of protection; the use of specialized footwear for rock, invented by Pierre Allain for the sandstone boulders at Fontainebleau south of Paris, which they brought back from their alpine summer seasons particularly in Chamonix. All this was passed on to the members of Manchester's Alpha Mountaineering Club, which superseded the Rock & Ice and in its turn initiated a new and major phase of exploration on a cliff that had by this time dominated British climbers' imaginations for more than thirty years. It was to do so for three more decades yet.

From a perspective of fifty years the new rock-climbs[207]

enjoyable since the collapse of its right wall in 1986 – a major rock-fall which scoured the slab, crushed many of its small holds to splintered fragments, and left the Western Terrace from which it starts a dangerous and rubble-strewn area.

207 The ascent of the Extremely Severe rock-climb of The Black Cleft – the

made on Clogwyn Du'r Arddu by the Alpha Club members seem not to mark any significant technical advance or raising of the standards. The hardest of them are much the same grade as the hardest from the Rock & Ice era, and the club's best climbers – Martin Boysen, Peter Crew, Barry Ingle, Richard McHardy, Paul Nunn – were operating at much the same standard as their predecessors had done (and in the case of Joe Brown, whose climbing career has been one of extraordinary longevity, continued to do). But what they did bring was a fresh eye, and perhaps from time to time a slightly more lax ethical viewpoint.

They produced numerous climbs – The Pinnacle Girdle, Serth, The Shadow, Scorpio, Daurigol, Bow Right-hand, Great Wall, West Buttress Eliminate, Pinnacle Arête and The Boldest on Clogwyn Du'r Arddu, and a group of new routes[208]

---

great corner immediately left of Longland's Climb – as a pure ice-climb by Martin Boysen and Barry Ingle in the exceptionally cold winter of 1962–1963 was revolutionary, and remained the hardest winter-climb on Snowdon until the two frozen cascades of Craig y Rhaeadr were climbed in the 1980s, by which time there had been a technical revolution in equipment for this facet of the sport.

208   These climbs – Plexus, Nexus, Black Spring and so on – involved extensive use of what climbers call 'gardening', by which is meant a stripping away of all loose rock and vegetation. Needless to say, this taking place in a National Nature Reserve has brought the sport into disrepute and conflict with other interests – the naturalists and botanists for example.

For a time the climbers were perceived as the greatest threat to the rare plants of Snowdon since the Victorian fern-collecting craze. My old friend Bill Condry – a mild man – used to loathe the activity of climbing with a vengeance for this reason, and would berate me continually for my involvement in it. However, agreements were reached and a more informed attitude now generally prevails among the scalers of rocks.

In the matter of agreement to avoid cliff-nesting sites of rare birds, too, respectful compromises have been reached, often through diplomatic work by the climbers' representative body, the British Mountaineering Council. And climbers themselves do seem to have become generally responsible and self-policing.

too on the rough, sound dolerite of the wings of Dinas Mot that is probably the best rock for climbing in Wales. The climbs were of exceptional quality, and are nowadays among the most enjoyable and popular on the mountain. But most of them used rather too many points of artificial aid – pitons, slings, even in one case an expansion bolt.[209] They used them to ascend lines that Brown's generation had retreated from rather than resort excessively to these means. And by the late 1960s another more puritanical generation was in action, cleaning up the cliff, obsessing about the accomplishment of 'free ascents' where no other help than a climber's own physique and mental control could supply was used. It could be argued that this generation was fortunate in arriving at a time when the development of means of protection on climbs was moving on apace, and climbing hence was becoming safer. The ridding of Clogwyn Du'r Arddu of its proliferating aid-points became a crusade from about 1967 onwards.

From this you may infer that an element of controversy had rooted itself among the climbing community; this was to develop over coming years into a healthy growth. In those years too, particularly as a result of advanced training techniques, an extraordinary sophistication in the equipment that was becoming available, from 'sticky-rubber' boots to micro-nuts and camming devices, habituation to the ever-more-extreme situations thus enabled, and the ubiquitous use of 'chalk'[210] allowed standards of difficulty to soar. Ever-larger

---

209   Two cases, actually – there is a line of bolts high on the right wall of The Black Cleft that was used on a particularly fatuous new girdle traverse of the West Buttress. This seems never to have been repeated, and given the animus bolts in Welsh rock arouse, perhaps it is better to leave without further mention.
210   Light magnesium carbonate in its climbing version, where it's used to keep fingers dry from sweat, which can cause them to skate off small holds

numbers of participants in the sport, as a result of increasing media attention, centres that offered climbing courses, and a proliferation of indoor practice climbing walls (that soon became an end in themselves and the venue for climbing competitions – something against which climbing's old guard was for a long time vehemently opposed) ensured that the available pool of ability had become immense.

The preoccupations changed too. Immense technical difficulty, but on a micro-scale, on craglets and glacial erratics where ropes and protection equipment and such-like impedimenta were unnecessary, became the focus. Tribes of hoodies wandered among them carrying their chalk-bags and huge black crash-mats, for all the world like so many overgrown dung beetles, or coracle fishermen looking in the wrong places for a river. 'Bouldering' – a play-aspect of the sport since the time of the Pen-y-Pass pioneers – was the name of this newly-most-popular version of the game.

It is surely a mistake to continue an historical account right down to the present day. The present is not yet history and we have no perspective upon it. Better, I think, to look for a concluding and summary event that ends a long and complex phase of development. The event I would choose happened 25 years ago from the time at which I write. It may well have been the most consummate and courageous lead ever made on British rock. Joe Brown thinks so, and so do I. The 'little master' who made it, Johnny Dawes, had learned his craft on the wall of the Fives court at Uppingham School – that social

---

vigorously used. It's also used pharmaceutically for stomach ailments, so if the effect of a climb on your bowels was too severe, medication was at hand. The chalk also reveals the location of holds and allows a degree of pre-programming of climbing sequences to take place, which is a distinct advantage particularly in very strenuous situations. Hence, some have seen its use as cheating …

wheel turning full circle? He called his climb The Indian Face. It has become iconic, is graded E9, 6c, takes the right-hand and smoothest section of the magnificent centrepiece wall on Clogwyn Du'r Arddu's East Buttress. In climbing parlance it is a 'chop' route – one from which a fall would almost certainly be fatal. Since the first ascent in 1986 it has seen three subsequent leads, none in better style than the original. That likely fatal consequence, along with its tiny, fragile holds and continuous high level of difficulty will militate against its ever achieving popularity:

> I went for the crux. The motion startling me like a car unexpectedly in gear in a crowded parking lot. I swarm through the roundness of the bulge to a crank on a brittle spike for a cluster of three crystals on the right; each finger crucial and separate like the keys for a piano chord. I change feet three times to rest my lower legs . . . I swarm up towards the sunlight, gasping for air. A brittle hold holds under mistreatment . . .

Long may it continue to hold: in reality; in his mind's multiple relivings of tenuous and irreversible moves into ever-increasing danger. On such moments, on such chance, are the great events of any history, even in so slight a thing as sport, eternally poised. And how fitting that Snowdon's greatest cliff witnessed this epochal one in climbing.

Envoi

The sunset, the grinding of atom against its neighbour atom, force against its neighbour force. Fortuitous, perhaps, but moulded now into this by its necessities and a long chain of use. Moulded now into a colour of paradise, then driven away again along illimitable change. And a little figure looks up out of his own preoccupation and catches perhaps something of the size. He, too, is nature. He knows the change, the decay and long births, the mills grinding . . .[211] — JOHN MENLOVE EDWARDS

We are nearing the conclusion of this narrative, but a mountain's story has no ending – or at least, not in human terms. Sometimes, sitting by Glaslyn and looking up at Clogwyn y Garnedd, perhaps in April when the 'small snow of the young lambs'[212] has masked out detail and accentuated the diminishing ellipses of worn-down strata that make up the pyramidal form of Yr Wyddfa, the wonder of this compacted and resistant rock, that was once at the bottom of a geological structure and is now its remnant top, comes home to me, and

---

211   From 'End of a Climb' by John Menlove Edwards, from the appendix of Edwards' writings included in *Menlove* (2nd edition revised, Ernest Press, 1993), p. 267.
212   *Eira bach yr ŵyn ieuainc* – a reliable early-spring phenomenon in the Welsh hills, known by this name to the shepherds with whom I worked forty years ago. (Welsh weather-terms have a folk-poetry all their own: *gwynt ffroen yr ych* – wind from an ox's nostrils; *gwynt traed y meirw* – wind off the dead's feet; and so on.) See also Chapter Four, note 101.

with it the immensity of the timescale involved in its having been left the highest now.

This book cannot hope to cover in anything more than briefest outline even the extent of human history and activity on the mountain. Whole libraries on the subject have failed to do that. To indicate the richness here is perhaps the best that writers about the mountain can hope to do. I'm acutely aware of having – like others before me – allotted disproportionate space in this book (and my life also) to the vainglorious triviality of climbing. But it has nonetheless brought gifts to me, and will do so for others yet to come. It is certainly the case that I have bestowed insufficient attention on what to me are now the overwhelming attractions of the mountain – its natural history, particularly the extraordinary riches of its relict arctic-alpine flora and the fascination of its bird-life.

In this I have felt profoundly conflicted: how much potential harm is done by telling of the exact locations of choughs' and peregrines' and ravens' nests? Or of where the saxifrages and the Snowdon Lily, the awl-wort and the saw-wort, *silene acaulis* and the holly fern grow? I could point to where you find these within ten feet of popular paths, and were I to do so, my dear dead mentor Bill Condry in my mind would be holding up as admonitory a finger as he often did in life. He would remind me of those predatory Victorian excesses; of the irresponsible erstwhile (I hope!) ways of my own climbing tribe. So find your own way to these treasures – for they are all here, and far more besides – with the help of the general books listed in the bibliography, which will inculcate the knowledge necessary in your search, and hence increase responsibility and respect. You will be the better for doing it that way.

On finding your way in the practical sense, it is no part of the purpose of this present volume to be a guidebook. Plenty of excellent examples of those exist, and for me to select from among them and recommend would only ruffle feathers. Their general standard is high. Also, the paths themselves, especially given reasonable proficiency with map and compass – a crucial skill in the mountain environment (I am too old to transfer my allegiance to GPS devices, and anyway am of the view that technology is not to be trusted and a good map pays re-reading more than any book) – are straightforward to find and follow in almost any conditions of weather. And often, of course, the crowds will show you the way. To my mind paths these days are oversigned and overcairned, so please don't think of adding to the latter's number – better, even, to knock a few superfluities over on your way, even though you may rouse the ire of overzealous safetymongers. They are for the most part quite unnecessary.

If I were to state my own preferences among the lines of ascent, I would have to say that all the paths to the summit have something to offer, whether it be refreshment at Halfway House (a long-established, locally-run institution that the National Park Authority in its wisdom made draconian attempts to do away with after a storm demolished it some years ago – I am glad to see it now thrives again in re-built form as a connection back to an older style of local initiative on the mountain than the preening architectural sleeknesses of Hafod Eryri), or the long level introduction by the Miners' Track into the heart of the massif.

Obviously I have favourites. I think the route from Rhyd Ddu with the final ascent along Clawdd Coch wonderfully spacious and airy in ascent or descent. The Snowdon Horseshoe from Pen-y-Pass over Crib Goch, Crib y Ddysgl, Yr Wyddfa and Y Lliwedd is the classic and definitive British mountain circuit outside Skye (though to my mind the southern horseshoe, from Bethania by way of Cwm Merch, Y Lliwedd, Yr Wyddfa and Clawdd Coch in descent has qualities that make it differently as fine). And the long approach that reaches Yr Wyddfa by way of Cefn Du, Moel Eilio, Foel Goch and Moel Cynghorion to join the Snowdon Ranger Path at Bwlch Cwm Brwynog is as satisfying a rolling ridge-walk as Wales provides, with the ultimate destination always in view on clear days.

The first section of this route, to Bwlch Maesgwm and back down to Llanberis again by the track along Cwm Brwynog, makes a good short winter circuit, as does the round from Pen-y-Pass to Glaslyn and up Y Gribin – a fine airy scramble – to return over Y Lliwedd. And the ascent of Yr Aran, the little outlier above Nant Gwynen, brings you to as wide-reaching and subtle a viewpoint as Eryri can provide. But the mountain is so extensive, complex and various that to carry on listing in this manner is a futile exercise, for you will want to devise your own routes of exploration once initial acquaintance has been made.

I'm acutely aware too that I have said little about the legislative and management issues that relate to this mountain environment. Nor have I praised the sterling work done by the statutory authorities, who have generally managed to preserve its character and integrity despite incessant pressure from often conflicting interests. Occasionally in the past they have been responsible for actions of questionable sensitivity – the army's overenthusiastic blasting in 1983 at the authority's behest of a bluff on the Pig Track to ease the path and prevent it spreading across fragile adjacent slopes of grass is a case in point, raising a crucial principle. But discussion of that principle needs tempering with awareness that this is a mountain upon which have been imposed the mines at Glaslyn, the mountain railway, the Cwm Dyli pipeline, Hafod Eryri. It is by no means an undespoiled environment, as chapters of this book testify.

That is no justification, in times when the rare value of its wildness is more than ever appreciated, for further damage being done to it in the name of any cause. Talking with Alan Jones, National Park Officer of the time nearly thirty years ago, he put the point to me with brutal and I think necessary frankness:

> The policy related to Snowdon basically is that we accepted that there were no means of curtailing the use of Snowdon by the masses rather than by the more committed mountaineers and mountain-walkers, and therefore, being the highest mountain in England and Wales and thus the one which everyone wants to climb, it had to be 'sacrificed' for the masses and we had to try and cater for the problems which they caused.

Endorse that point of view and you risk the wrath of the outdoor purist. But this is the *realpolitik*. Snowdon has palpably become a victim of its own magnificence, and I believe that the means employed in the attempt at preserving that magnificence have in general been justified, far-sighted, and minimally intrusive. Concepts like management of recreational facilities, the rule of career-conservationists, and warden-service policing sit ill perhaps with the old anarchies of the hills in which my generation of climbers particularly rejoiced; yet in this instance, history has surely proved them inevitable, and beyond that valuable.

In the last few weeks I've read in the national news with a slight degree of amused ambivalence about the owner of a Vauxhall Frontera who twice attempted to drive up the mountain by the Llanberis Path, and twice had to have his vehicle rescued from it (once it was brought down on a flatbed maintenance truck by the Mountain Railway). 'Something I wanted to do before I was forty,' he pleaded in self-exculpation. Maybe he was taking his clue from the gypsy woman Sinfi Lovell in Theodore Watts-Dunton's 1898 novel *Aylwin* (in which it could be argued that Snowdon is the main character), who said of this route that 'You may ride up the Llanberis side in a go-cart'.[213] I doubt he did more damage than the proliferating charity 'challenge' walks that – always for the best of causes – continually 'conquer' the peak.

Some have frothed about this Frontera driver's irresponsibility. I wouldn't wish to see it happening again, but am reminded that in the 1960s the Automobile Association's *Drive* magazine carried a feature on Don Whillans riding his motorbike to the top of Ben Nevis; that at much the same period, along with other hoodlums, I would regularly race up on motor-bikes from Llanberis to the old Clogwyn Coch mine barracks after work for evening climbs on Clogwyn Du'r Arddu; that once, on the back of Al Harris' Greaves scrambler, I rode all the way along the ridge from Moel Eilio to the Snowdon Ranger path, over the cliff and back down the Llanberis Path. It ill becomes old men like me, whose pasts will scarcely bear the weight of scrutiny, to grow sanctimonious.

All this, anyway, is somehow incidental to the way Snowdon roosts in our individual consciousnesses. Memories garnered from experiences of the mountain are what gleam most brightly – even the mundane ones, which grow by association. The taste of the cup of Horlicks some kind man of the hills with whom I'd entered into conversation on the way up from Snowdon Ranger bought me, in the summit café that snowy

---

213   Theodore Watts-Dunton, *Aylwin* (Oxford World's Classic, 1929), p. 397.

Easter day of my first acquaintance with the mountain over fifty years ago, still lingers on my palate, as does the concern with which he set me on my right way down.

I look back on all the cloud-inversion days on Crib Goch, scrambling across pinnacles rising not from a world of the human everyday but from the cloud-sea, so that they were places apart.

I think of the many sunset descents down western flanks with the Eifionydd hills in front so eloquently graceful they seemed like lines of music, and two burnished seas beyond them at either hand.

I remember the voices of wren and stonechat scolding at the ermined stoat that loped across the scree by Llyn Teyrn. I thrill to the ravens' metallic echoes around Clogwyn Du'r Arddu, and the hiss of air through a peregrine's pinions as he stooped for a pigeon by the little lake in upper Cwm Glas one bright summer forenoon, the thump on the turf of the rock-dove's severed head, the downward waltz of the feathers, the resonant ensuing silence of even a small and witnessed death.

From another day comes back the sensation of arriving head-level at a ledge 400 feet up the cliff and burying my face in a dew-jewelled mound of flowering moss campion that throbbed with a mauve, self-generated light as I climbed unroped and alone up Spillikin on the Pinnacle Face of Du'r Arddu. I remember the cool, scented wetness against forehead and cheek, the fragility of those spicules by which I'd balanced up to this ledge, the lovely waved ochres in the rock-wall behind, the delicacy of stepping over to it without wetting slick soles of climbing shoes on the moisture-beaded plant, the deathly immensity of the drop beneath. Moments like this remind continually of our lives' capacity for ecstasy, and its close companion joy.

Also comes back memory of climbing the White Slab with my son Will when he was fourteen or fifteen: the absorption in the ascent – rope-work, protection, the delicacy of each move up the long slab-pitches, sharp small holds at my fingertips or crisping into the rubber of my boots. Alongside this there was the resonance of how atmosphere of this mighty place was impacting on my child as it had done on me decades before, his exultancy, and how the thrill of that had rung through a descent down the Llanberis Path illuminated by sunlight streaming through the *bwlch*.

How brightly that memory glows – all the more so since Will's death. And there are memories too of times early and late when the whole cliff has glowed with the sunlight it gathers early and late as I settled down into my sleeping bag and watched on summer nights and mornings from the grassy hollows on the far side of that dark lake of the fairies. I marvel, too, at the lucky chance that life accorded me in time spent here under the wise, quiet, wry tutelage of Bill Condry, finest of all writers on the natural history of Wales – the delight in a friendship that, far from fading, I value ever more dearly for the knowledge and example it brought. There are boulders, crannies, that I return to each spring and summer in pilgrimage now to see how saxifrage and roseroot and Snowdon Lily fare, because Bill bestowed their whereabouts, rarity, significance and immeasurable worth into my awareness.

Sometimes too there steals into my mind the sense of the rhythm of kicking crampons into the hard snow above Glaslyn on a bitter winter's day, the metronome crunch of each step syncopating with the tick of my ice-axes picking into the slope above, the sun rising through a hazy mist above the Capel Curig Pinnacles, light expanding, blooming and intensifying along the Nant y Gwryd as I climbed out of blue frozen shadow to stand on the sunrise summit, and a solitary silver-mew importuned querulously for breakfast there.

Auden wrote, on the death of the poet Yeats – who missed his chance for Snowdon, Winthrop Young refusing to invite him to Pen-y-Pass on the grounds that his dreaminess might have been a danger to himself and his companions – that 'the poet became his admirers'.

It is so with this mountain. Something of Snowdon will surely infiltrate into the being of everyone who comes here. May it long sustain you all, and may you too value it at its true worth; which is infinite:

Fe ddaw crawc y gigfran o glogwyn y Pendist Mawr
Ar lepen yr Wyddfa pan gwffiwyf ag Angau Gawr.

Fe ddaw cri o Nant y Betws a Drws-y-coed
Ac o Bont Cae'r-gors pan gyhoeddir canlyniad yr oed.

Fe ddaw craith ar wyneb Llyn Cwellyn, ac ar Lyn
Y Gadair hefyd daw crych na bu yno cyn hyn . . .

Fe ddaw cric i gyhyrau Eryri, ac i li
Afon Gwyrfai daw cramp fy marwolaeth i.

Nid creu balchderau mo hyn gan un-o'i-go', –
Mae darnau ohonof ar wasgar hyd y fro.[214]

214 From 'Bro', T. H. Parry-Williams, *Myfyrdodau* (Gwasg Aberystwyth, 1957) p. 120.

Select Bibliography

In certain areas, the contemporary publishing fashion – as exemplified by the *Granta* 'new nature writing' project – seems to be for bibliographies of inordinate length, perhaps to pad out the girth and intellectual credentials of volumes otherwise slim on substance and experience. My sardonic eye has noted a tendency to egregious error in these, which suggests in turn to my native scepticism that perhaps the greater part of the titles listed remain unread. I detect the taint of social enlistment here. Or perhaps merely of academic *diktat*. On whether these are proof of inauthenticity, or merely of personal insecurity, I would not dare speculate. They seem to me the cultural equivalent of those four-wheel-drive behemoths that some visitors imagine necessary to traverse Welsh roads – all for show, seldom if ever used in the way for which they were designed. For this book, I want to limit the list to the essential and foundation texts for background and further reading. Anyone who is seriously interested in the topics covered should anyway be able to find their way back to more detailed discussion of matters of interest through references in the footnotes for each chapter.

HISTORY AND FOLKLORE

John Davies, *A History of Wales* (Penguin, 1994). The standard and authoritative one-volume history.

D. E. Jenkins, *Bedd Gelert: Its Facts, Fairies and Folk-Lore* (Porthmadog, 1899). Hens' teeth don't come into it! This one will cost you, if you can find it. Worth remortgaging your house for the rare information it contains.

R. Merfyn Jones, *The North Wales Quarrymen 1874–1922* (University of Wales Press, 1982). A lucid and brilliant work of social and industrial history that gives the clearest insight into the life of communities surrounding Snowdon at the turn of the nineteenth century.

Dewi Jones, *The Botanists and Mountain Guides of Snowdonia* (2nd edition, Gwasg Carreg Gwalch, 2007). An exhaustively-researched account from an exceptionally knowledgeable local enthusiast in the classic autodidact tradition of this crucial aspect of the mountain's history. It comes from Myrddin ap Dafydd's marvellous local press Gwasg Carreg Gwalch – the 'press of the falcon's rock'. (The rest of Myrddin's publishing list also repays study.)

David Blick, *The Old Copper Mines of Snowdonia* (3rd edition Landmark, 2003). Another informed enthusiast's treatise on an important topic.

NATURAL HISTORY

There have been two volumes on Snowdonia in Collins' magisterial 'New Naturalist' series. Both are worth having.

F. J. North, Bruce Campbell and Richenda Scott, *Snowdonia: The National Park of North Wales* (1951) runs to nearly 500 pages and is, it scarcely need be said, the more comprehensive of the two. Rather dated now.

W. M. Condry, *The Snowdonia National Park* (1966), however, is individual in its treatment, encyclopedic in its knowledge, and written in as limpid and graceful a style as befits the region. A classic of its genre, it will also cost you less than 'North, Campbell and Scott'.

John Raven & Max Walters, *Mountain Flowers* (1956) in the

same series is perhaps the best general introduction to study of this fascinating subject, though its coverage of Snowdon is by no means detailed.

Mark Cocker, *Birds Britannica* (Chatto, 2005) is a beautifully-written and wide-ranging book for the non-specialist that includes sections on all the mountain birds. It is worth supplementing with two other titles that treat exclusively of these latter:

Derek Ratcliffe, *Bird life of mountain and upland* (Cambridge University Press, 1990) is as balanced as you would expect from this great authority, whilst his *The Raven* (Poyser, 1997) is the best British study of Snowdon's tutelary bird-spirit, covering every aspect from its place in legend to its current marked population-increase. Long may it prosper here!

THE TOURS

Pennant, Bingley and Borrow are all three indispensable – see footnotes in chapters 5 and 6 for publishing details. Hard to come by, the first two especially so.

LITERATURE

This is curiously sparse on Snowdon ground.

Aylwin (1898) by Theodore Watts-Dunton is the habitual recourse of those racking their brains for a relevant novel, and a strange and entertaining Victorian melodramatic romance it is. Watts-Dunton was a young friend of George Borrow in that great eccentric's later life, and the two share a love of gypsies and all things outdoors. The portrait of Snowdon in *Aylwin* is rather as it might have been painted by Picasso in his Cubist period – features recognizable, but endearingly re-arranged, and animated by the flitting and fleeing thereover of various gypsy girls, wise Romany sybils, lovelorn young men and the like.

For more modern novels, there are several detective fictions by ageing climbers – 'Glyn Carr' (Showell Styles), Gwen Moffat (the 'Miss Pink' mysteries) – set on the mountains which appeal to some tastes. Elizabeth Coxhead's *One Green Bottle* was a *succès de scandale* in its time and seems merely worthy, and unlikely, nowadays. More recently Simon Mawer's *The Fall* and Russell Celyn Jones' *An Interference of Light* are novels very much in the U.E.A. 'creative writing' mode and have scenes set on the mountain, as well as much mechanistic coupling, both heterosexual and gay. Neither convince in terms of character, setting, knowledge of activity described or period detail.

The best fiction set around Snowdon is in Welsh. To compare *Chwalfa* by the Llanberis writer T. Rowland Hughes (you'll find his birthplace plaque a hundred yards from Pete's Eats, up Goodman Street on the left) with the Celyn Jones novel – they both take as underlying theme the same historical event – is to recognize the vastly superior humanity, writing skill and knowledge of the Welsh text (of which, unfortunately, there is no recent English translation).

In terms of poetry the matter is very simple. There is *The Prelude* in both its versions; and far better than either, there are the Welsh lyrics of T. H. Parry-Williams, which are haunted by the rocks and lakes and ridges of Snowdon, and in their metaphysical quest are as resonant through all the situations of our lives as only the greatest poetry can be. And they are as untranslatable in the pithy, gnomic strength of their echoing lines.

Finally there is folk tale, of which the acknowledged oldest surviving Welsh example, *Culhwch ac Olwen*, will take you to the summit of our mountain and in doing so explain much of the legendary texture around it. You will find it as one of the 'Four Independent Native Tales' included in the collection known as *The Mabinogion*, and my strong preference here is for the 1948 translation made by Gwyn Jones and Thomas Jones, which makes use of a register somehow appropriate to the events it describes, over more recent and self-consciously scholarly versions. It was published by Everyman in 1949, and is still quite easily available.

THE CLIMBERS

H. R. C. Carr & George Lister (eds.), *The Mountains of Snowdonia* (2nd edition, Crosby, Lockwood, 1948). A remarkable collection of essays for its time and still useful if you can find it, with excellent contributions from Sir John Lloyd, Kennedy Orton and others.

Noyce, Sutton and Winthrop Young, *Snowdon Biography* (Dent, 1957). Comprises three extended essays by the individual authors. The one by Winthrop Young is a late reprise of his mythopoeic project, stately as ever; Sutton's 'The Greased Pole' is distinctly quirky and perhaps the finest long essay on climbing history yet written; Wilfrid Noyce's concluding literary essay is elegant, and good on the minor Victorians (Kingsley *et al*) who perhaps should have been mentioned in the main text, but weren't – look them up here if you must, and if thereafter you need to hunt them down, try the dustier kind of ancient second-hand bookshop with appropriately musty proprietor. The novels were still current during Noyce's adolescence, but have faded rather since then. The whole volume has long been a favourite among climbers. Probably due for reissue, and possibly worth it.

Alan Hankinson, *The Mountain Men* (Heinemann, 1977). A thorough-going party-line account from familiar sources of the earlier pioneers before the Great War, by a very competent writer.

Crew, Soper & Wilson, *The Black Cliff* (Kaye & Ward, 1971). A climbing history of Clogwyn Du'r Arddu by significant participants. Racy and competitive.

Jim Perrin, *Menlove* (Gollancz, 1985).

Steve Dean, *Hands of a Climber* (Ernest Press, 1993). Biographies which cover the lives and time of the two great Welsh-based climbers of the 1930s, Menlove Edwards and Colin Kirkus. My later book, *The Villain* (Hutchinson, 2005) did the same for Don Whillans, whilst providing a semi-scurrilous parallel-text social history of climbing between 1950 and 1985 in footnotes. If ever a poisoned chalice were proffered, and accepted, it was this commission – the deconstruction of hero-legend is never a wise project to undertake.

R. Merfyn Jones, 'The mountaineering of Wales, 1880–1925' (*Cylchgrawn Hanes Cymru / Welsh History Review*, Vol. 19, no. 1, June 1998), p. 44–67, is an exemplary treatment by this outstanding Welsh historian of mountain activity around Snowdon during the early period of the sport.

ANTHOLOGY

Ioan Bowen Rees (ed.), *The Mountains of Wales* (2nd edition, University of Wales Press, 1992). This has been a bedside book of mine for twenty years, and seems now more judicious, eclectic, balanced, entirely enjoyable and surprising than ever – you could skip the rest, present book included, and just make do with this one volume.

MAP

Ordnance Survey 1:25,000 Outdoor Leisure 17, *Snowdon & Conwy Valley areas*. The most redolent, informative and evocative text of them all, despite suspect nomenclature here and there and shady militaristic provenance. Perhaps best read in conjunction with the Irish dramatist Brian Friel's great play from 1980, *Translations*.

MAGISTERIAL OVERVIEW

Jan Morris, *The Matter of Wales: Epic Views of a Small Country* (Oxford University Press, 1984). That Wales is home to the finest writer on travel in the English language is cause for celebration – here she brings her passion and eloquence to bear on the history and atmosphere of Wales, and leaves us profoundly in her debt.

Acknowledgements

A book such as this depends on far more than the sources acknowledged in the text. Its earliest impetus derived from those who successively inspired interest in all the differing levels of its subject matter. Peter Crew – one of the pre-eminent rock-climbers of his era and the most significant among a generation of Welsh archaeologists – and I first discussed the idea for it over forty years ago. From him I assimilated my slender knowledge of his subject.

To the inspired teaching and tuition of Gwyn Thomas, to whom the book is dedicated, I owe an interest in the mythology, early history and literature of the mountain. Two more fine teachers at Bangor – the late Dr. Enid Pierce Roberts and Professor R. Merfyn Jones – one formally, the other through his written work and friendship (I must thank him also for his eloquent and generous foreword to this volume) gave on the one hand an appreciation of the near-indefinable quality of Welshness, on the other a moving sense of the mountain's industrial communities.

Many other teachers from inside or outside academia have brought wisdom, knowledge, fine example: Joe Brown, Bill Condry, Dr. Iestyn Daniel, Dewi Jones, Jan Morris, Dr. Angharad Price, the late Ioan Bowen Rees, Evan Roberts. So too have friends and fellow-writers: Mark Cocker, Ed Douglas, Paul Evans, Niall Griffiths, Chris Kinsey, Horatio Clare, Gwyneth Lewis, Robert Minhinnick, Sian Northey, the late Showell Styles, Ray Wood. The National Library of Wales staff has responded to requests with unfailing courtesy, and the proprietors of Browsers' Bookshop in Porthmadog – a heartening and civilized survival in an age of amazonian degeneracy – surprise time and again with their promptness and efficiency.

Tony Shaw, friend and companion of many early climbs, placed his extensive mountaineering library at my disposal and was indefatigable in transmitting copies of rare journal articles.

To the Writers' Centre for Wales and its remarkable director Sally Baker-Jones, my gratitude and affection are unstinting – working with her, her staff and students has been an infinitely rewarding experience over many years.

My thanks are due to the Banff Centre in Alberta where much preparatory work was done through the grant of a Fleck Fellowship there. To individuals with whom I have shared walks, climbs and times on and around Snowdon, a list of names – from which no doubt the lesions of age would exclude many – is too scant a reward for the riches they brought. Let the book itself be their recognition.

I thank all at the fine old Welsh institution of Gomer Press (to be published by which is always a privilege). Three names in particular deserve to be singled out: my old college friend Mairwen Prys Jones was involved with this book from its inception; Francesca Rhydderch's intelligent reading and deft editorial skills have been a revelation; and the support, guidance and expertise of Dylan Williams are as indispensable as they are congenial. To work with this trio has been more friendship than task.

Finally, there are those closest to me. Their names in a world that operates all too often *sub specie mali* are too precious to publicise here. They know who they are. Their forbearance and generosity of spirit I recognize with profoundest gratitude. In time-honoured writerly formula, whatever merits this book may possess are gift and property of all the above. Its failings are entirely my own.